THE WRIGHT SPACE

D0100330

THE WRIGHT SPACE

Pattern and Meaning in Frank Lloyd Wright's Houses

GRANT HILDEBRAND

University of Washington Press ▼ *Seattle*

11 10 09 08 07 06 05 04   9 8 7 6 5

University of Washington Press
PO Box 50096
Seattle, WA 98145–5096, U.S.A.
www.washington.edu/uwpress

Library of Congress Cataloging-in-Publication Data
Hildebrand, Grant, 1934–
    The Wright space : pattern and meaning in Frank Lloyd
Wright's houses / Grant Hildebrand.
        p. cm.
    Includes bibliographical references.
    ISBN 0–295–97108–8
    1. Wright, Frank Lloyd, 1867–1959—Criticism and
interpretation. 2. Architecture, Domestic—United States—
Themes, motives. 3. Architects and patrons—United States.
4. Space (Architecture). I. Title.
NA737.W7H48   1991   90–12154
728'.37'092—DC20   CIP

The first printing of this publication was supported in part by
interest on the capital fund established through a challenge
grant from the National Endowment for the Humanities, a
federal agency.

For Miriami

Contents

Figures

Preface

Thanks are owed to many.

Domino's Farms Activities invited me to give a talk in Ann Arbor in April 1986, in which these thoughts first acquired some semblance of organization. Since that time Domino's, and especially archivist Kathryn Crawley, have been helpful beyond measure.

Monetary support was extended by the College of Architecture and Urban Planning and the Graduate School Research Fund of the University of Washington.

Lydia Miner typed the earliest versions of this and then, perhaps in desperation, taught me to do it myself by introducing me to the mysteries of the Macintosh.

Photographers Ann Eaton, Pedro Guerrero, Mike Hulahan of Hedrich-Blessing, David Kapps, Balthazar Korab, Scott Leff, Ellen Nibbelink, Julius Shulman, Christian Staub, and Ezra Stoller/ESTO have been most graciously helpful. My sons Peter and Matthew have also assisted with various photographic tasks.

Shirley Courtois, Ann and Leonard Eaton, Norman Johnston, Douglas Kelbaugh, Peter Miller, Jeff Ochsner, and Claus Seligmann slogged through the manuscript at various stages, offering advice and encouragement. Joseph Clark, friend and biologist, patiently endured what must have seemed to him some very amateurish discussions on principles of evolution. I should also thank those readers who most helpfully responded to the Press. Such persons are supposedly anonymous, but three of them—Jay Appleton, John Savo, and Henry Matthews—discarded their anonymity to talk to me about the work directly and most helpfully. I thank them all for their gracious counsel.

Another reader suggested that all plans of Wright's houses ought to be drawn anew for this book. I regarded that suggestion without enthusiasm; some forty-odd plans were at issue, and Wright's plans are of a wondrous complexity. But I owe that still-anonymous reader real thanks; an arduous task was also a blessing. Many previously published plans of the houses dis-cussed herein are inaccurate, occasionally severely so; redrawing thus has meant some detective work, but it has provided an opportunity to correct at least some of the more glaring problems. Still, these plans are by no means the equivalent of measured drawings of the houses as built. That task still needs doing but is entirely beyond the scope of this book, and is in some cases, e.g., Taliesin, simply impossible. In that case, and in others as well, there is often an element of conjecture, and no doubt errors remain; I can only hope they are minor. I believe these plans to be more nearly accurate than any similar published collection, but it would be wrong to make any further claim. In all cases except the Coonley house, the intention has been to show the design as it existed at the time of first occupancy; features proposed but not originally built, as for example the pool at the Hanna house, are omitted, as are subsequent changes. Scale and compass indications, rare in published plans, are given, except that compass indications are omitted for three unbuilt projects.

In addition, however, the redrawing of these plans brought home, as nothing else could have done, the full range of spatial and formal characteristics this book describes. On many occasions I found myself fleshing out the text and even making major changes and additions as a result of the drafting.

It was clear early on, however, that drawings of a more diagrammatic sort would be enormously useful to an understanding of Wright's spaces, and for that task I was entirely out of my depth. William Hook, a friend, an architect, and a delineator of wonderful artistry, took time away from his livelihood to create the diagrammatic drawings of the key houses, and participated in the detective work and graphic decisions for the plan drawings as well. He has contributed research, perception, criticism, and artistry to this work; I owe him thanks beyond measure.

In the winter of 1988 two colleagues, psychologist Judy Heerwagen and zoologist Gordon Orians, allowed me to join them in offering a seminar on aesthetics and evolution, in which we developed many of the thoughts that underpin this book. We were doubly fortunate in having Jay Appleton as a participant at several of the sessions. I thank all three for stimulation and support. Warren Lloyd was a graduate student in that seminar; he contributed a paper on the Japanese house, which was helpful to that discussion as it appears in chapter 1, and he and Jan Fredrickson assisted William Hook and myself with several plans and diagrammatic drawings. Patrick O'Hare, in the same seminar, developed a paper on the Alhambra that brought the appropriateness of that structure to my attention.

The cooperation of owners and curators of the houses has been most helpful. I particularly thank Edith Anderson, Gus Brown, Jeff Chusid, and William and Mary Palmer. Virginia Ernst Kazor, curator of Hollyhock House, generously made the house available; she also read the manuscript and offered many factual clarifications. The Affleck house is now owned by Lawrence Technical University; Dean Karl Greimel kindly provided photographs, and several years ago hosted an open house there for the Cranbrook ACSA seminar, at which time I was able to renew my familiarity with the house. I also thank Mr. and Mrs. Stuart Roberts, wherever they may now be. Years ago, as owners of the Cheney house, they were warmly hospitable when two colleagues and I were doing an NSF-funded movie of the Robie house; Christian Staub's photographs of the Cheney interior were taken at that time.

Naomi Pascal, Julidta Tarver, and Audrey Meyer of the University of Washington Press have been wonderful all along. Not the least of their contributions was to put the manuscript in the hands of Lorna Price, the most patient and skillful editor one could hope for.

The problem in having all this splendid help is that there can now be no one but myself to blame for errors and omissions.

THE WRIGHT SPACE

The effects you see in this house are not superficial effects. . . .

Frank Lloyd Wright, *Architectural Forum*, 1938

Introduction

This book comes from the chance meeting of two thoughts. The first has to do with a problem— a lingering question, really—about Frank Lloyd Wright's houses.

In both early and late life Wright had an enormous number of domestic clients; among noted architects almost certainly a record number by a wide margin. They came to his drawing board in droves, and, having seen through to completion their adventure with him, they were, by and large, ecstatic about what they got. Evidence of this, and not the sole evidence, is that many of these clients subsequently returned to Wright for another house, and sometimes more than one. In *An Autobiography* Wright even tells of two houses that "were bought back again by the same people who had built them and sold them, because they said they could not feel at home in any other."[1] Given the source, one might approach the comment with caution, yet Robert Twombly, a careful and balanced biographer of Wright, notes that "as questionnaires and interviews establish again and again, his clients love their homes, indeed, are more than ordinarily enthusiastic, and leave, if they have to, with considerable reluctance."[2]

And then there is the response of the general public, harder to document but sometimes brought home with dramatic clarity. Anyone who has taught or attended an introductory class in modern architectural history for a lay audience will know that when a slide of Le Corbusier's Villa Savoye or Mies van der Rohe's Tugendhat House goes on the screen, some explaining is in store, but when Fallingwater appears, the class is all attention within, quite literally, one second. The appeal is immediate and pervasive, and the same observation can be made of on-site responses to this house, as is suggested by Edgar Kaufmann Jr.'s query: "Why does a house designed by an architectural individualist for the special purposes of a special client appeal so much to the public in general?"[3]

And there is, of course, an enormous body of attention to Wright at the professional and critical level. The literature on his houses is voluminous, and almost without exception it gives them a monumental place in the story of architecture, both for their revolutionary formal, spatial, and technical inventiveness, and for their sheer evocative magic.

Yet few houses of equal fame have embodied more conspicuous faults. Many of Wright's plans defy reasonable furniture arrangements,[4] many frustrate even the storage of reasonable and treasured possessions.[5] In many cases, severe problems afflict the architectural fabric: leaking roofs, unserviceable detailing, even structural inadequacies.[6] A number of the houses were over budget to a degree that challenges belief.[7] And, one must add, there were problems of personality as well: it is a matter of record that many of Wright's clients found him arrogant, careless, slow, and misleading, and were not by any means always amused by his temperament.[8] And there are more vague and subjective difficulties, for the sheer power of these houses as dramatic exercises in space and form can intimidate the more varied and spontaneous acts of ordinary daily life: how does one have a casual conversation in the Robie house dining room, or hang a cherished delicate picture in a Usonian?

Normally such pervasive problems would finish an architect's career almost before it started. Yet Wright's houses have offered some quality capable not only of transcending their formidable shortcomings but of engendering a uniquely widespread devotion. Something about them, obviously, has more than redeemed their multitudes of sins.

The conventional wisdom is that the houses have been liked, even loved, because they have been found to be in some way extraordinarily beautiful; attention has then turned to an interpretation of the ways in which that beauty has evolved and been manifested. Wright himself tried at great length to explain that evolution and manifestation through references to a belief in the organic, a sympathy with nature, the art and craft of the machine, the countenance of principle, the sense of shelter, the destruction of the box. Art historians have proposed analogies to natural forms or to contemporary, primordial, or exotic architectural examples; they have analyzed abstract compositional processes and devices; they have offered explanations about the liberation of space; they have suggested the metaphor of expansive democratic life. Such studies have helped us to grasp the characteristics of Wright's houses, and to speculate about how they came to be; thus they have assisted our understanding of the creative process and the resultant artifact. But they have not been of equal help in explaining the appeal, and especially the lay appeal, of Wright's houses, because the characteristics they describe have never been shown to account for the compelling, pervasive, and immediate responses that the houses engender. Do any of those characteristics have such power? If so how, and why? If not, what does, since *something* obviously does?

That, then, was the first thought.

The second thought seems, on the face of it, quite unrelated.

Since 1978, when Jay Appleton spoke at the University of Washington, I have been intrigued by his work in theory of landscape aesthetics. Appleton is an English geographer; with debts to John Dewey and others, he is the author of what he calls a theory of prospect and refuge, which he most fully presented some fifteen years ago in a book entitled *The Experience of Landscape*.[9] Put in inadequately brief terms, Appleton's argument is that there is a deeply seated, genetically driven, human predilection for conditions of prospect and refuge within landscape settings. By *prospect* Appleton means a condition in which one can see over a considerable distance, and by *refuge* he means a place where one can hide; in combination they reinforce one another, creating the ability to see without being seen.

This combination once had survival value, for in choosing it Homo sapiens could hunt successfully without being, in turn, successfully hunted. But as with other survival behaviors, eating and copulation being the obvious examples, this habitat-selecting is enacted just for the inherent pleasure it yields, without conscious recognition of survival function. Thus Appleton argues that a juxtaposition of prospect and refuge conditions is basically and of itself pleasurable to our species, and so occurs repeatedly as a condition of choice in landscape settings.

Though Appleton has made no extended attempt to apply his theory to architecture, such an attempt has long seemed to me to offer a rich field for further work, since it holds the possibility of describing and exploring issues of spatial choice at a more significant level than has been offered by any other design-related theory. It can also make the enviable claim that in the years since its first appearance, it has received a fair amount of empirical substantiation;[10] thus, while no one, least of all Appleton himself, would wish to claim that it represents immutable truth, nevertheless it has been carried somewhat beyond the stage of speculation.

With the lingering question of the attraction of Wright's houses on the one hand, and Appleton's work on the other, it occurred to me that the properties of the one seemed to reflect the properties of the other. I recalled that some of Wright's houses contained architectural dispositions analogous to the preferred landscape dispositions discussed by Appleton. A closer reexamination led me to believe that of the houses Wright designed after 1902 almost all held an extraordinarily rich array of these analogies, at several hierarchical levels—and did so through a complex and repetitive composition of elements unique to him in his time. I began to recognize that Wright had developed with consistency and richness an architecture that stimulated powerful, genetically driven responses of Homo sapiens.

At that point it seemed worthwhile to consider relevant literature of the last decade or two that has examined other preferred conditions of aesthetic experience. This literature is extensive and not always conclusive.

But one position, current for a long time as an undemonstrated theoretical stance, now seems to be garnering empirical support. It is that preferred aesthetic experiences of many sorts, including preferred architectural experiences, tend to be relatively rich in both complexity and order.[11] And this conjunction of characteristics has also proven receptive to a biological rationale similar to that offered by Appleton; it has a survival value together with an inferred a priori pleasure stimulus. Exactly what *order* and *complexity* mean in a specific architectural application is not entirely clear, since they are relative, but they are, at least on the face of it, terms that are eminently applicable to Wright's houses. To these characteristics I would add only two others that play a minor and less frequent role in Wright's work. These are what Appleton refers to as *hazard*, and what Stephen Kaplan, especially, has termed *mystery*.[12]

Therefore, in this book I am going to consider the ways in which Wright's houses offer a uniquely rich array of fundamentally appealing conditions of prospect, refuge, complexity, order, and, to a much lesser extent, hazard and mystery. I believe that an understanding of the ways in which Wright's houses manifest these conditions helps to explain the devotion they have engendered. I emphasize that I offer this not as the sole explanation of their appeal, but as one way of thinking about that appeal. It is a truism, but true nevertheless, that a work of art is amenable to more than one interpretation. This one can coexist peacefully with others; I would hope it might complement and enrich them. I would further maintain that the characteristics of prospect, refuge, complexity, and order are illustrated with sufficient profusion and regularity in Wright's houses to constitute a defensible and internally consistent argument, while his remarkably prolific domestic practice—over 300 executed houses[13]—offers an unusually extensive range of examples and, through their sheer numbers and popularity, some corroboration of their configurational value.

The interpretation that follows, then, seems to me to be largely defensible and helpful, and is one in which I have a degree of belief. As to purpose, I cannot do better than to paraphrase Appleton's purposes of more than a decade ago: I seek to bring the argument to a level of plausibility at which other scholars competent to pursue further inquiry, including a wealth of empirical inquiry, might find here a framework based on sufficient prima facie evidence to warrant their attention.

Wright's life was long, complex, rich, multifaceted, uneven, and endlessly fascinating. A book purporting to deal, in any finite way, with the effects of his work rather than its causes must keep a steady focus. I am more concerned with the values that may accrue to Wright's configurations than with the origins of those configurations. Therefore I have generally avoided the large causal issues of his sources and motivations, about which, in any event, a great deal has been said already. I make no attempt to recount material from the vast number of personal and professional biographies he has engendered (more, I believe, than any other architect) except as such recounting is necessary to the reasonable flow of the argument. At the same time I must admit that I have found it hard to be an absolute purist in this regard: in the case of Taliesin, and to a lesser extent the California work, some reference to personal circumstances has seemed unavoidable, and the discussion of Wright's pattern seemed incomplete without at least a brief outline of where it may or may not have come from.

Does this interpretation have a creative dimension? Are the characteristics of Wright's work described here capable of further creative exploration? In the last chapter I discuss some ways in which this may be possible and attempt to illustrate the point through a few pertinent examples selected from the apparently quite different work of some current architects—although these examples, and many others, deserve far greater attention than I can give here. Nevertheless, Wright's houses seem to me to be the place to begin, because the correspondence between prospect and refuge, complexity and order, seems to be evinced in them with unique strength and consistency.

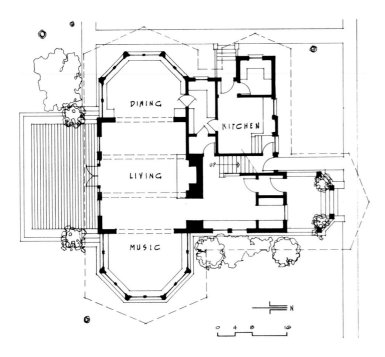

1.1 Warren Hickox house, Kankakee, 1900. Lower floor plan. The fireplace is the black U-shaped mass located at the approximate center of the plan, as it will be in most of Wright's houses hereafter.

1.2 B. Harley Bradley house, Kankakee, 1900. Lower floor plan.

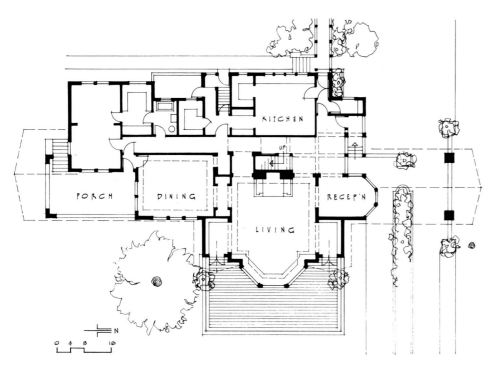

1. The Pattern

In 1893, at the age of twenty-six, Frank Lloyd Wright left the offices of Adler and Sullivan to launch his own practice. Over the next seven years he produced a number of houses that demonstrated his already considerable abilities: the Winslow house of 1893, the Williams house of 1895, the Heller house of 1897, the Husser house of 1899, and at least two ventures in period styles, the Blossom house of 1893, and the Moore house of 1895. All were adept pieces of design and have long been so recognized. But in the context of his long career, these houses are atypical in that they do not represent variations on any established theme, but rather are autonomous individual designs in which Wright seems to have been investigating a wide variety of spatial arrangements and formal treatments. These early houses were more a search than a discovery.[1]

Then, in 1900, Wright began to develop in his houses a particular repetitive configuration of their key elements: the entry, the fireplace, ceilings, solid and glazed walls, openings to adjacent interior and exterior spaces, and terraces. Within two years, he developed this configuration to a canonical state that informed the vast majority of his residential work for the rest of his life. For lack of a better term, I would like to call this repetitive configuration of domestic architectural elements Wright's *pattern*. Wright's reasons for creating and then remaining loyal to this pattern were almost certainly intuitive, but recent work in many related fields now enables us to ascribe to it an explicit humanistic worth.

In 1900 Wright produced four house designs of extraordinary interest. Three, the Warren Hickox and Harley Bradley houses in Kankakee, Illinois, and the first *Ladies' Home Journal* project[2] (figs. 1.1–1.3) each have a single fireplace at the center of the plan. Wright had done this before; the Winslow house is an example.

But he had not done it consistently: the Husser and Heller houses, for instance, each had two noncentral fireplaces, and in both, the living room fireplace was on an outside wall. In the three houses of 1900 Wright handled the fireplace in a repetitive way. It is at the center of the house; it also establishes and opens to the internal edge of the living room. On each flank the living room opens to the contiguous spaces: dining and music, dining and reception, and dining and library respectively. Opposite the fireplace in each scheme is a wall of windows and french doors; beyond is a terrace of generous size serving both as an extension of the living room and as a viewing platform for the land beyond.

1.3 Project: "A Home in a Prairie Town" for *Ladies' Home Journal*, February 1900. Lower floor plan.

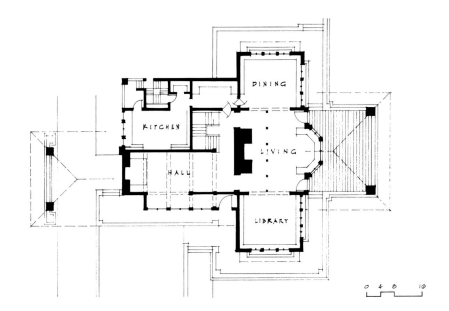

In the fourth important design of 1900, a second house for *Ladies' Home Journal* called "A Small House with Lots of Room in It" (fig. 1.4), Wright enriched the arrangement by providing two fireplaces, one for the living room, one for dining.[3] As in the other three houses, these fireplaces are located at the center of the plan and at the internal edges of the rooms they serve. Each has an adjacent screen and seat on the flank which creates a kind of half-inglenook; the sectional perspective of this house published at the time showed a lowered ceiling over this area. The organization is asymmetrical. The openings to contiguous spaces are more complex; the dining room and the entry seem to slide away from the edges of the living room fireplace. Terraces are shown opening from both living and dining rooms.

An almost identical organization of elements appears in the house actually constructed for Ward W. Willits[4] in 1901–1902 in Highland Park, Illinois (fig. 1.5A). Differences in plan from the second *Ladies' Home Journal* scheme are primarily in nuance: Wright has given up the polygonal projection of the living room; vast rows of casements and french doors are used from both the living and dining rooms to their terraces; ceilings are lowered over both fireplaces; and the terrace off the dining room has a more complex and dramatic geometry. On the upper floor of the Willits house (fig. 1.5B), the master bedroom repeats the organization yet again. A fireplace lies at the inner edge of the space, with a half-inglenook seat to one side; as in the major spaces below, a low ceiling occurs over this area with a higher ceiling forward of it. Glass and french doors are opposite, and a terrace lies beyond.

Thus, the *Ladies' Home Journal* projects and the Hickox, Bradley, and Willits houses show the evolution of a spatial and formal theme in which architectural elements are repetitively composed in similar ways. Nevertheless they, as well as Wright's earlier houses, still lack a characteristic vital not only to his subsequent houses but to virtually all his subsequent architecture, domestic and otherwise.

The major spaces of these five houses, like those of most other multistory houses, including all of Wright's earlier ones, are surmounted by a floor directly above, on which bedrooms and baths are located. For this reason, and given Wright's fondness for proportions that emphasized the horizontal (see fig. 1.6), the ceilings of the major spaces on the lower floor had to be relatively low and more or less flat. Some modest manipulation of the ceiling plane is possible in such a situation, and in

fact Wright did so in each of these houses, but the ability to juxtapose and dramatize low and high spaces is necessarily limited by the floors above. The result is clearly evident in the low, flat-ceilinged living rooms of the Bradley and Willits houses (figs. 1.7–1.8). Wright's next major house (and the work of his entire subsequent career) suggests that he could not accept this limitation, and was determined to find a means for a much more dramatic modeling of the ceiling plane.

In a scheme such as the Willits house he might have found that means by omitting the front upstairs bedroom and opening the living room right up to the roof, thus making it a two-story space—although to give the dining room a similar opportunity, another bedroom would have had to be sacrificed. (In fact Wright proposed just such an alternative for the first *Ladies' Home Journal* scheme, noting the loss of the two bedrooms, but he did not use this approach in actual constructed work until several years later.[5]) He might also have found his way by simply increasing the height of the main floor, to give a larger vertical dimension within which to model the ceilings. But such an increase would have compromised the horizontal emphasis of the overall composition, and so cannot have had much appeal for him.

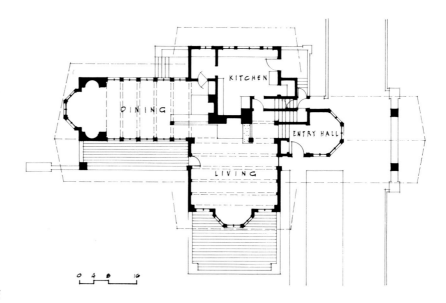

1.4 Project: "A Small House with Lots of Room in It" for *Ladies' Home Journal*, July 1900. Lower floor plan.

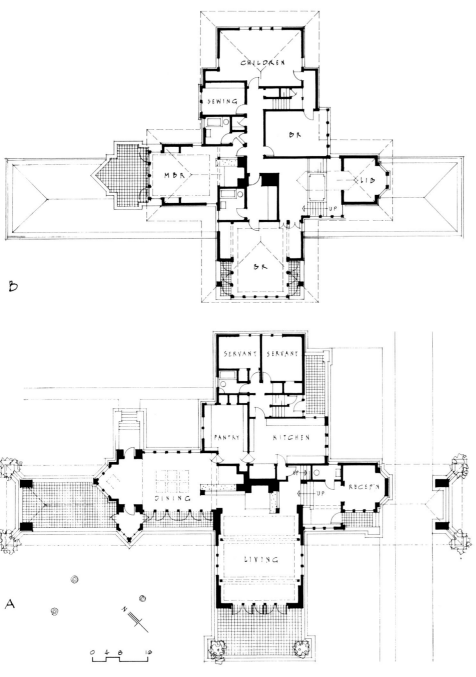

B

A

CHILDREN

SEWING

MBR

BR

LIB

BR

SERVANT SERVANT

PANTRY

KITCHEN

DINING

RECEP'N

LIVING

UP

UP

N

0 4 8 16

1.5A–B Ward Willits house, Highland Park, 1901. Plans: A. Lower floor. B. Upper floor. Compare the organization of the lower floor with fig. 1.4, and note also the similarity of organization between the living room and the master bedroom, at left in the upper floor plan.

1.6 Willits house. Perspective from the street. The living room and its terrace are at center, with bedrooms above.

1.7 Bradley house. Living room.

1.8 Willits house. Living room. In both this and the Bradley house the ceiling, lying under a floor of bedrooms above, is flat and relatively low in comparison with Wright's later houses.

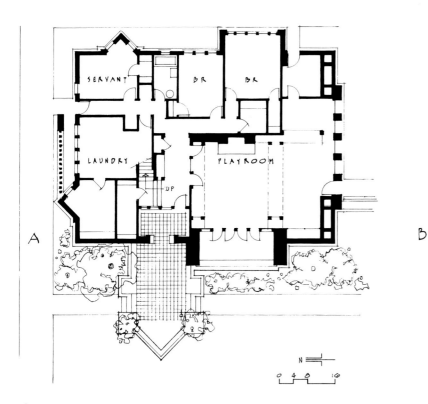

A

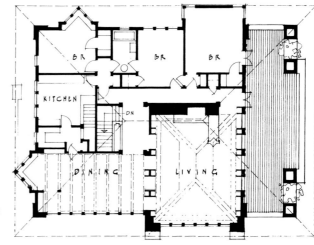

B

Instead he approached the problem by a radically different path. In the design of the house for Arthur Heurtley in Oak Park, done perhaps just a few months after the Willits house, he took the first and decisive step by reversing the overwhelmingly prevalent organization of multistory houses. At the Heurtley house, the entry occurs on a floor given over not to the major spaces of the house but to bedrooms and a children's playroom (fig. 1.9A). Wright has located the major spaces, the living and dining rooms, on the floor above, which is the topmost floor of the house. These spaces, substantially elevated above the surrounding terrain, are reached by a twisting stair ascending a full story (fig. 1.9B). By this radical means, and for the first time in his work, Wright placed the major spaces of the house directly under the roof, with no superimposed floor. This condition became all but universal for him. In work done over the next four years of his career there were a few exceptions; thereafter, it is almost axiomatic that if the major spaces are not directly under the roof the building is not by Wright.[6]

The advantage of this condition is apparent in its first usage.[7] For while still keeping the low horizontality of each stratum of the Heurtley elevation (fig. 1.10), it gave Wright his chance to model the upper surfaces of its major spaces in a really significant way (fig. 1.11). These spaces, the living and dining rooms, open into the roof's volume and borrow their configuration from it. In this way they achieve a drama of contrast between low edges and high center not attained by Wright in any earlier work. He has called attention to the condition in this first application by picking out the geometry of the roof planes with a wood trim, unusually heavy even for Wright, and by marking the apex with a false skylight leaded in shapes emphasizing the diagonals that result.[8]

1.9A–B Arthur Heurtley house, Oak Park, 1902. Plans: A. Lower floor. B. Upper floor. Living and dining spaces are to the front; the terrace is at far right.

1.10 Heurtley house. Exterior from sidewalk. The broad sweep of windows above the entry arch is that of the dining room; the living room is to the right; at the extreme right, under the broad roof, is the terrace.

1.11 Heurtley house. Living room with fireplace and half-inglenook. The dining room and stairhead are to the left; the terrace (now enclosed) is beyond the windows at far right.

The upper floor plan of the Heurtley house in other respects roughly derives from the main floor plan of the Willits house. The single fireplace, in the living room, is in a like location, and is flanked on the south by a similar half-inglenook seating promontory whose enclosing character is emphasized by tall terminating cabinetwork. The living room terrace is laterally displaced, lying south of the seating promontory, and is seen through windows and is accessible through french doors from the flank of the room.[9] The dining room has been moved forward in plan so that it becomes a part of the street façade; it therefore lacks a separate terrace, but opens through a colonnaded, glazed wall to the living room. But the location of these major spaces on the upper floor has led Wright to make the path to them much more elaborate than at the Willits house; one enters into the porch itself, then a dogleg to the front door, then several more turns up a twisting stair, then more turns at the top.

What, then, are the fundamental compositional characteristics of the Heurtley house? The major spaces are elevated well above the terrain they overlook. The fireplace is withdrawn to the heart of the house and to the internal edge of the room it serves. Its withdrawal is emphasized by a low ceiling edge and flanking built-in seating and cabinetwork. The ceiling forward of the fireplace zone sweeps upward into the roof, echoing its form. The distant edges of the ceiling then return to a low elevation like that near the fire. There are interior views to contiguous spaces seen beyond architectural screening devices. Glass and glazed doors are located on walls distant from the fire. A generous elevated terrace lies beyond. The exterior consists of deep overhanging eaves, an evident central chimney, broad horizontal groupings of window bands, and conspicuous balconies or terraces. The connection from exterior to interior is by means of a long and circuitous path.

This is Wright's pattern. It occurs in its entirety for the first time in the Heurtley house, and is comprised of those thirteen characteristics. It would be wrong to claim that all these characteristics are found in all of Wright's subsequent houses, but the truth is not far short of that: for the next fifty years all his major houses, except only the Ocatillo camp and Taliesin West, will have at least ten of these characteristics; many will have all thirteen. Thus, this pattern in various permutations is the informing arrangement of all the great Prairie houses, Taliesin, the California houses of the 1920s, Fallingwater, and the Usonians.

Are there other domestic architectural precedents known to Wright that could have suggested to him either the totality of this pattern or individual aspects of it?

Wright's organization of the house around the central fire is analogous to that of many simple dwellings before the days of central heating systems. An apposite example likely to have loomed large in Wright's mind would be the early colonial American house. But such an example offers a precedent only in bald terms, for in the colonial house, the fireplace was a simple practical urgency, and all characteristics of its treatment were driven by that urgency. Thus, the fire was central in order to distribute the heat to surrounding occupied spaces, and the seating was often contiguous with the fire to gather the family close to the heat source. And beyond those elementary similarities to Wright's configuration, there are no others, nor can it be pretended that Wright was in any way driven by the same practical motivations.

A more recent and more specific fireplace-laden American house, probably known to Wright through his employer and hero Louis Sullivan, was H. H. Richardson's Watts Sherman house of 1874, at Newport, Rhode Island. That house has several fireplaces, and all are dominant features of the interior, modeled with the energy that Richardson could so wonderfully summon; they are fitting inspirations for Wright's own dominant fireplaces. Yet that house also has limitations as a precedent for Wright, since its main fireplace is in the very high living hall, and each of the others is at the end of the room it serves, under a ceiling undifferentiated from that of the rest of the room.

Fireplaces were also emphatic features in houses of the Shingle Style. Wright had been introduced to this style through the Lloyd-Jones family chapel at Spring Green by Lyman Silsbee, and even more directly, a year or two later, through his first architectural employment with Silsbee in Chicago, before his years with Adler and Sullivan. Wright drew a lot from the Shingle Style in his early years; a number of the houses he did for Adler and Sullivan derive from it, as does his first house for himself, in 1889, in Oak Park. But the Shingle Style also has limitations as a source for Wright's treatment of the fireplace. Occasionally, as for example at "Shingleside" of 1880–81 in Swampscott, Massachusetts, by Arthur Little, the fireplace is withdrawn into a low-ceilinged space with an inglenook of built-in seating to one or both sides;[10] and such an example might well have suggested a markedly similar treatment early in Wright's career in his own Oak Park house. But in the Shingle Style, the fireplace is often located within a high space, as in the Robert Goelet house of 1882–83 in Newport, by McKim, Mead and White.

So while Wright may have got the general idea of the central fireplace from its practical location in colonial American houses, and may have picked up the idea of the inglenook from occasional examples in the Shingle Style, neither offered any pervasive, compelling, or specific model for his way of handling its context, nor his ubiquitous use of it long after it had lost its earlier utilitarian purpose.

What of the heavy overhanging eaves? The early colonial American house certainly did not offer any model for these. Nor did the houses of the Shingle Style; quite the opposite, in fact, for one of their most characteristic features is a closely tailored eave line which interrupts as little as possible the expression of a continuous surface of wall and roof. Similar points might be made regarding the broad horizontal expanses of window.

Nor is there a single example in the Shingle Style of major living spaces directly under the roof. One can argue of this feature, of course, that any house of one story automatically possesses it, including some of the simpler smaller houses of colonial America (or anywhere else, for that matter), and therefore its source is obvious and ubiquitous. But Wright did not come to it by that path. From 1893 to 1911, every one of his major houses is multistoried;[11] and a multistory house with major living spaces located on the uppermost floor directly under the roof is as rare in the general realm of American domestic architecture as it is in examples in the Shingle Style specifically. It is equally rare in the broader spectrum of Western domestic architecture generally.[12] Nor does the Italian *piano nobile* arrangement work very well as a source. It might just possibly have stimulated in Wright the idea of an elevated living floor, although even that is not likely, given his transparent hostility to the Renaissance. But what argues against it even more strongly is that the *piano nobile* scheme normally carries a third floor of rooms above the main floor, and so neither provides nor suggests the advantage of dramatic spatial modeling that Wright sought and obtained by elevating the living floor to a position directly under the roof.[13]

The generous elevated terrace of the pattern finds some precedent in the "piazzas" of the houses of the Shingle Style, and for that matter simply in the general American tradition of the front porch. Yet here, too, there are essential differences. Wright's terraces invariably open quite broadly and directly from the spaces they serve, and invariably they are kept entirely separate from the entry sequence by the interposition of a considerable distance.[14] In these respects they differ from the piazzas of the Shingle Style and from the conventional American front porch as well. In fact they are more like the verandas of the traditional Japanese house than they are like any Western precedent.

And here we open up once again the old question of Wright's relationship to Japan.[15] Do any of the features of Wright's pattern, or any of his canonical relationships among these features, find parallels in Japanese architecture? Crisp conclusions remain elusive, but putting the question in this way may at least yield some fresh observations.

Wright's personal architectural practice had been under way for twelve years before he actually visited Japan in 1905. But it has long been recognized that in 1893, the very year in which he launched his practice, he could have seen and probably did see Japan's Ho-o-den pavilion at the Chicago World's Columbian Exposition. Of this structure Grant Manson long ago observed that "beneath an ample roof—a powerful expression of shelter—and above the platform on which the temple stood, was the area of human activity."[16] Here clearly is a possible precedent for Wright's own "ample roof" at least, and perhaps more as well—though it should be noted that the pavilion did not offer a precedent for a ceiling rising into the volumes of the roof, because it had flat false ceilings. Dimitri Tselos has also noted the possible importance of the Nippon Tea House at the exposition, whose roof forms may have suggested those of the Prairie house.[17] As far as we know, these are the only two instances of Japanese architecture that Wright could have seen before 1905.

But at another and admittedly far more speculative level, there is a relationship between Wright's pattern and the architecture of Japan—for if we take the broader context of Japanese architecture generally, and compare it with Wright's pattern in all its characteristics, striking parallels emerge. The *tokonoma*, the most cherished element of the Japanese house, often bears analogies to Wright's fireplaces. Both are usually at the heart of the house, enclosed within clay walls; both are typically under a low ceiling; and the management of the surrounding spatial configuration is also similar. The floor is typically elevated above the terrain it overlooks. Views are available between contiguous interior spaces. Forward of the *tokonoma*, as of the fireplace, the ceiling rises, often into the roof's volume. Opposite in each case, under a low ceiling edge, is a broad horizontal expanse of transparent surface, which opens to an elevated terrace or veranda over which the heavy eaves loom. And there are other parallels between much of Japanese architecture and some less frequent characteristics of Wright's houses (which, therefore, I have not included within the pattern): the framing of white or near-white panels with dark, naturally finished wood trim, the subdued quality of the light; the absence of ornamentation deriving from historic, or at least western, precedent. But I have particularly used the word "parallels," not "sources," in dealing with this subject. In spite of a lot of work on the question over many years and by many scholars,[18] we still do not know, and may never know, just what of Japanese architecture was familiar to Wright through publications, drawings, or descriptions, when in 1902 the juxtaposition of the above characteristics appeared for the first time in his work.[19] Thus we simply cannot say whether Wright's affection for Japan was based in part on a sympathy for spatial configurations he found by happenstance to be analogous to his own, or whether his pattern was in part inspired from those Japanese configurations in some occasional or indirect way.

In any event, that pattern has no American precedent whatever, nor for that matter any precedent in the Western world. Nor is it found in the work of others during Wright's lifetime, not even among his colleagues and disciples including those of the Prairie School.[20] Therefore, it seems fair to say that as a totality, it is particular to Wright, and is either of his own devising or was, perhaps, in part a remarkable reinterpretation of Japanese precedent occasionally and distantly seen but profoundly comprehended.

Nowhere in his voluminous writings did Wright describe the pattern specifically. This is not especially surprising. Such things develop as often by intuition as by conscious intent, and even when they are as pervasive as this, they may remain in the realm of the designer's subconscious. There is no evidence that the pattern was

other than just such a subconscious predilection for Wright. He did on occasion touch on some elements of it: he wrote of his pleasure in seeing "the fire burning deep in the solid masonry of the house itself,"[21] and of a *"sense of shelter"*[22]—in italics—with the broad overhanging eaves no doubt in mind. He often referred to his work as the destruction of "the box,"[23] by which he meant the opening of vistas between rooms, and likewise to the outdoors by means of the broad horizontal expanses of window. And he noted the enrichment of prospect to be had from an elevated viewpoint, presumably something like the raised living spaces and terraces of these early houses: "And I saw that a little height on the prairie was enough to look like much more. Notice how every detail as to height becomes intensely significant. . . ."[24] But that is about all. Nor have historians on Wright mentioned the pattern in any specific way, though many describe something of its general character. A comment by Christian Norberg-Schulz is typical:

Traditionally the human dwelling had been a refuge for the individual and the family. Wright wanted rootedness *and* freedom, and thus he destroyed the traditional 'box' and created a new interaction between inside and outside. . . .[25]

And so he is led to conclude that Wright "opened up his plans to make them interact with the environment, at the same time as he created an inner world of protection and comfort."[26]

But if we are to ask why this duality of effect that the pattern provides should be of any humanistic importance—and that is a question worth asking—then another comment by Norberg-Schulz is more suggestive of a fruitful line of inquiry:

Figural architecture, then, does not consist of casual inventions, but of *typical* elements which may be repeated, combined and varied. We have already suggested that the typical elements are not just a matter of convention, but represent basic ways of being between earth and sky. They are given with the world. . . .[27]

Is this true of the repeated, combined, and varied elements of Wright's pattern? Can they be shown to represent "basic ways of being between earth and sky"; are they in some describable sense "given with the world"?

2. Complexity and Order, Prospect and Refuge

Whatever the words *human* and *nature* may mean, they have often been used in discussing Wright's architecture. I intend to use them too, but not in the customary way. By relating his architecture to things human I do not intend a vague romanticism. Nor in the use of the word "nature" do I suggest what biologist Nicholas Humphrey calls "naive naturalism,"[1] that is, I will not infer that parts of Wright's buildings resemble specific forms found in nature, nor emphasize that he wove plant materials into his architectural configurations.

I mean something broader but also more specific. I want to examine correspondences between Wright's pattern and the characteristics that we now believe human beings, preconditioned by nature, select in their habitations. To do this it is necessary to consider what particular characteristics human beings select—to examine if and how, in Norberg-Schulz's words, there are conditions of some sort that are "given with the world" as "basic ways of being between earth and sky."

Can any such conditions be identified? Do they exist? Not everyone will agree on this; one writer has recently put forward this view:

The establishment of society can be seen as the establishment of order through conventions, or more specifically, the establishment of a language through symbolic codes. Before order, before language, there exists a primal chaos where there are no rules for marrying, building, eating.[2]

But I would argue, and I think most biologists and anthropologists would agree, that this cannot be entirely true. Obviously in the lower animals, in the absence of language, there exist quite indispensable "rules" for "marrying, building, eating," to ensure survival. This is equally true of Homo sapiens, and with us, too, such rules functioned to ensure basic survival in those generations—who knows how many?—that preceded language.[3] Nor can it be maintained that our emotional makeup is dependent on either learning or language: "One does not learn to feel afraid or to cry any more than one learns to feel pain or to gasp for air. . . . Five emotions can be elicited at birth. . . . There is no evidence to suggest that feelings are necessarily preceded by a cognitive process."[4] Language clearly follows upon

such predetermined behaviors but does not precede them. For to argue that man in his earliest moments acquired, used, and linguistically transferred information about what to eat, how to procreate, and—more to our purpose—what to select as appropriate habitation, clearly is not credible. Such prelinguistic predilections, furthermore, "given with the world" and dependent upon genetic determination, persist quite independently of their survival value; they inform responses throughout the history of a species. This point is clearly expressed by Peter F. Smith: "We come into the world already equipped with an elaborate set of mental programmes which establish probabilities as to the way we shall react within given environmental situations."[5] In Homo sapiens the responses that are informed by such prelinguistic or nonlinguistic programs include some responses that we commonly think of as aesthetic in nature, responses that underlie the beauty we find in many art forms.

As recently as 1984 the distinguished art historian E. H. Gombrich endorsed the application of just such a point of view in dealing with some pervasive characteristics of the decorative arts: "My belief in a 'Sense of Order' . . . is based on an evolutionist view of the mind. I believe . . . that such a view has become inescapable since the days of Darwin."[6] Yet the idea that our sense of beauty might have a biological basis apparently even predates Darwin. Humphrey notes what he believes to be its origins:

Seventy years before Darwin published *The Origin of Species*, the Scottish philosopher Thomas Reid, in 1785, suggested how a modern biologist might proceed:
"By a careful examination of the objects which Nature hath given this amiable quality [of beauty], we may perhaps discover some real excellence in the object, or at least some valuable purpose that is served by the effect it produces upon us. This instinctive sense of beauty, in different species of animals, may differ as much as the external sense of taste, and in each species be adapted to its manner of life."[7]

And this same line of thought was pursued at eloquent length early in the twentieth century by John Dewey, especially in his *Art as Experience* of 1934:

The nature of experience is determined by the essential conditions of life. While man is other than bird and beast, he shares basic vital functions with them and has to make the same basal adjustments if he is to continue the process of living. Having the same vital needs, man derives the means by which he breathes, moves, looks and listens, the very brain with which he coordinates his senses and his movements, from his animal forebears. . . . Human beings . . . had needs that were a demand for the building and were carried to fulfillment in it; . . . the one who sets out to theorize about the esthetic experience embodied . . . must begin with it in the raw.[8]

That one can "theorize about the aesthetic experience" by beginning "in the raw" depends on and derives from an obvious fundamental principle of evolution implicit in the above paragraphs. Species, including our own, have survived by engaging in behaviors contributory and essential to survival. Eating appropriate foods, copulating and caring for offspring, and selecting appropriate habitation are all instances of this. But such activities are not undertaken as strategies consciously thought through for survival objectives. Rather, survival results through natural selection of species which find an intrinsic pleasure in a preponderance of activities with survival value. The English geographer Jay Appleton puts this point very well:

[The creature] enters the world "programmed," as it were, to seize the advantages offered by the environment while avoiding its disadvantages. . . . This pattern of actions is indispensable. They *must* be put into operation if the creature is to survive, and this means that there *must* be some mechanism which ensures that they are. That mechanism is what we call, for want of a better word, "pleasure." There are plenty of other words like "desire," "drive," or "libido" which one may find employed in the literature. In plain language we do all these things on which our survival depends *because we want to.* That is the force which impels us.[9]

Therefore, as a generality, it can be said that if one can identify unlearned behaviors with survival value, one can also reasonably postulate that such unlearned behaviors are based on equally unlearned, genetically determined pleasure stimuli.

In recent decades, increasing attempts have been made to identify characteristics that humans innately prefer in natural and manmade environments, and to understand these characteristics in terms of some biological basis derived from the above rationale. These attempts have been made in many fields: behavioral and environmental psychology, biology, philosophy of aesthetics, anthropology, geography, and perhaps others,

the different fields losing their distinctions in this context.[10] Presumably there are an indeterminate number of such innately preferred characteristics. Those that have engendered widest agreement to date are given different terms by different scholars; it seems to me they can be reasonably grouped under the headings *complexity and order, prospect and refuge, hazard,* and *mystery.* Of these, complexity and order constitute a mutually complementary pair, as do prospect and refuge, and these two pairs of characteristics are the ones I want to introduce in this chapter; hazard and mystery can be more easily dealt with separately at a later point.

There is now considerable empirical evidence to corroborate the long-standing belief that aesthetic experiences, including those of preferred environments, seem to exhibit some combination of "diversity, structural complexity, novelty, incongruity, or surprisingness,"[11] in conjunction with some perceived order or resolution. Appleton says that "there seems to be a dichotomy [in preferred environments], which I think is found in all the arts, between, on the one side, order, regularity, simplicity and harmony, and, on the other, disorder, irregularity, complexity and discord."[12] Peter F. Smith puts the same point crisply: "It is now widely accepted that the basis of aesthetic experience stems from the interaction between chance and order, complexity and redundancy."[13] The point is easily illustrated in music or poetry, and also in architecture. Many explanations have been offered for the Parthenon's appeal; the complexity-and-order approach works as well as any, and perhaps better than most. Like all Greek temples, the Parthenon has an obvious and pervasive order; yet it is the only Doric temple to bring into play the complexity of all the so-called "refinements"—double contraction, curvature of both stylobate and entablature, entasis, enlargement of corner column diameters, and inward inclination of all four façades—whose presence, I think most would agree, is essential to the appeal we find in it. One could equally well illustrate the point with the Gothic cathedral, whose form was contrived, if analogies to scholasticism have any validity, especially to cohere a rich complexity within a pervasive order.

What biological argument can explain the appeal of this conjunction? One of the earlier ones of which I am aware is John R. Platt's article of 1961 entitled "Beauty: Pattern and Change";[14] a more recent and particularly lucid discussion is found in an essay of 1980 entitled "Natural Aesthetics," by Nicholas Humphrey.[15]

Humphrey's rationale uses rhyme as a starting point. Rhyme, Humphrey says, can be described as "likeness tempered with difference";[16] *Jill*, in rhyming with *hill*, is like hill in some ways, different in others. This, Humphrey argues, is exactly what we like about rhymes, and at a more sophisticated level is why, in part, we enjoy poetry as an aesthetic experience. Humphrey notes that music, in its repetition and variation of melodic themes, can be analyzed in a similar way as a structure of likenesses and differences, as can many other aesthetic experiences. He further argues that our predilection for this "likeness tempered with difference" has a biological basis; there is a survival value, indeed an imperative, in the ability to discern categories of things on the one hand, and differences within them on the other. Animals (including the human animal) must be able to recognize their own species to survive, but within their own species must be able to recognize mother, brother, male, female, friend, and enemy. Species success also depends on an ability to recognize a general group of environments capable of sustaining life needs; within this large group it is helpful to distinguish between those that can sustain such needs especially well and those whose sustaining potential is weak. At a more specific level, one must be able to distinguish from the general type of habitation one's own personal habitat and the habitats of a number of other known individuals of one's species. Humphrey argues that given the pleasure basis of survival behaviors we, as a surviving species, derive a built-in delight in such categorizing and differentiating. He extends this notion to explain, among other human oddities, the collector, who finds pleasure in accumulating endless variations of a particular stimulus type, and can be shown to do so just for the sake of the variations and the commonalities.[17]

From this, it is a short step to an explanation of the familiar observation that experiences or artifacts consistently ranked very high in aesthetic value usually exhibit high levels of both complexity and order. The complexity engages our search for variations of stimuli; the order reassures us that these stimuli share a commonality; and we find in the juxtaposition an enduring aesthetic delight, whether in poetry, music, or architecture. Architectural examples such as the Parthenon or Chartres are usually considered "high art." But vernacular or popular examples that are used most often to demonstrate aesthetic value can also be shown to possess a large measure of the same duality of characteristics.

Thus complexity and order, found in or designed into our surroundings, allow us to act as collectors of a large variety of phenomena which are also perceived as cohering. As we both order our collection and distinguish within it, we satisfy instincts that, from the beginning of our species, have been pleasurable. The reader familiar with Wright's work will already have seen correlations that deserve some examination.

Another body of thought in a cognate design field has an even more central relation to Wright's work. I have already cited two comments on complexity and order by the English geographer Jay Appleton, but the focus of his attention has been directed toward a different issue. While complexity and order are common to many of the arts, Appleton's main theoretical thrust has been toward a matter pertinent only to the spatial arts and their surrogates. There, however, he finds it to be of considerable, even essential value:

If I looked at a park laid out by Capability Brown and compared it with one of the great set-pieces of Andre le Notre or one of his followers, or with the near-wilderness exploration-grounds of the Picturesque, it became clear that the basic dichotomy between order and regularity on the one hand and disorder and irregularity on the other was of immense importance, but equally that this dichotomy could not alone explain my preferences.[18]

Thus, in 1975, in a book entitled *The Experience of Landscape*, Appleton outlined what he has called prospect-refuge theory.[19] In developing his position Appleton has drawn on various sources including the writings of John Dewey mentioned above. As the title of his book indicates, Appleton began with landscape as a vehicle for analysis; to that end he has explored a vast resource of landscape design, landscape painting, and landscape literature. He argues that these evidences of pleasurable response to landscape conditions consistently illustrate certain repetitive characteristics. These repetitive characteristics he calls *prospect*, by which he means a place with unimpeded opportunity to see; and *refuge*, by which he means a place of concealment. These are mutually complementary, and can be summed up as the dual characteristics in the phrase "to see without being seen." The essential conditions are that the setting must suggest and provide a refuge in which the occupant cannot easily be seen; that from the refuge the occupant must be able to identify and move to a prospect setting; and that the prospect setting must suggest and provide an unimpeded outlook over a considerable distance. Though Appleton did not at the time try to develop empirical verification for this theory, others have since done so.[20]

Appleton also offers a biological rationale, for he points out that as with complexity and order, the selection of juxtaposed conditions of prospect and refuge confers a vital advantage in species survival. Species, Homo sapiens included, that intuitively choose settings which allow seeing without being seen are thereby enabled to hunt successfully without being successfully hunted, and so survive and flourish. But, again, the intuitive pleasure motive that drives such a choice must logically precede any grasp of its functional value. The choosing of such settings, then, must be driven by an intuitive, immediate pleasure that is felt in the command of prospect and the containment of refuge. Such a pleasure, genetic to our species, is therefore independent of the functional utility of the setting and persists quite independently of our need to call on that utility.[21]

Since this pleasure in prospect and refuge settings is a continuing part of our genetic heritage, Appleton is able to draw on recent poetry, literature, and painting to illustrate such settings. Examples of prospect in poetry or painting are often broad meadows or great sweeps of water, invariably relatively brightly lit. In one exquisite poem cited by Appleton, Sidney Lanier's "The Marshes of Glynn," the poet is drawn to "the edge of the wood" where prospect appears as "the vast sweet visage of space," the "world of marsh that borders a world of sea."[22] But prospect may also be found in views across uneven terrain, whose hills may suggest other powerful prospect-claiming viewpoints. Seen from such elevations, prospects become especially strong, as view is extended to a more distant horizon and the viewer perceives the prospect from a dominant position. Thus prospect is intensified not only by sweep of view but by elevated vantage point. Manmade features, towers especially, may also symbolize prospect by offering a dominant position and extended view. Towers on hills thus offer two mutually reinforcing prospect symbols; Appleton calls such mutual reinforcement by like symbols the condition of *reduplication*.

As the complement of prospect, the refuge concept is of paramount importance, "one of the most fundamental in the symbolism of environmental perception. It finds extreme expression in the search for the nesting-place. If safety can't be secured, and if in consequence, the individual organism ceases to function biologically,

then all other desires become, for that individual, biologically irrelevant."[23] In Lanier's poem, refuge is the deep wood that precedes the "visage of space," the wood of "Beautiful glooms, soft dusks in the noon-day fire,—/ Wildwood privacies, closets of lone desire, / Chamber from chamber parted with wavering arras of leaves—." Such refuge conditions—Lanier's shadowy grove, or pocketed, contained spaces such as ravines, or in the extreme case caves, all of these always in relatively subdued light—such conditions hold an extraordinary power in conveying the possibility for hiding and, therefore, for safety.

Though Appleton does not cite it, one of the tidiest literary descriptions of the joining of prospect and refuge conditions is found in Charles Dickens's *Bleak House*. Like Lanier, Dickens establishes his setting near the edge of a wood, one of the most prevalent of natural prospect-refuge conjunctions:

We had one favourite spot, deep in moss and last year's leaves, where there were some felled trees from which the bark was all stripped off. Seated among these, we looked through a green vista supported by thousands of natural columns, the whitened stems of trees, upon a distant prospect made so radiant by its contrast with the shade in which we sat, and made so precious by the arched perspective through which we saw it, that it was like a glimpse of the better land.[24]

All the elements are here: the sheltering grove, with its subdued light and its screen of "columns," all keeping the viewer unseen; the "arched perspective" through which is seen the contrasting open and brightly lit expanse beyond, for which Dickens even uses the term "prospect"—and the intensely pleasurable human response to it all, "like a glimpse of the better land."

In the next paragraph of this narrative, however, we are introduced to a firmer refuge, and one which brings into the argument an architectural example:

. . . the storm broke so suddenly—upon us, at least, in that sheltered spot—that before we reached the outskirts of the wood, the thunder and lightning were frequent, and the rain came plunging through the leaves, as if every drop were a great leaden bead. . . . As it was not a time for standing among trees, we ran out of the wood. . . . and made for a keeper's lodge which was close at hand. We had often noticed the dark beauty of this lodge standing in a deep twilight of trees, and how the ivy clustered over it, and how there was a steep hollow near, where we had once seen the keeper's dog dive down into the fern.

Thus this lodge offers a haven against heat and cold, sun and, in this case, storm. In so doing it takes us back to primordial purposes, for architecture, and particularly the dwelling, has its very beginnings in refuge, was invented most fundamentally for that purpose. It also serves to protect the inhabitant's privacy, and his possessions including food stores. Such is the essential function of the dwelling.

But the lodge in this narrative not only shelters Dickens's heroes. It appears to them as a symbol of its ability to do so long before their practical need of it; "standing in a deep twilight of trees," its symbolism reduplicated by the "steep hollow near," it is a thing of "dark beauty" to them. So we can make a distinction between practical utility and symbolic or aesthetic value—for as an aesthetic experience, "what matters is not the *actual* potential of the environment, to furnish the necessities for survival, but its *apparent* potential as apprehended immediately rather than calculated rationally."[25]

The building by its very existence conveys a signal of its refuge potential, thus is more or less automatically not only refuge-provision but also refuge-symbol; Appleton mentions buildings as universally carrying this symbolism. But as a totality, a building can present additional clues that enrich its capacity to be read as refuge. Appleton notes particular features that serve as refuge-clues: "windows, alcoves, recesses, balconies, heavy overhanging eaves, all these suggest a facility of penetration into the refuge. Even if actual access is not practicable the suggestion of accessibility can stimulate the idea of refuge."[26] As a building presents these and perhaps other refuge-clues, it not only provides refuge but conveys in enriched terms its pleasure-arousing potential for doing so. And refuge-clues are not limited to the exterior. Spaces within the building that impart a strong feeling of containment contribute to a sense of refuge. Windowless corners, spaces closed on three sides, spaces of small dimension with low ceilings and prevalent solid walls, declare themselves as protective pockets of retreat. Halls and stairways, especially when narrow and low, bring wall and ceiling surfaces close to the body and so suggest protection and enclosure.

And yet the building, like its predecessors the grove and the cave, is not refuge alone. Almost always, in one way and another, it will offer some suggestion of prospect as well—will be not only a haven, but one from which one can survey the surrounding terrain. Pros-

pect from within a building must be obtained by some kind of opening. Here, too, the functional provision operates automatically as symbol or clue; a window unavoidably announces the potential of prospect from within. But this bald clue also can be enriched, thereby enlarging its aesthetic value. Some means for doing so are those already mentioned for cluing penetrability into refuge: balconies or terraces outside windows are immediately understood as prospect-providing platforms; heavy overhanging eaves suggest leading the eye to view, pointing the way outward to horizon; windows of unusual width or occurring in groups signal the availability of panoramic prospect across a broad arc of terrain.

And just as refuge can be a characteristic of not only the house as a whole but also its interior parts, so too with prospect. The opening of one room to another provides an interior prospect; it is clarified, signaled, and enriched when there is some marking of the distinction between the spaces, a reminder that one is looking not just across one space but from one space into and perhaps through another. Vistas through hallways opening to more distant windowed spaces can also provide related conditions of interior prospect.

Thus, when a house combines strong refuge signals, inside and out, with strong prospect signals, inside and out, it may be argued that it provides conditions that human beings are preconditioned by nature to select as pleasurable in their habitations. It is in this sense that the words *human* and *nature* can have more than romanticist value.

One can find examples of these conditions in houses throughout history. The Mycenaean megaron comes to mind: its cella, windowless on three walls and with central hearth, provides an internal refuge-space from which one sees through the column screen the more brightly lit porch which in turn opens toward the courtyard and, in the distance, the prospect of the Argive plain. The Hall of Mirrors at Versailles is a famous and extreme example of a prospect-claiming room, while the bedrooms of this same building, as refuge spaces, typically contain the bed within a windowless low alcove. The Elizabethan country house with its projecting glazed bays suggests rich panoramic prospect from within, while the terraces of later English houses, Harewood for example, are dramatic external prospect-claiming features.

The Alhambra offers an extraordinarily clear example of the juxtaposition of prospect and refuge in its well-known and well-loved Court of the Lions (fig. 2.1). From the deeply shadowed, surrounding arcades whose columns can be understood as the tree trunks of Dickens's narrative, and whose spandrels above invoke the leafy bowers of a glade, one looks out to the contained meadow where—and here the example is almost too literal—the animals are gathered around the water source. One looks from the dark concealing refuge to the brightly lit hunting ground, seeing without being seen. Behind is the even more secure refuge of the darker interior recesses under the *muqarnas* glades. The Alhambra is an especially interesting example because, from a certain point of view, it is a building with un-usually specific meaning: it incorporates symbols and messages exclusively pertinent to Islam and the history of Islam. And yet—and this is the intriguing point—at another level, its appeal can be felt without knowing anything at all about its culturally specific meaning. For as an eloquent example of prospect-and-refuge juxta-position, its beauty is not a matter of acculturation or cognitive reasoning but rather of universal and immedi-ate emotional response. In this sense its appeal is not to Moslem but to Homo sapiens.

All this, of course, assumes that characteristics of value in landscape analysis can have archi-tectural analogies. This assumption perhaps cannot be proved—indeed, as Appleton points out, his arguments can hardly be proved in the usual sense, even in the case of landscape. But the idea of an archi-tectural analogy is, on the face of it, a hypothesis worth pursuing. Surely if it is to be tried, the house is the building type with which to begin, since selection of prospect and refuge conditions is, after all, selection of habitat, and that is what houses are. And surely among houses, those of Frank Lloyd Wright are the ideal start-ing point. For as Walter Creese has recently observed, "among American architects of any time, Frank Lloyd Wright was the most committed to architecture as it ap-plied to nature and the landscape."[27] Thomas Beeby echoes this: "It is commonly held that the buildings of Frank Lloyd Wright fuse with their specific sites and demonstrate an organic link with the forces of nature. Wright himself suggests that the forms of the landscape are mysteriously related to the configuration of his buildings."[28] It may be possible to make the relation

ship less mysterious. For in Wright's houses, the fea-tures that signal and provide refuge and prospect are consistently deployed with richness and emphasis. Fur-thermore while the megaron, Versailles, Harewood, and the Alhambra include a few such features, Wright's work, even at an early date, included a unique profu-sion of them, usually reduplicated and at several hier-archical levels, and this proved to be true of his entire career.

2.1 The Alhambra, Granada, Spain, 14th–15th century. The Court of Lions, showing the refuge of the shadowed grove, with the prospect of the bright meadow beyond, and the animals gathered around the water source.

That Wright was intuitively especially attuned to prospect and refuge juxtapositions is suggested by one of his early works, the Romeo and Juliet windmill done in 1897[29] on the hilltop above what later became his home, Taliesin, near his birthplace in central Wisconsin (fig. 2.2). Its hilltop location, natural enough for a windmill, carries with it the potential for dramatic prospect. It is also an instance of reduplication, since both hilltop and tower suggest and offer the prospect condition. All this is, so far, more or less unavoidable and therefore unremarkable. But the way in which Wright seized the prospect potential and at the same time provided refuge clues and opportunity takes this structure entirely out of the usual family of windmills. Appleton maintains that the "sense of exposure is dominant in the windmill, invariably a prospect symbol because it is functionally required to reach upwards into the moving air. . . . The refuge aspect, though present, is suppressed."[30] But this is not the case at Romeo and Juliet. As its eminence declares its prospect role, so the deep roof near the top, sheltering a dark void, signals refuge. Thus, in addition to its windmill function, Romeo and Juliet is a climbable and habitable tower, at the top of which is the belvedere,[31] within which the human observer, obscured within the shadows of the deeply eaved roof, looks outward from the magnificent prospect-enhancing elevation, seeing without being seen.[32] Thus Romeo and Juliet provides actual conditions of both prospect and refuge and also provides strong architectural signals of its ability to do so. This dual symbolic and operational provision would seem to overshadow entirely its windmill function.

But whatever Wright's emphasis on it, this structure was a minor opus in his career. It serves only as an introduction to the characteristics that underlie his architecture, and it reveals them in ways that are simplistic by comparison with what was to come. To develop the issues of complexity and order, prospect and refuge, in a more substantial way we have to begin again with Wright's pattern, and with the building that first embodies it, the Heurtley house.

2.2 The Romeo and Juliet windmill, near Spring Green, Wisconsin, 1897.

3. The Prairie Houses

The houses Wright designed in the Oak Park years, and especially those done between 1901 and his departure for Europe in 1909, have long been known as the Prairie houses; the term can be debated, but it has found its way into common usage. The *Ladies' Home Journal* schemes, the Hickox and Bradley houses, and especially the Willits house have each been put forward at one time or another as the first example of the type.[1] But the configuration I have called Wright's pattern, which is vital to all his Prairie houses after Willits and in fact to all Wright's subsequent houses throughout his career, first appears in its entirety at the Heurtley house. Therefore there is good reason for taking it as the first fully mature Prairie house; it is also the obvious starting point for probing the value of the pattern.

As seen from the sidewalk the Heurtley house presents clear signals of refuge (fig. 1.10). The dual bands of windows, the deep overhanging roof, and the "balconies," that is, the terrace at upper right, the loggia at lower center, and the porch with its promontory, all clearly and strongly modeled features, are ideal instances of the those suggested by Appleton as stimulating the idea of refuge. And so is the arched entry; carrying an unavoidable suggestion of a cave mouth, its refuge inference is reduplicated by the protective masonry porch and the screening plantings in the urns at the porch corners. Yet several of these features also signal prospect. The "balconies," the horizontally prolonged window bands, even the prowlike modeling of the generous elevated porch, all clearly convey the availability of a multitude of panoramic outlooks.

One enters the Heurtley house by moving toward the rear of the lot, turning sharply right and ascending the porch with its planted urns (figs. 1.9A, 1.10, 3.1). One then turns to the left to pass through the cave-mouth entry into the protective masonry mass of the house, then up the twisting ascent of the stair to the major spaces of the upper floor, having negotiated from the sidewalk ten right-angle turnings, a 9-foot change of vertical elevation, and a considerable horizontal distance. And here it may be worth noting that at least two of the turnings and 25 feet or so of horizontal distance could easily have been avoided had Wright chosen to do so, for the entry walk could have led straight to the front door, as it had at the earlier Winslow, Williams, and Thomas houses, as well as Wright's own Oak Park house. Thus, the entry to the Heurtley house is not only long and complex, it is deliberately so. Such an entry experience is analogous to the entries of the earliest known special human habitations, for the prehistoric caves of Spain and France have just such lengthy and circuitous routes to set their special chambers at a distance from the outer world of hunter and hunted.

Having pursued this elaborate path to the special place, one arrives at the massive fireplace with its flanking built-in seating (figs. 3.1, 1.11). It is tempting to continue to use the cave analogy to describe this fireplace zone, and there is strong precedent for doing so. Vincent Scully, among others, has especially reiterated it: "The Heurtley house is an earth-pressing mass and a dark cave, with a deep, low entrance whose arch is echoed by that of the central fireplace within. The interior space is a cave."[2] Thomas Beeby makes some related observations with reference not only to the Heurtley house but to the Prairie house generally:

> The dim light of the interior also suggests the perpetual twilight of the underworld or that of a shallow cave. The entire arrangement heightens this sense, for the continuous flow of space is detailed to accentuate the horizontality of the surfaces, evoking the stratification of the rock walls of a cave formed by erosion. The continuity of finish between wall and ceiling approaches the monolithic material distribution familiar in caves. This illusion is further heightened by the rising slope of the ceiling planes toward the center of the rooms. The overall impression is that of the sheltering confines of the prenatal condition of the womb that is symbolized by the void of a cave.[3]

Such a term, and such a space, are of themselves powerfully suggestive of refuge: "Caves, chasms, ravines, in short any orifices which allow a creature to enter physically into the fabric of the earth, are obviously potent refuge symbols . . . the cave is the most complete general purpose sanctuary provided by nature."[4] But the word "cave" can suggest not only a refuge but also a cold, damp, and even terrifying setting. What is essential to overcome these associations and make the cave amenable to human refuge is the potential for light and warmth, for which an indication of some provision for fire is an obvious means.

Obvious, yet not so obvious. Heretofore we have been discussing responses which, so the argument has gone, are intuitive, genetically programmed into our being; we do not learn them, nor is rational reflection involved when those responses come into play. But is the choosing of a space with the potential for a fire also intuitive? That is harder to show. But in Wright's houses the potential for fire is invariably indicated by a fireplace, as at the Heurtley house—and here, in terms of the intuitive and the learned, the issue is clear. An understanding that the typical western fireplace is actually a place for a fire certainly must be learned—surely only a person who knows western architectural conventions could interpret it for what it is. Nevertheless, within western tradition, there is equally no doubt that the meaning of the form is learned by virtually everyone, and at a very early age. It is likely, therefore, that in the western world the fireplace is pervasively understood, on an all but intuitive level, as a valued complement to the refuge, of which the cave or its architectural surrogate is an example. Probably largely for this reason fireplaces have a widespread popularity, not only in Wright's work, where they are universal, but in western dwellings generally, long after the loss of their practical value as an essential heat source.

What distinguishes Wright's work in this regard is the unusually emphatic declaration of the potential for fire. For just as the cave inference at the Heurtley house is strongly declared both inside and out, so the potential for fire is also strongly declared, on the exterior by the overscaled dominant chimney, on the interior by the strong modeling and generous dimensions given to the fireplace. It is also strengthened by reduplication, since it is held within a containing pocket of space, withdrawn to the low zone of the ceiling and with the half-inglenook seating alongside (figs. 1.9B, 1.11). The fireplace and its setting thus mutually reinforce the refuge condition. "An inglenook creates the image of a special warm enclave, for its function is intuitively clear: with seats built in along the walls, it is just large enough for a few people to gather close to the fire's radiant warmth."[5] This area, treated in this way, thus becomes at small scale an *interior refuge* zone, contrasting with the remainder of the room of which it is a part.

Forward of the fireplace the ceiling rises into the volume of the roof (fig. 1.11). This is the key to Wright's modeling of spaces as juxtapositions of low and high volumes: by making the major spaces contiguous with the roof at the Heurtley house, he changed the ceiling planes in a really significant way. And this in turn gave

him a spatial device of considerable value. Our perception of degree of spatial enclosure is affected more by the proximity of the ceiling plane than by any other characteristic: bringing it down generates a sense of containment; moving it up generates a sense of release, and it is more effective for either purpose than like movements of wall planes.[6] Thus, at the Heurtley house, the low ceiling edges contain, the high center releases, and the effect is gained by the most powerful means for doing so; the refuge of the low, contained fireplace zone is powerfully complemented by the open field of space forward of it. In spite of Wright's emphasis on the importance of the horizontal, he perceived the value of this vertical spatial manipulation, so much so that it became a nearly universal feature of his work.

In the Heurtley house, as in Wright's houses from 1900 onward, the living room is opened to contiguous spaces, in this case the dining room and the entry hall (fig. 1.9B). This kind of arrangement is generally called an open plan, and Wright, it is generally agreed, originated it. In so doing he invented an important means for the manipulation of prospect and refuge. Appleton notes: "If the eye makes a spontaneous assessment of the environment as a strategic theatre for survival, this must include some assessment of the opportunity for movement between the various key positions in the prospect-refuge complex."[7] Wright's open plan is the essential device—and a device unavailable to prior domestic architecture—that makes possible the offering of such an assessment within a residential interior of modest size. But in his work, with the Heurtley house as a good early example, the open plan is not just a larger unarticulated space. To the north, the edge of the living room is marked out by four columnar elements (figs.1.9B, 1.11). Through three of the resultant intervening spaces, views are available into the dining room; the remaining two spaces open into the entry hall. These columnar elements and the views they frame between them bear noting. They make the interior experience analogous to that of looking past the trees at the edge of the forest to view the meadow or the grove beyond. For in looking from the stairhead toward the living room, or from living to dining room, one does not just look across different zones of a single space, but rather from one demarcated space into another, the columnar elements establishing the boundary through which vista is seen. I would like to call this condition, and permutations of it, *interior prospect*.[8] It provides yet another powerful complement to the containing characteristics, the interior refuge, of the fireplace zone.

3.1 Heurtley house. Diagrammatic drawing by William Hook.

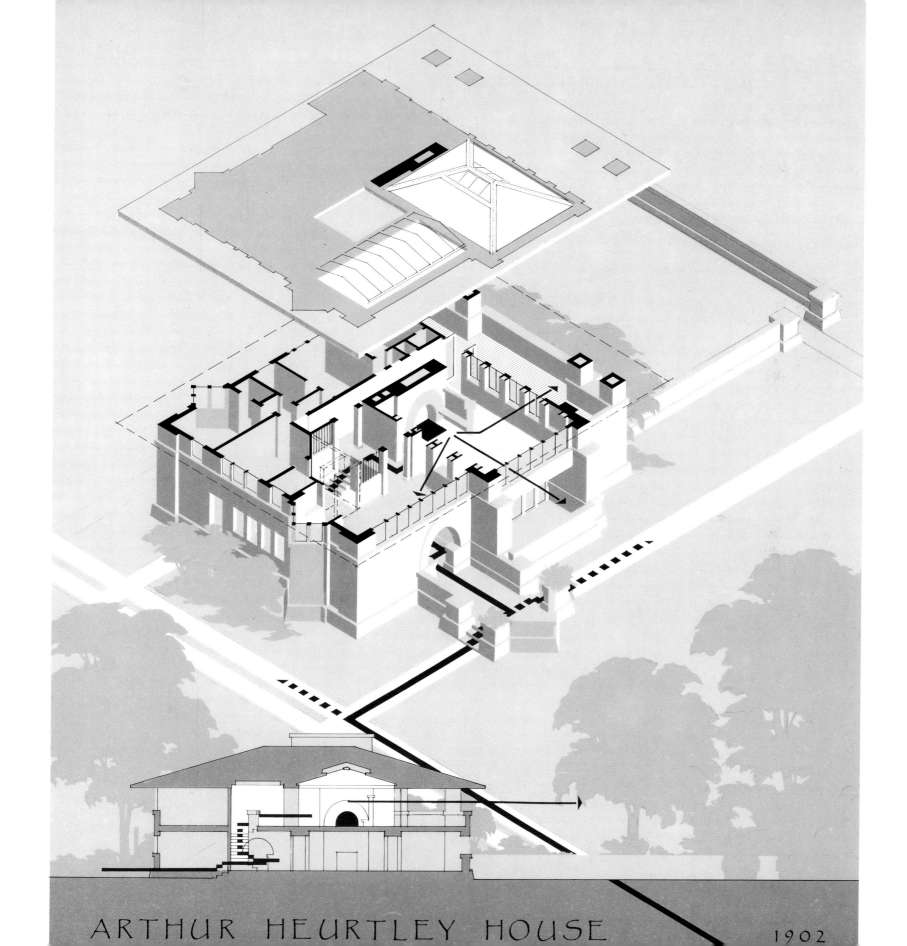

ARTHUR HEURTLEY HOUSE   1902

At all edges of each of the spaces, the ceiling returns to a low elevation, which is emphasized by a continuous band of dark trim. These continuous low edges reassert the idea of the totality of the house as a refuge. At this level of interpretation, the bands of windows and the french doors are a release to the larger external prospéct. In this release, the terrace south of the living room has a dual role. Terraces in Wright's work are typically generous; thus they symbolize prospects in themselves, understood from the interior as external architectural meadows open to light and air. At the same time, they are viewing platforms for the landscape prospect beyond. From just such a platform, the inhabitant of the Heurtley house, seeing without being seen, commands the vast midwestern prairie—or, more realistically, as much of it as can be symbolized by the suburban lawns and trees of Oak Park. It is the Romeo and Juliet condition carried to an infinitely richer state.

And here, of course, is another advantage Wright gained in putting the major spaces, including the terrace, directly under the roof, for they are thereby elevated above the level of the prairie's surrogate, the Oak Park lawns. Wright often expressed a fondness for being close to the plane of the earth, and in many of his houses before Heurtley, the main floor really is: this is true of the Winslow house, the two *Ladies' Home Journal* schemes, the Hickox and Bradley houses, and to a lesser degree the Willits house. But it is the exception after Heurtley. Typically thereafter, either the main floor is in some way elevated within the house (as at Heurtley), or the house itself is placed on elevated ground, so that the view outward is toward a landscape well below floor level.[9] Such an elevated platform implies a considerable and intuitively understood strategic advantage, since one looks down upon the surrounding terrain and anything that inhabits it. Elevation also offers an enrichment of prospect value, since it increases the distance to the horizon and thereby the depth of view. Grant Manson has put the point beautifully, specifically with regard to the Heurtley house: "The occupants look out over the landscape with that sense, so agreeable in a flat country, of having a vantage point."[10] Appleton agrees: he says of landscape conditions that "elevation of the viewpoint also enhances its prospect value."[11] But Wright himself hinted at much the same point: "I saw that a little height on the Prairie was enough to look like much more. Notice how every detail as to height becomes intensely significant."[12]

The Edwin Cheney house of 1903–1904, also in Oak Park, offers to the street prospect and refuge clues similar to those of the Heurtley house: the deep eaves, the glass, and the "balcony," the terrace with its flanking walls, which in its own way proclaims both prospect and refuge, and which, as we will see, is an essential element for both (fig. 3.2).

At the Cheney house, however, there is no indication whatever of the location of the front door, the first instance of an extraordinary downplaying that marked Wright's houses from this date onward. Previously he often had done a splendid job of giving architectural presence to the front door; even at the Heurtley house this is true.[13] At the Cheney house, the glass and the overhangs may suggest penetrability, but the house protects its actual access through ambiguity (the dual walkways), masking (the screening of view to the door from the street), and convolution. Turning 90 degrees off the sidewalk and taking the proper right-hand walkway, one ascends five steps (figs. 3.2–3.4). Ahead is a walk of perhaps 30 feet, heading straight to the back yard, then a right angle turn to the left, up three steps, a walk of 12 feet or so, but still not directly toward the door, then up two more steps and under the eave.

3.2 Edwin Cheney house, Oak Park, 1903–1904. Perspective from the street; the entry walk is at the far right.

Another right-angle turn and another, and the door—
an unassuming door—is reached. The approach has
entailed perhaps 75 feet of walking, eleven risers, and
360 degrees of turning. Having traversed this long
sequence one arrives, again, at the very heart and
core of the house (fig. 3.4). The secure haven has been
penetrated to its very center by circuitous processes of
transition navigable, or so it seems, only by the initi-
ated, and no threat will ever find the way.[14] As in the
Heurtley house, the Cheney house entrance has analogies to the entry sequences of prehistoric caves, in
which the ornamented ceremonial chamber was also
reached by long convoluted passageways that ensured
and dramatized the privacy and remoteness of the
special place.

One reaches this special place to discover its fireplace, representing warmth and light, ahead on the
right (fig. 3.4). Withdrawn behind the edges of the adjacent dining room and library, it lies under a low flat
ceiling of considerable extent (figs. 3.4–3.5). To right
and left, this zone is flanked by book-lined walls
(though there are small "windows" to the hall); these
walls and the extensive low ceiling define an interior
refuge more firmly contained and therefore stronger
than at Heurtley.

The ceiling planes of the living room forward of the
fireplace refuge again echo those of the roof above. But
unlike Heurtley, these ceiling planes continue uninterrupted to right and left into dining room and library,
uniting the three spaces and inviting the eye into them,
enriching the reading of an interior prospect condition
between them (fig. 3.6). Vertical and horizontal articulating elements again appear, and their role, already
noted at the Heurtley house, is important. They serve
as reminders that one is not simply in an oversized
space, but looks from one defined space toward another. At the edges of the ceiling, and especially in the
zone of the french doors leading out from the living
room, the height returns to that of the fireplace refuge
and, like the fireplace refuge, includes an area of flat
ceiling (fig. 3.7). The continuous low edge is again emphasized by heavy trim. Thus, within the house itself,
as at the Heurtley house, there is a microcosm of the
refuge-prospect sequence, while in a larger sense the
whole interior, with its emphatic low edges all around,
is declared as a refuge.

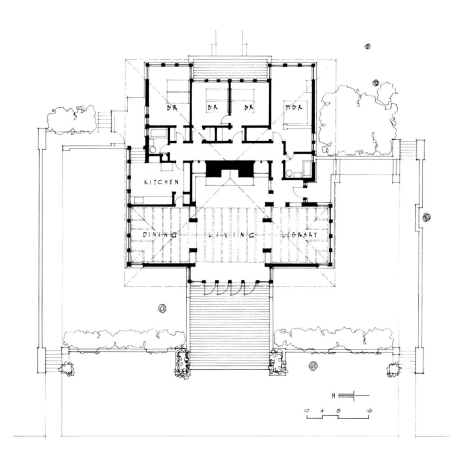

3.3 Cheney house. Plan.

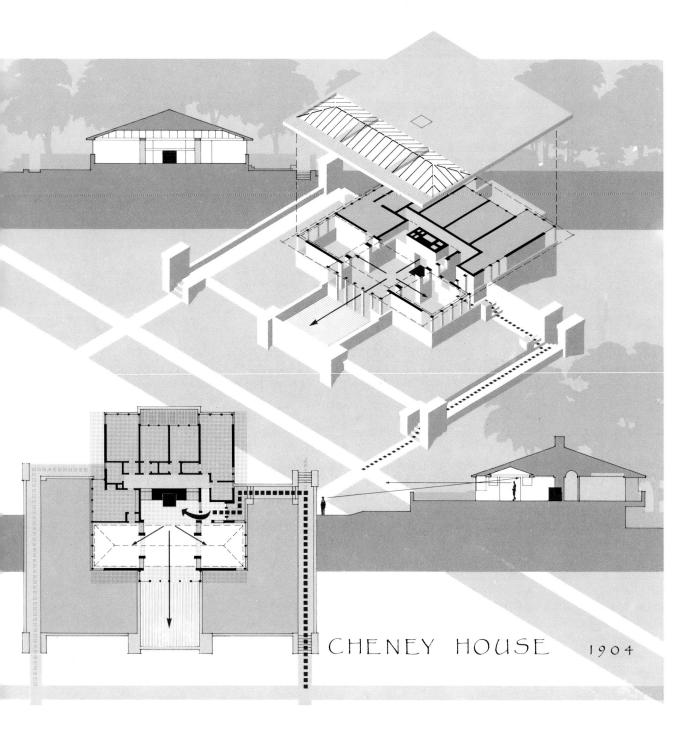

CHENEY HOUSE 1904

3.4 Cheney house. Diagrammatic drawing by William Hook.

3.5 Cheney house. Interior refuge: the living room fireplace area. The fireplace is deeply recessed under the low ceiling and is pocketed by book-lined walls to either side. The entry is at right.

3.6 Cheney house. Interior prospect: vista from the living room to the library. The entry and fireplace are to the left, the terrace is to the right. The ceiling continues uninterrupted through the entire forward part of the house, while the intervening vertical and horizontal elements clarify the spatial subdivisions. Behind the camera a similar vista opens to the dining room.

3.7 Cheney house. Living room from the fireplace toward the terrace. The terrace is reached through the leaded french doors under the lowered ceiling edge.

3.8 Cheney house. View north from the terrace.

The sense of the entire house as a refuge is reinforced by the leaded and stained windows, used here and in most of Wright's houses of the Prairie period. Plain unornamented glass, when seen from the exterior in typical daylight conditions, is opaque; therefore the occupant within the building cannot be seen from outside.[15] Nevertheless, one feels exposed behind a wall of glass, no matter what the intellect says is the case. Hence the importance of the leaded and stained glass of the Cheney house, and the other Prairie houses that precede and follow: it conveys immediately and without cognitive intervention the sense that one is hidden from view. Thus it converts the screening characteristic of the glass from a phenomenon understood through reasoned cognition, over time, to a phenomenon grasped intuitively and immediately. One senses that one is hidden in the dark recesses behind the foliage and the branches of a grove.

If the house as a totality is to be understood as refuge, the french doors opposite the fire open out to an undeniable prospect condition, that of the elevated exterior terrace as an architectural meadow (figs. 3.4, 3.8). Here, too, there is a development beyond that of the Heurtley condition. At Heurtley the terrace is entirely covered by the great roof whose eaves project well beyond; at Cheney the roof, a concise square, overhangs the french doors only slightly. As one moves out onto the terrace, therefore, the prospect is expanded not only laterally but vertically. And this also yields a contrast in light quality not available at Heurtley: as one moves from the Cheney living room out onto the terrace one moves from dark to light. Darkness, as Appleton notes,[16] is associated with not being seen and therefore with refuge, while light is associated with seeing and therefore with prospect. Thus this manipulation of the roof not only releases sky views as one moves forward onto the terrace; it also intensifies the contrast in light quality between the darker interior refuge and this more brilliant exterior prospect. Here, too, Wright had an intuitive sensitivity to the value of this condition; hereafter his terraces typically will be partly roofed, partly open to the sky.

It also bears noting that this terrace is not directly analogous to the typical American front porch. This observation holds true for the Heurtley terrace and those of many of Wright's previous houses as well. But at the Cheney house the difference is less obvious, and therefore more in need of discussion, since at Cheney the terrace occupies a location, in relation to both house and site, that is clearly similar to that of the typical

porch. The difference, and it is an important one, is that the terrace is in no way a part of the entry sequence; its surface is in fact withheld from view until the completion of a long path of penetration through the very heart of the house. Thus the terrace, as an architectural surrogate of the meadow, is not entirely like its natural prototype. It, like the rest of the house, is removed, bounded, and protected, clearly but subtly set apart from the world of the chase; it is a symbol of that world, yet is itself safe and secure. This lengthy separation of the terrace from the entry path will be found in all of Wright's subsequent major houses.[17]

Having pushed the major spaces up under the roof at the Heurtley house, Wright brought the pattern closer to the earth at the Cheney house. The house has a basement, but it is recessed in the earth, visible only at the back. The main floor is established at about five feet above sidewalk grade; in spite of its low, earth-hugging appearance, the main spaces of the Cheney house are substantially elevated above the surrounding terrain to garner the prospect enhancement that that condition provides. But since the Cheney house is nearer to the sidewalk than either the Willits or Heurtley houses, and since, like them, its street-facing wall is largely glass, Wright here had to solve a problem of privacy. By bringing the terrace wall out toward the sidewalk, and by locating the coping of its solid brick parapet over seven feet above sidewalk level,[18] Wright controlled the sight line from the near sidewalk so that it intercepts the lower edge of the leaded glass in the french doors to the terrace (fig. 3.9). This brick parapet wall originally extended across the entire lot (see fig. 3.2), ensuring privacy to the whole house and from diagonal as well as frontal views. This was essential, of course, to the development of refuge within a small, low house near a city street. Yet, standing anywhere in the living room, one sees the trees and houses on the opposite side of the street, so that prospect is retained. The occupant sees without being seen.[19] Appleton has said:

The modern, centrally heated flat or maisonette affords a far better protection against meteorological hazard than the more primitive shelters of earlier days. But where large windows face streets, squares or public open spaces, and especially if the internal structure of the house is based on the "open plan," the physical protection provided against the weather may not be matched by the visual protection against the eye of the intruder. The refuge may be effective as "shelter" but ineffective as "hide."[20]

3.9 Cheney house. Diagrammatic section showing sight lines toward and from the living room.

This is not true of the Cheney house, even though it is an early example of the open plan and has large windows facing the street. Wright manages to have it both ways. In so doing he realizes a condition described by Colin St. John Wilson, who, paraphrasing Adrian Stokes, says: "It is uniquely the role of the masterpiece to make possible the *simultaneous* experience of these two polar modes; enjoyment at the same time of intense sensations of being inside and outside, of envelopment and detachment, of oneness and separateness."[21]

There is still more to be said of the configuration of this house, and especially as Wright portrayed it in relation to the site. The exquisite rendering by Marion Mahony (fig. 3.2) is an excellent example of the way Wright chose to have his houses portrayed. Norris Kelley Smith has observed that "a spacious openness exists around and in front of the building but not . . . behind and beyond it. The house is made to appear at once embraced by its natural setting and opened to it."[22] There is a certain obviousness in making a presentation drawing this way, as it shows the building clearly and sets it against an appealing ground, and for this reason many architects will show siting in a roughly similar way. But Smith is correct in calling attention to it in Wright's case, for with Wright the characteristic is unusually strong and consistent, especially after 1902. And for him it was more than just a convention of presentation. Wright meant it as an indication of how vegetation was actually to be managed. With the later Hollyhock House, sited on a rather bare Los Angeles hill,

such a planting program was carried out by the owner, with Wright's enthusiastic approval, to make the building look like the drawing; still later he urged just such a planting scheme on Mr. and Mrs. Paul Hanna, without success.

The Cheney rendering shows plantings that no doubt in part preexisted. But the effect in all cases is to enfold the refuge portions of the house in the primordial refuge of nature, the grove at the edge of the meadow, while the prospect components of the house reach forward from the hiding place to project into the prospect-space of the meadow. Thus, Wright's preferred rendering of siting locates the inhabitant, at least in intention, at "the edge of the wood" to which Sidney Lanier was drawn, and to the place where Dickens placed his characters (see p. 31). It is also exactly the location that Stephen Kaplan's recent empirical studies identify as the place of intuitive human choice: "It becomes clear that neither being out in the open nor being in the woods is favored. These opposing vectors would tend to place the individual right at the forest edge. Ecologists point out that such an area is the richest in terms of life forms; it is likely to be the safest as well."[23]

Let us for a moment regard the Cheney house from another point of view. In chapter 2 I noted that in the study of environmental aesthetics there is some degree of agreement about preferences for some combination of complexity and order, and that this can be accounted for in part, at least, as a manifestation of survival behaviors genetic to our species.

Complexity clearly is a characteristic that can be found in the path of movement into and through the Cheney house. The path toward the front door is far more complex than that of the ordinary house its size. Four right-angle turnings must be negotiated to reach the front door; once inside, another three occur before one faces the fire or the terrace (figs. 3.3, 3.4). Yet this point lies on the centerline of a symmetrical composition, and one is conscious of its doing so (fig. 3.5). In addition, the numerous turnings all have been of 90 degrees, and have been indicated as such by architectural emphases at every point (see fig. 3.4). The ceiling planes, whose slope is exactly that of the external roof planes, recall the first views of the house. The trim at the ceiling edge is of the same height and dimension as the external eave under which one passed on entry. Thus, this complex path also possesses and declares an order and culminates in a resolution and reestablished clarity of orientation.

Complexity can also be regarded spatially: are we in a single, bounded space or is there a complex and ambiguous relationship of spatial interpretations? Clearly the Cheney organization is the latter. The living room is declared by the fire recess (figs. 3.4, 3.5) and by the range of french doors, and by the paired columns that intervene between it and the dining room and library, leading us to regard those rooms as subspaces to the living room. But as the eye moves to the ceiling, dining room, living room, and library are one; the subspaces, which do not partake of this ceiling volume, are the fire nook and the french-doors bay (figs. 3.4, 3.6). Yet all are bound together by the heavy dark wood trim at the ceiling edge, the thickest trim of the entire interior, which both integrates and articulates. Thus, an extraordinarily complex spatial organization is seen to possess an extraordinary order. This is architectural rhyming, to use Humphrey's term, the repetition of like characteristics joined with unlike.

The house for the Avery Coonleys was done perhaps three years later than the Cheney house. It is much larger, and its plan far more extensive (fig. 3.10). As at Heurtley and Cheney, Wright has raised the main floor (fig. 3.11), which is reached by the usual twisting passage and ascent. One enters this rather grand palazzo under the porte-cochere (fig. 3.12) through a door of utter modesty. A stair lies ahead, and above it light filters in from the sky, drawing the eye upward. At the top of this stair vistas open to left and right, down narrow low passages leading to pavilions of light. One turns to the left, then navigates two more left turns, to arrive at the living pavilion (figs. 3.11, 3.13). The fireplace, off the left flank, is at the living room's inner edge, and in this case is pocketed by the high railings that edge the stairs to either side (fig. 3.14). The pocket thus created is lined with books below and (originally) the arboreal mural on either side of the brick fireplace. From this, the grand ceiling rises, congruent with the roof planes above.[24] Walter Creese has recently remarked that "the ceiling panels may represent the spreading clouds of the prairie sky, or the branches of Olmsted's trees."[25] Perhaps they are both. The space, considered as a hierarchical enlargement of the fireplace cave-refuge, thus becomes, as a totality, a gentler grove-refuge, in which the lighted edge panels and the skylights of the adjacent hall ceilings suggest the light of the sky sifted through the branches of the grove. Such an interpretation is conveyed from within by the house itself, for the ceiling planes are felt to be only inches away from the leaves and branches, the sun and the rain. Here we can feel, perhaps more clearly than before, another reason for Wright's placement of the major rooms directly under the roof. Within this interpretation, the appropriateness of the arboreal mural flanking the fireplace is obvious.

Like the preceding houses, the Coonley house has an open plan; the eye is easily carried outward from the living room to the extended hallways and skylit stairwells (figs. 3.13, 3.15), although actual movement is held away from the fireplace pocket. The hallways articulate the linkage between spaces, as did the horizontal and vertical dividing elements of the Heurtley and Cheney houses. Vincent Scully has described the sense of movement through the Coonley house: "The separate pavilions are interwoven by long, heavily framed corridors, and the low ceilings sail on seemingly endlessly . . . ,"[26] a description that recalls yet another comment by Appleton:

The rich alleys and byways provide us with vistas which every now and then widen into little panoramas . . . like woodland paths leading between glades, each of which, as soon as we enter it, becomes yet another vista leading on to the next opening. . . . Here we are back with Konrad Lorenz in the Vienna Woods, pausing before we ". . . break through the last bushes and out of cover on to the free expanse of the meadow" to gain "the advantage which it can offer to hunter and hunted—namely, to see without being seen."[27]

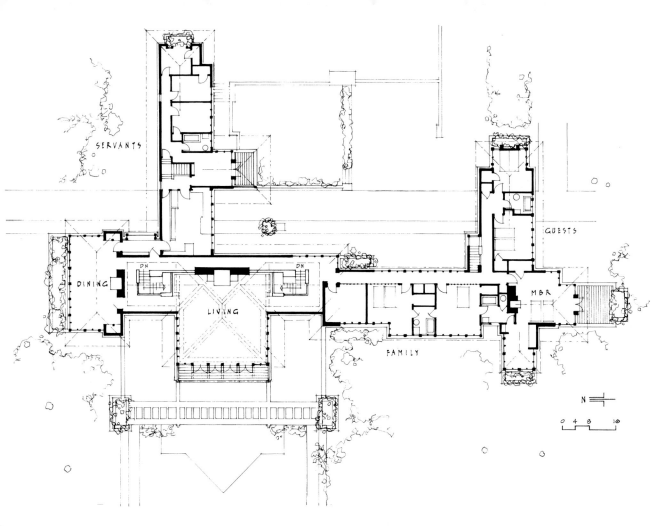

3.10 Avery Coonley house, Riverside, 1907. Upper floor plan. Entry is from the floor below, at the base of the stair which leads up to the left of the living room.

3.11 Coonley house. Diagrammatic drawing by William Hook. *Opposite*

3.12 Coonley house. Approach to entry, in the right wall of the porte-cochere.

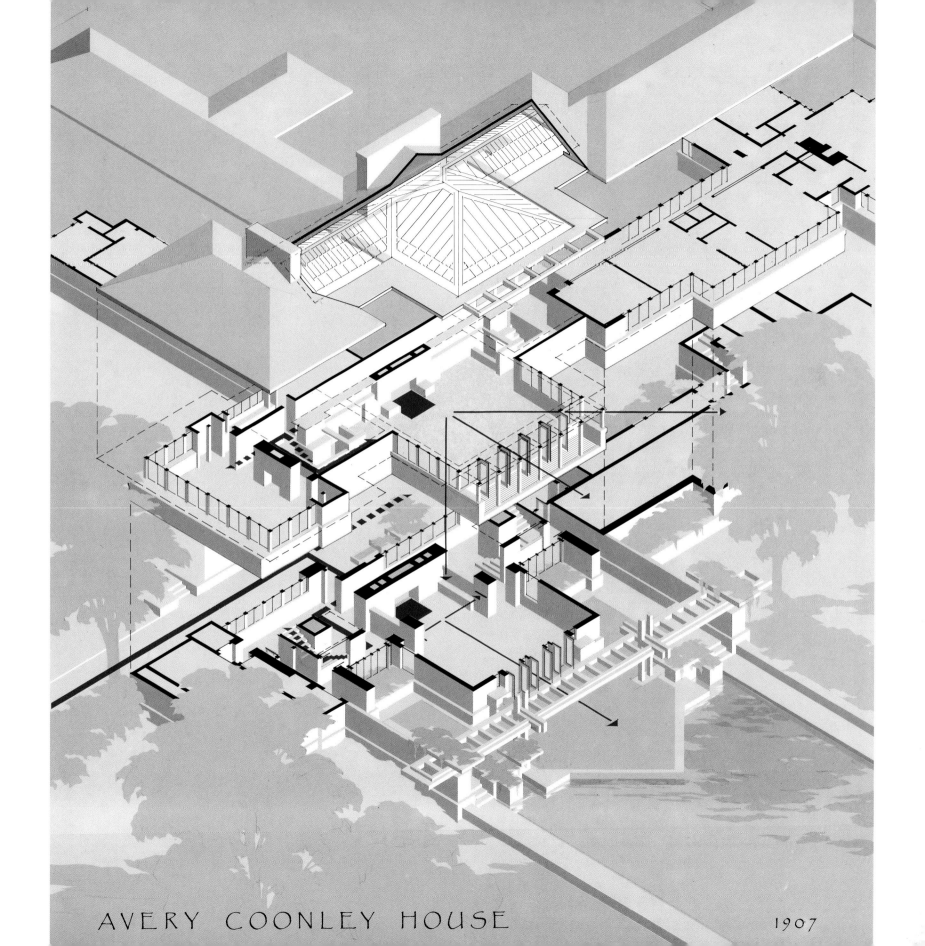

AVERY COONLEY HOUSE 1907

3.13 Coonley house. View from the stairhead looking toward the living room. The fireplace is at left. The horizontal "beams" just ahead, cousins to those of the Cheney house, are reminders that we look across a spatial seam between the corridor and the living pavilion beyond. (These "beams" may also serve as tension ties restraining the thrust of the roof structure; see n. 24.)

3.14 Coonley house. Living room looking toward the fireplace. The corridor to bedrooms is at right. The wall to either side of the fireplace does not extend to the ceiling; the ceiling hovers over both the living room and the hall beyond, and is seen to do so.

3.15 Coonley house. Living room. The interior refuge of the fireplace is at right; interior prospect to the dining room is straight ahead. Views to the pool and garden open at left.

3.16 Coonley house. Living room view to the prospect of pool and garden, and Riverside beyond.

Opposite the fire, at the edge of the ceiling, three walls of the usual leaded and stained glass open from the prospect-enhancing elevation of the living room to the extensive grounds, with Olmsted's Riverside beyond (figs. 3.11, 3.16). Yet originally there were windows beyond, not french doors, and only modest planting boxes beyond, and no terraces. It has always seemed to me that as the exterior of the house appears in its original form in early photos, the terraces are much missed; and lacking french doors to open the space, the refuge induced in the interior by the usual means must have been inadequately countered by prospect symbols and opportunities. Wright may have felt this, too, because eventually he added the pergola to suggest horizontal extension of the floor plane toward the horizon (fig. 3.17), and later still he removed the planting boxes and replaced the windows with floor-to-eave french doors (as shown in fig. 3.16) leading to a real, although small, terrace. Thus the final version realizes the pattern completely and with unprecedented richness.

The master bedroom at the terminus of the long bedroom wing is, like that at Willits, a miniature version of the pattern (figs. 3.10, 3.11, far right). This master bedroom was the one space of the original scheme to have had a terrace, in early drawings called a porch, which, like Cheney, is open to the prospect enrichment of the sky.

Thomas Beeby has recently discussed the relationship of Wright's work to nature, and in particular nature as found in the central Wisconsin valley of his childhood. Beeby mentions no specific house as an example; but one passage seems to have the Coonley house in mind. His description complements those of Scully and Creese and is also consistent with a prospect and refuge interpretation:

The house is lifted out of the dampness of the Earth, with the living areas on the second level. This allows views from the house above the ornamental plantings of the understory and through the open tree trunks, passing below the canopy of leaves overhead. The experience of entry is the equivalent of climbing above the thicket that grows along the river's edge, escaping the brambles and insects, to catch the breeze and look down on the smothering lushness of the valley. The plants growing on the ledges along the house bring to mind the vines growing among the trees and provide the sense of being hidden in a secret overlook, buried in vegetation. The space on the exterior that is formed between the understory and the forest canopy is carried inside the house through the vertical mullions that signify tree trunks and the lineal trim that defines the interior space of the house. The glazing is broken down into ornamental leaded casements that obscure vision. Colored glass patterns represent the leaves and flowers of the shrubbery that is found at the edge of a forest or grove where the added light there creates a wall of foliage. Skylights are also cut through the ceiling volumes allowing filtered sunlight to flicker into the hollow of the house. The entire structure becomes a grove surrounding the masonry altar of the hearth. The canopy of trees protects its initiates from the burning sun and devastating winds of the prairie, where there is no shelter from nature.[28]

The complexity of the Coonley house is evident in most of its characteristics: the circuitous entry path exceeds by far the complication of Cheney; the geometrically involved ceilings are articulated with a maze of trim; the plan itself is a profusion of zigzagged corridors and discrete pavilions. Yet the order is equally evident and similar to that of Cheney. All ceiling planes, whatever their configuration or complexity, share a continuous and common lower edge emphasized by continuous and emphatic dark trim (figs. 3.14–3.16). As at Cheney, this trim is at exactly the height of the external eave and is of similar dimension and coloration, so that it not only coheres the interior experience but refers it to a dominant exterior feature as well. The sill line is also repetitive and is emphasized, and many other horizontals repeat and interweave. The plan of the Coonley house also reveals another order, that of a controlling grid of squares which establishes all major locations and dimensions.[29] The role this grid plays is not perceivable in all cases in the finished building. But it is clearly evident as the module that determines dimensions of windows and doors, and since those elements are repetitive and profuse, one is continuously reminded of the underlying modular order of the house. Thus the Coonley house is an especially rich example of the architectural rhyming already illustrated at Cheney, a measured encountering of experiences which share some characteristics and differs in others—a set of variations on repetitive stimuli.

3.17 Coonley house. Exterior from the pool and garden toward the living room. The pergola is in place, but the french doors shown in fig. 3.16 are not yet installed at the time of this photo.

Wright's other great terminal masterpiece of his early period is generally taken to be the Frederick Robie house of 1908–1909 in Chicago.[30] In it the pattern recurs, although it lacks one interior element, and from the prospect-refuge point of view is less rewarding than Coonley.

The Robie house exterior (fig. 3.18) maximizes prospect-refuge clues. Balconies and terraces run the length of the house and beyond; alcoves and recesses abound; overhangs are enormous; glazing appears as if continuous. The chimney mass, more evident and more massive than at Heurtley, Cheney, or Coonley, signals the presence of the refuge fire at the core. But none of the street frontage is really penetrable. Like the Cheney house, one has to find a hidden entry (fig. 3.19A); like the Heurtley and Coonley houses, one has to ascend to the heart of the refuge.[31]

The Robie house fireplace is free-standing; unlike the Cheney or Coonley houses, no spatial pocket is defined by flanking full or partial walls (figs. 3.19B, 3.20). Wright used free-standing fireplaces rather often in his early period; other examples are the Gridley, Evans, Hardy, Martin, and Tomek houses, the latter a prototype of the Robie house. The effect in all such cases is to weaken somewhat the refuge characteristic, as it is more difficult to group sitting provisions around the fire. But at the Robie house, the urge toward spatial unification, presumably, also led Wright to continue the living room ceiling and south wall conditions through to the dining room without interruption, even parting the fireplace mass itself to allow the ceiling plane to be seen as continuous. This meant that the usual lower ceiling edge over the fireplace could not happen here. And therefore the fireplace is doubly limited in its ability to suggest a refuge. Perhaps as an attempt at compensation, Wright provided his by now familiar seating promontory, projecting from the north pier of the fireplace and creating, as usual, a kind of half-inglenook. Today this half-inglenook is gone, but even when in place (see fig. 3.20), it cannot have been fully effective, as it faced, and was rather close to, the continuous glazed french doors to the south. In the dining room, the enclosing character of the high-backed chairs and pylon-cornered table (fig. 3.21) is partial compensation, and perhaps intuitively was intended to be so, creating a room within a room, a refuge within openness for the family at mealtime.

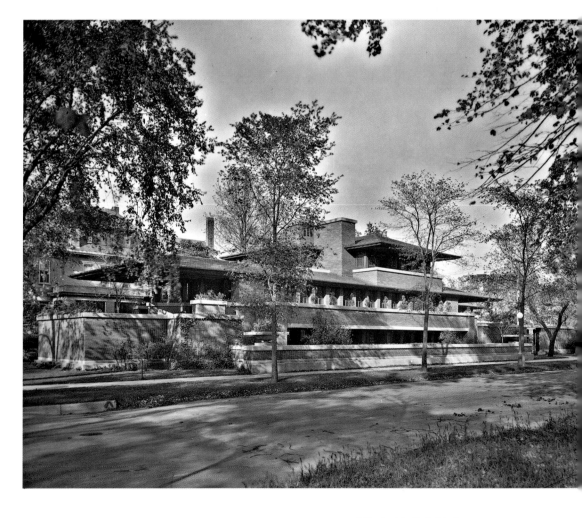

3.18 Frederick C. Robie house, Chicago, 1909. Exterior from the southwest.

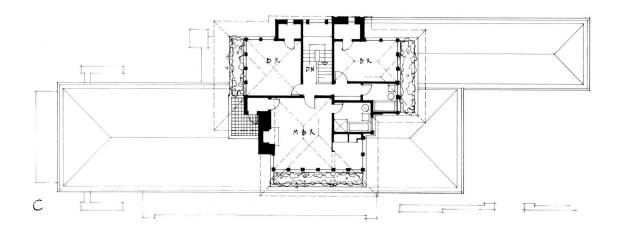

C

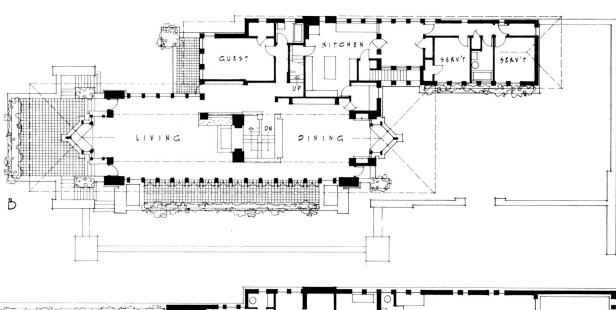

3.19A–C Robie house. Plans: A. Lower floor. B. Main floor. C. Upper floor.

B

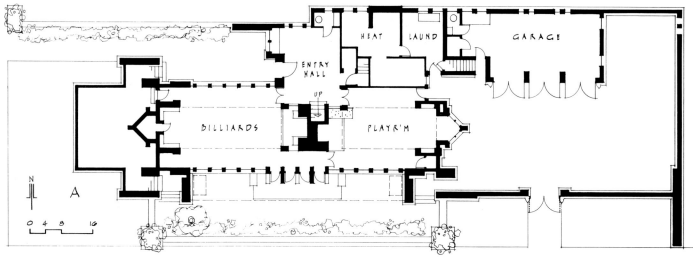

A

0 4 8   16

The containing ceiling rises, as usual, at the center, with low edges. The french doors to the south and the prowlike projection to the west lead to the terraces. Both of these are, as usual, only partly roofed, and one of the memorable experiences at the Robie house is to go out to either of these and feel the power of release from the pressure of the low soffits to the expanse of the sky and trees. This experience must have been even more powerful in 1909, when the planter boxes, now empty and forlorn, would have softened a prospect which in those early days extended all the way to the old Exposition midway two blocks to the south.

Like the Cheney house, the Robie house is close to a city street. Thus privacy, provided at Coonley by the sheer size of the site, here had to be dealt with again by manipulation of the architectural material. Robie himself put it tersely: "I wanted to be able to look out and down the street to my neighbors without having them invade my privacy."[32] Wright, working again through careful attention to section, managed this issue with precision and elegance (fig. 3.22). The parapet wall of the south terrace, solid as at Cheney but unlike Coonley, is disposed to intercept exactly a sight line from the center of the near sidewalk; a view from that position reveals only the wood trim of the tops of the french doors, and no glass at all of the main floor spaces. This can hardly be accidental, as the planter forward of the upstairs bedroom does exactly the same thing, to the inch.[33]

The Robie house, then, was an exquisite platform for prospect, and, taken as a whole, was meticulously managed to provide refuge from a busy public thoroughfare. But the smaller refuge within the house, the zone around the fireplace, is atypically weak in the context of Wright's work generally. Gaston Bachelard, writing before Appleton, describes the mood of refuge in his book, *The Poetics of Space*. He first quotes Henri Bachelin, describing his childhood house:

At these moments, I felt strongly—and I swear to this—that we were cut off from the little town, from the rest of France, and from the entire world. I delighted in imagining . . . that we were living in the heart of the wood, in the well-heated hut of charcoal burners; I even hoped to hear wolves sharpening their claws on the heavy granite slab that formed our doorstep. But our house replaced the hut for me, it sheltered me from hunger and cold; and if I shivered, it was merely from well-being.

Bachelard himself continues:

Thus, the author attracts us to the center of the house as though to a center of magnetic force, into a major zone of protection. . . . He has only to give a few touches to the spectacle of the family sitting-room, only to listen to the stove roaring in the evening stillness, while an icy wind blows against the house, to know that at the house's center, in the circle of light shed by the lamp, he is living in the round house, the primitive hut, of prehistoric man.[34]

3.20 Robie house. Living room looking toward the fireplace. This early photograph shows the half-inglenook seat. The stair and dining space are beyond the fireplace.

3.21 Robie house. Dining room. The original dining furniture in place; the view is through and beyond the stair and fireplace mass toward the living room.

It is just this sensation that is so easy to project into the Cheney and Coonley houses, and so difficult to feel at the Robie house. The fireplace zone is too open, an island rather than a cave.

Nor is there the fluid ambience of Coonley. It is a cliché that the Robie house is a free and open spatial exercise, and from one point of view there is truth in this. But it is a stiff freedom, more rigorous and more relentless than at Coonley. Few discussions of the Robie house consider its interior as a setting for human living. It is to William Jordy's credit that he does so, and he hints briefly at its difficulty: "Of all his [Wright's] interiors, that of the Robie house is one of the more difficult for many to appreciate. A little cramped, and among the most insistently modeled, it is difficult to imagine it congenially furnished."[35] Nor is it possible to experience the Coonley sensation of moving along woodland paths from glade or glade, since the theme of corridors and pavilions does not occur, and the hardlined rectangularity of the living-dining ceiling is not softened by dappled light from the sky as it is in the corridor extensions of the Coonley ceiling (though the electric lighting at the edges of the Robie ceiling, behind the grilles, has a little of the same effect). Nor does the Robie master bedroom have the experiential richness of that of the Coonley house. It is reached by an uninteresting stairway; the bedroom fireplace is bald by comparison, and the actual terrace is almost an afterthought, tucked behind the scenes on the west of the chimney mass, neither seen from nor enriching the room itself (figs. 3.19B–C).[36]

Was it for these reasons that, in spite of the unmatched drama of the Robie exterior, Wright claimed the Coonley house as his own favorite of those early years, the "most successful of my houses from my standpoint"?[37] This comment may puzzle those who have not examined the interior conditions of the two houses closely. But seen in terms of complexity and order, prospect and refuge, Wright was right: the Coonley house is the perfection of his early pattern.

54

3.22 Robie house. Diagrammatic section showing sight lines.

related series of houses of this period, all on
steep hillside sites, have a story of their own in
modifying the pattern. The first of them, the
Thomas Hardy house of 1905, in Racine, is the subject
of one of the most famous of Wright's drawings, the
orientalized view from the lake, which so dramatizes
the precipitous character of the site (fig. 3.23). Such a
site meant a real problem for the pattern: the terrace
could not extend from the living room opposite the fireplace without cutting off the view downward, in this
case to the lake. The Hardy house is a wonderfully vertical composition of spaces, unusual in Wright's domestic work and especially so at this early date. He modified the pattern in a way that is exactly appropriate.
The terrace is displaced downward in the spatial stack-
ing, opening opposite the fireplace of the lower dining
room rather than that of the living room (figs. 3.24A,
3.25), and so more or less maintaining the pattern. The
living room lacks the horizontal extension of its floor
plane, but since the terrace is seen from any point near
the windows, there is partial compensation, and the
prospect to the lake is ensured.

The W. A. Glasner house of about the same year, in Glencoe, also dealt with the problem of a hillside view toward which the living room faces. But unlike the Hardy house, all major spaces of the Glasner house are more or less axially disposed on one level. The Glasner house therefore uses a terrace displaced to the east as an entry porch, although it is unsatisfactory—awkward, almost grotesque as entry, and so small that it has no hope of counting as prospect (fig. 3.26). Its only redeeming feature is that it avoids blocking the living room view (fig. 3.27). There is also a much larger "veranda" opening from the opposite end of the living room, but it is reached by a long corridor, and is not sensed as an extension of the living spaces—nor does it garner a similar view. The intended but unexecuted "tea house" surely was Wright's attempt to provide a vital, alternate, prospect-claiming feature to counter the inadequacies of the terrace and veranda, though the tea house also would have failed to provide Wright's usual contiguity between terrace and major space.

Unsatisfactory as the Glasner approach is, it leads on to a number of houses which use a lateral disposition advantageously. The well-known Isabel Roberts house of 1908 in River Forest (fig. 3.28), and its larger progeny, the Frank Baker house of 1909 in Wilmette, both use a lateral terrace to keep distance from the street; unlike the Cheney or Robie houses, both have floor levels near grade, so that privacy could not be had by parapet manipulations.

A laterally disposed terrace was also proposed for the great McCormick project of about 1907 (fig. 3.29). The site, a magnificent lakeside bluff, was similar to that of the Hardy house. Blockage of views from main spaces would have been unthinkable. The enormous terrace was therefore to have been placed between the living and dining pavilions, with access from each through the connecting loggia.

This configuration of terrace conditions can be compared with that of the Cheney, Coonley, and Robie houses as evidence of Wright's site-specific management of prospect.

3.23 Thomas Hardy house, Racine, 1905. Perspective from the lake.

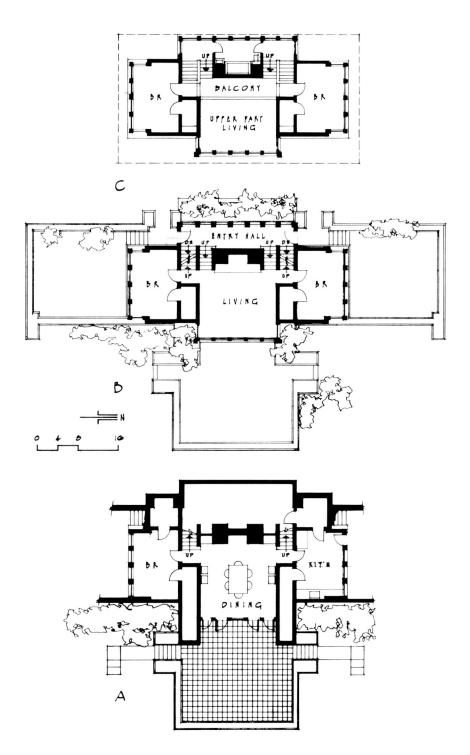

C

B

N

0   4   8   10

3.24A–C Hardy house. Plans:
A. Lower floor. B. Main floor.
C. Upper floor.

A

3.25 Hardy house. Perspective from below the terrace

3.26 W. A. Glasner house, Glencoe, 1905. Main floor plan.

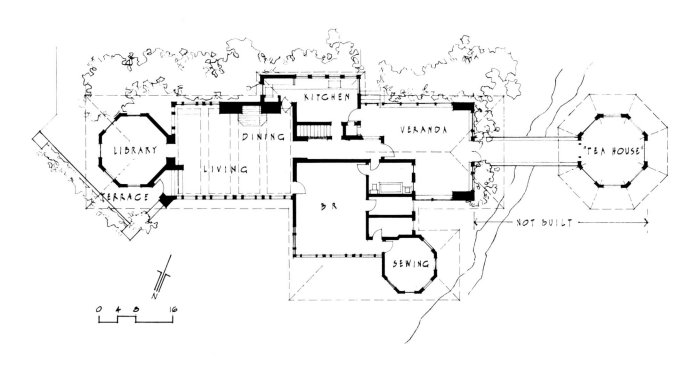

3.27 Glasner house. Perspective; entry at far left.

3.28 Isabel Roberts house, River Forest, 1908. Main floor plan.

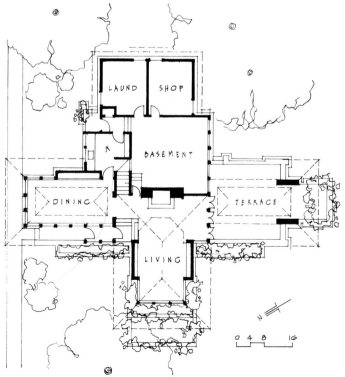

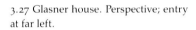

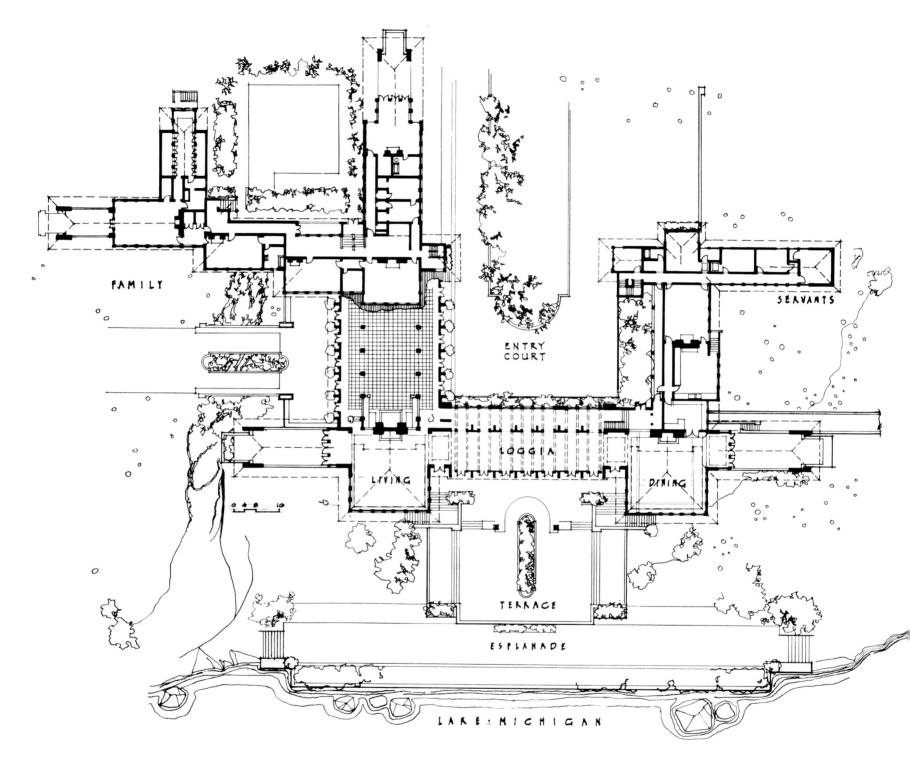

FAMILY

SERVANTS

ENTRY
COURT

LOGGIA

LIVING

DINING

TERRACE

ESPLANADE

LAKE·MICHIGAN

3.29 Project: Harold McCormick house,
Lake Forest, 1907. Plan.

Thus, in the years from 1900 to 1902 Wright resolved, and from 1902 pervasively employed, a typical composition of domestic architectural elements consisting of both exterior and interior repetitive features. Nine houses manifesting this pattern, and five more that show its development, have been cited. They include all those commonly considered to be Wright's major houses of that period, with just three exceptions, the Susan Lawrence Dana house of 1903, in Springfield, the Darwin Martin house of 1906, in Buffalo, and the Mrs. Thomas Gale house of 1904–1909, in Oak Park. In all three, the living room lies under a second story of rooms above (which in the case of the Martin house yields a decidedly low living room ceiling)—and the Dana house presents a straightforward entry from the sidewalk. Otherwise the pattern typical of Wright's houses after 1902 occurs in these houses as well. In various permutations this pattern continued to inform his work after his flight from Oak Park in 1909, and remained a constant through his career.

Why was this pattern pervasive in Wright's work? Was he not, after all, designing for a variety of clients, and should this not have yielded alternate patterns quite different from this repetitive one? In fact, few architects design in radically different ways; almost all compose in ways that persist from one client to another despite personal differences among clients. There is nothing particularly insidious about this. An architect is usually chosen because of his way of designing, and this is especially true when that architect has a strong personal direction. With Wright, however, we have a special case in which this phenomenon is intensified. For Wright was consciously aiming for an archetypal model of dwelling—his innumerable references to the typical conditions and aims of the Prairie house type make this unarguable[38]—and such an archetype can only be sought through development of such repetitive characteristics. Norris Kelly Smith makes a similar point in observing that Wright's houses were really for himself,[39] for in the sense that he was defining the archetype in his own terms, this is true.

The extraordinary value of this pattern, I am suggesting, lies in its uniquely close, rich, and complex correspondence to fundamental human spatial and formal preferences, "given with the world," in Norberg-Schulz's phrase, as "basic ways of being between earth and sky."

Was Wright conscious that he consistently deployed the characteristics on which this correspondence depends?

He often and eloquently alluded to his interest in the relationship between order and complexity: "Truly ordered simplicity in the hands of the great artist may flower into a bewildering profusion, exquisitely exuberant, and render all more clear than ever."[40] This kind of comment occurs with sufficient frequency in his writings to indicate that it was a continuing and conscious foundation for his designing, though there is no evidence—as indeed one would not expect any—that he understood the fundamental biological basis of its wider appeal.

On his feelings about prospect and refuge conditions in his work, there is less to go on. He did write of a sense of shelter, and of the value of the fire, and of elevation above the prairie (as noted in chapter 1), and on one obscure occasion commented that man "first lived sometimes in trees and sometimes in stone caves."[41] But nowhere did he bring these characteristics together in a cohesive statement of spatial intentions in approximately these terms; he is silent on the value of the long and circuitous entry, the lowered ceiling over the fire, the raised ceiling forward of it, the views to contiguous spaces, the terrace, the glazing that links it to the major spaces. We are left to conclude that he believed these characteristics were essential—our evidence for this, of course, lies in their consistent deployment—but that he understood this importance intuitively rather than consciously.

It seems most reasonable, therefore, to believe that Wright found, through the pattern, a way of embodying almost to perfection characteristics for which he had a strong but primarily intuitive affinity.[42] He was an unparalleled composer of spaces, and in a series of designs from 1900 to 1902, he discovered such a satisfying way of composing them that it became thereafter his canonical way. The pattern became for him a repetitive device whose appeal, he seems correctly to have sensed, would be both widespread and powerful.

4. Taliesin

In September of 1909 Wright left his wife Catherine and their six children, and with Mrs. Cheney went to Europe, to Fiesole, to see through its Berlin publication the monumental Wasmuth portfolio of his work. On his return in October of 1910, he began to build near his Wisconsin birthplace a home for himself and Mrs. Cheney (soon divorced, to live the brief remainder of her life as Mamah Borthwick). He named this new home Taliesin, after the Welsh boy-hero-bard whose name derived from his "radiant brow."[1]

A house is always a refuge against two generalized and impersonal threats. One is climate, against which the house protects by means of its walls and roof, its hearth, and its ventilating sash (and the less symbolic modern surrogates, central heat and air conditioning). The other threat is the intrusiveness of communal society. The house protects against this by the obvious means of walls, roof, and doors and also by subdued interior light conditions, by curtains, and often, in Wright's case, by leaded and faceted stained glass windows. Trees and shrubs can also be means to protect against societal intrusion, and were often exploited by Wright. The extensive site of the Coonley house and the sight-line manipulations of the Cheney and Robie houses are other sophisticated means to the same ends.

4.1 Taliesin, near Spring Green, Wisconsin, 1911–. View from the south. Living spaces are at center of the photo; the valley is at right with its bounding hills in the distance.

Wright built Taliesin as refuge against these universal threats; he also built it as refuge against two threats which were more specific and personal. The first of these was external, a focused societal hostility, as he saw it, toward himself. The second was internal, an inner sense of disorientation and confusion.

Our evidence for Wright's state of mind at this time is a series of conferences and correspondences with the press,[2] and his recollections as they appear in *An Autobiography.* The latter have the disadvantage that they were written down some two decades after the event, and with Wright the passage of time typically did not lend accuracy. But Norris Kelly Smith argues, I think correctly, that in this case distance was necessary, and that we are justified in taking seriously Wright's later reflections.[3] In any event, what emerges at this time in

Wright's life is a mixture of many feelings. Defensiveness is paramount but is heavily laced with his usual combativeness. (At this time he had cast, as a mantelpiece for Taliesin, the symbol of that oddly chip-on-shoulder family motto of the Lloyd-Joneses: "Truth Against the World.") One can also find in his words guilt,[4] isolation, frustration, pride, and confusion. Through it all is a poignant need to be understood, poignant because of its obsessive repetition, and also because he understood himself least well at this time. Twenty years later he could say as much: "Weary, I was losing grip on my work and even my interest in it . . . now it seemed to leave me up against a dead wall. I could see no way out. . . . I did not know what I wanted."[5]

4.2 Taliesin. Approach drive, with the roof of the porte-cochere ahead.

So Taliesin had to be refuge against more immediate threats than those facing the usual house. It is not surprising that refuge symbols and refuge provisions are dominant in it. It was to be a retreat, tranquil, deep-rooted, unassailable, where Wright could pursue a new life with his beloved and could also rethink his professional and philosophic stance. In his own description of the homecoming, Wright used the word "refuge" and a number of synonyms:

My mother foreseeing the plight I would be in had bought the low hill on which Taliesin now stands. She offered it to me as refuge. Yes, a retreat when I returned from Europe in 1911. I began to build Taliesin to get my back against the wall. . . . I turned to this hill in the Valley as my Grandfather before me had turned to America—as a hope and haven.[6]

The house was built encircling the side of the hill, getting its own back to the wall (fig. 4.1). Wright's comment about Taliesin's hillside siting is famous: "I knew well that no house should ever be *on* a hill or *on* anything."[7] What often passes unnoticed is that he was inconsistent about this.[8] The Romeo and Juliet windmill at Taliesin, which Wright himself said "took its place on the hill,"[9] is a trivial exception and not a house, anyway—but the same cannot be said of Hollyhock House of 1920, "in full stature on its hill,"[10] nor of the Hardy, Little, Ennis, Pauson, or Morris houses among others. Obviously the issue was one of circumstance, not of canon. At Taliesin the hilltop was inappropriate, perhaps partly because of Wright's sense of its sanctity, but partly because at that time he needed to have his—and therefore its—back to the wall, for which purpose the hilltop could not work. Therefore he chose the hillside around which the living spaces were ranged.

The house built on this hillside changed over time, especially after 1925, when Wright's changed personal circumstances led to major alterations. Thus few living observers have experienced the early Taliesin. In understanding it we are dependent on plans and photographs, tricky evidence for any architecture and especially for Wright's.[11] But if we are to understand this most important building in his career, these are the evidences we must use. They tell us of a building consistent, rich, and appropriate in its management of prospect but far more importantly of refuge. It is also a gentler, more intimate, and more freely composed house than any other of Wright's work.

A clear reading of the total form of the exterior is precluded at Taliesin by its own complexity and by the dense vegetation of the hillside into which this complexity is interwoven: "The finished wood outside was the color of gray tree-trunks in violet light. The shingles of the roof surfaces were left to weather silver-gray like the tree branches spreading below them."[12] The dominant image at Taliesin always has been an image of roofs, roofs emerging randomly from the hillside vegetation, a repetition of gentle shingled surfaces, "the slope of the hills their slopes."[13] The deep overhanging eaves were all at a uniform level (except, of course, the monitors perched on the ridges), forming an absolutely continuous eave line, and one very close to the earth on the hillward side. The eave fascia was deeper and simpler than in previous work, emphasizing its continuity. Whatever else the original Taliesin was, gliding over all were these insistently sheltering roofs ranged along the hill among the trees (figs. 4.1–4.3).

The only competing features were the vertical masses of stone. These were the chimneys, which reduplicated the refuge symbolism. Wright eloquently described their refuge-signaling role: "The chimneys of the great stone fireplaces rose heavily through all, wherever there was a gathering place within, and there were many such places"[14] (figs. 4.2–4.4).

4.3 Taliesin. View toward the southeast, across the roofs and the courtyard. The original approach ran from right to left behind the foreground trees and under the entry porch at center.

4.4 Taliesin. Looking east across the inner court.

4.5 Taliesin. Looking northwest along the courtyard. The roof behind the studio chimney had been revised by the time of this photo; compare with fig. 4.3.

4.6 Taliesin. View northeast through the entry porch to "the edge of the wood" lying somewhat beyond, from which the land falls away to the valley.

Thus, as the house was originally approached, from the south (figs. 4.1, 4.2), refuge was signaled by the hillside to the west, the grove ahead, the sheltering roofs among the trees, and the stone pylons marking the "gathering places within." Prospect signals, on the other hand, were almost nonexistent until one moved forward, under the low porte-cochere, at which point there was a contained vista to the left, although it was a restatement: stone fireplace pylon and continuous eave to the right, stratified stone walls reiterating the hillside to the left (fig. 4.5). Ahead, framed by stone pylons and the refuge of the ever-present low roof, was the distant horizon of the valley, with the magnetic inference of intervening prospect. One moved forward, then up four low steps between the pylons, and under the darkness of the low roof (fig. 4.6). Then, beyond the release of its northern eave, lay a broad stone terrace open to the sky, splendidly presenting the prospect of Wright's ancestral valley (fig. 4.7). Yet even here one would have been able to see without being seen, for intervening between terrace and view was a grove of mature trees—analogous perhaps to the articulating features of interior prospect at the Cheney house, but at Taliesin also hiding the viewer from the valley below.

Thus, this condition was unlike that indicated in the drawing of the Cheney house (fig. 3.2), in which the house, in Wright's perception, is placed at the very edge of the forest, with its prospect features projecting into the meadow. At Taliesin the house is withdrawn behind the forest edge; the forest closes around it and the hiding place is itself hidden.

The entry sequence of Taliesin, from the southernmost approach to the final screened view of the valley, would have been a rich one for any who experienced it. We have the comments of visitors as diverse as Eric Mendelsohn and Alexander Woollcott, who were profoundly moved by the early Taliesin and whose reactions would have been molded by this first spatial sequence.[15] But it was likely to have been seen as most extraordinarily meaningful to Wright himself, not only by being the refuge he needed but by richly seeming to be so, holding the participant through a series of refuge-signaling forms until the prospect was reached—a prospect, framed and filtered through the old trees, of the hill-contained valley of Wright's clan, itself a refuge in a still larger sense.

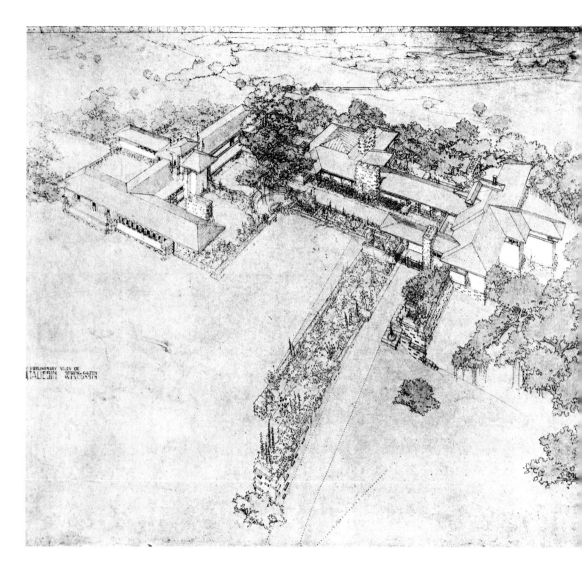

4.7 Taliesin. Perspective looking north.

At the right edge of this terrace, tucked deeply under the low eave, was the entry to the living room, behind the fireplace mass and its seating promontory which together immediately reasserted refuge once again (figs. 4.8–4.10).

This fireplace was one of four included in the original scheme, a number equaled only in the Dana house among Wright's executed houses up to this time. All of Taliesin's fireplaces tucked their backs to the hillside-oriented wall. They are the first fireplaces in which Wright used stone, a natural choice since, as Wright says, it was the constituent of "the hills around about"; it "lay in strata like outcropping ledges in facades of the hills."[16] Still, in this refuge which he built for himself at a time in life when he felt embattled, the choice was especially appropriate. Stone may be used in a rough near-natural state, less modeled by the hand of the workman than brick and therefore capable of an even stronger suggestion of cave-refuge, recalling our earliest habitats. At Taliesin it associates, as Wright clearly wanted it to, with the tan sandstone strata of the nearby hills and river valleys from which it was extracted. It was least worked in the fireplace breasts, great slabs of irregular outline and surface that appear as primeval dolmens, spanning what seem, even more than in Wright's earlier work, to be cave fires (fig. 4.10). (Thomas Beeby cites a number of dolmen-suggestive features at Taliesin, including the heavy roofs of the entry sequence, poised on stone piers, as well as the fireplaces. He considers the entire house analogous to a dolmen, "man's first spatial construction—a fabricated cave."[17])

4.8 Taliesin. Plan as of 1911–14.

4.9 Taliesin. Diagrammatic drawing by William Hook.

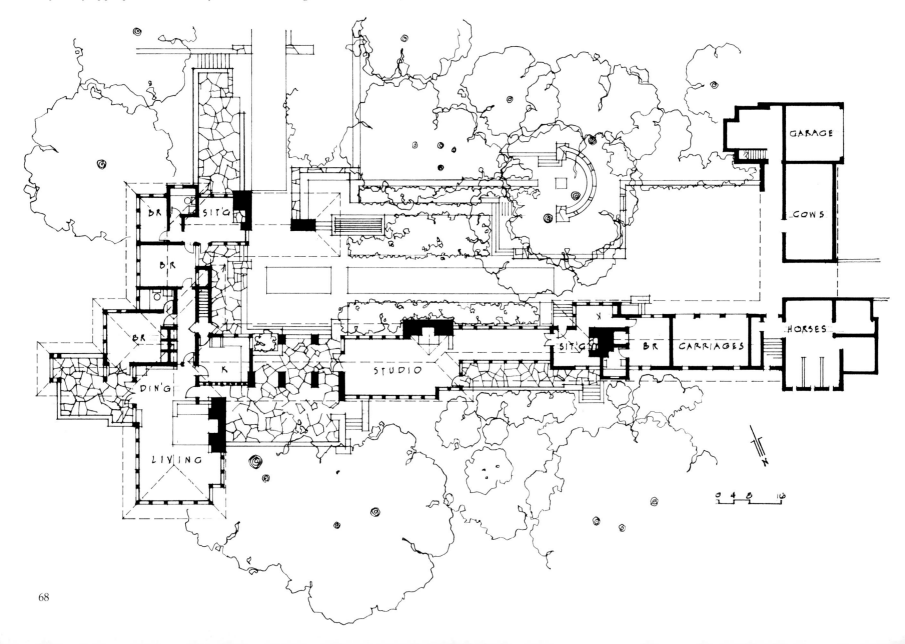

68

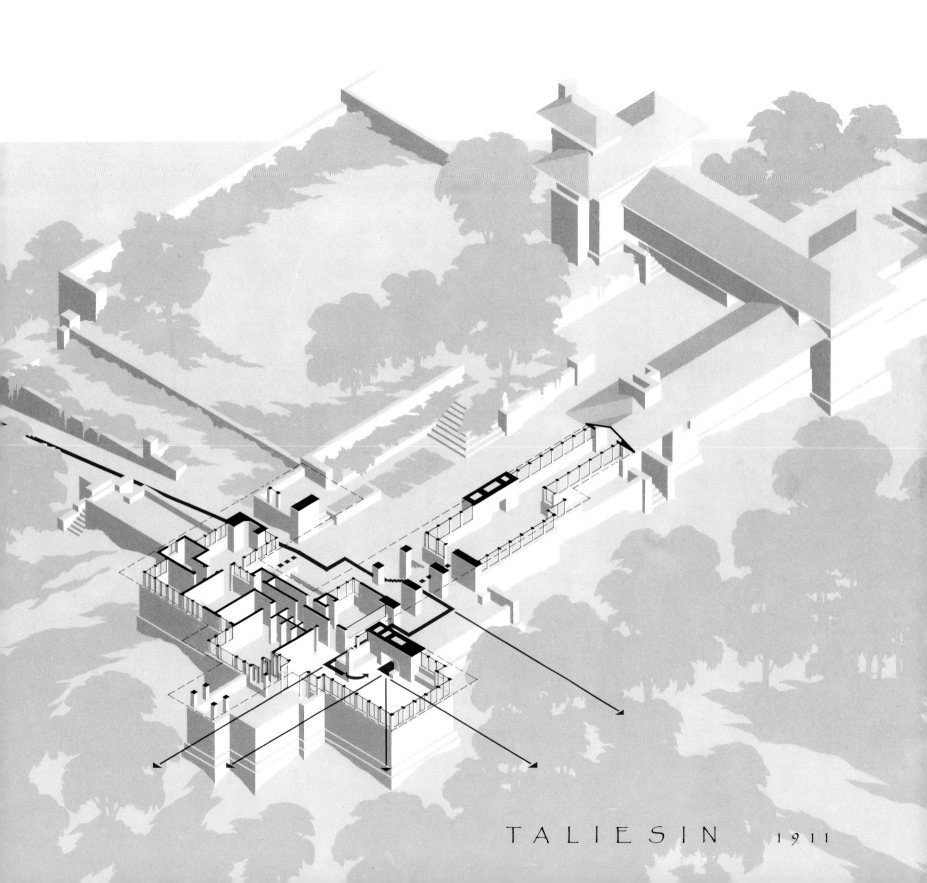

TALIESIN   1911

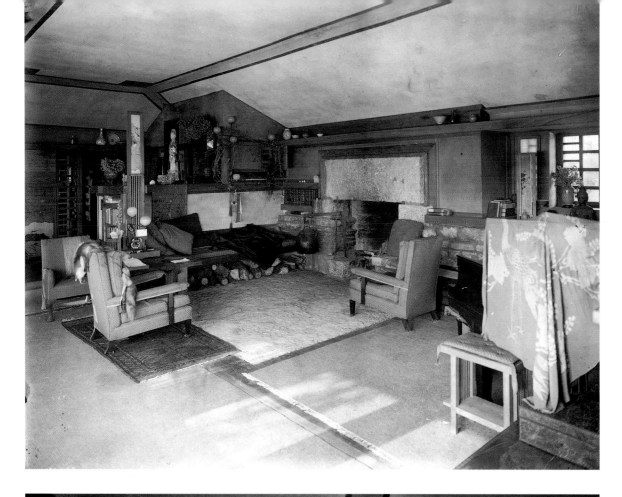

4.10 Taliesin. Living room looking toward the fireplace. The entry is at left, behind the half-inglenook seat.

4.11 Taliesin. Living room looking southwest. The entry is at far right; the terrace is reached through the opening at far left.

The living room fireplace, under the low ceiling edge, is flanked by the seating promontory with partial wall, the primary "gathering place within." The stone hearth extends forward of the fire the full length of this promontory, comprising a floor area of about 7 by 8 feet. It, too, is of roughly hewn stone, its dimensions and texture reinforcing the image of a cave fire.

Old photographs (figs. 4.10–4.12) show the seating promontory ending in two light wooden pylons on which are hung Japanese prints or scrolls, their long vertical format carrying the eye toward the ceiling. Today, after many remodelings, this ceiling is congruent with the now-raised roof plane, but originally it was much lower and its central portion was flat because of collar-ties to the roof joists to eliminate thrust against outer walls. Both the sloping and the horizontal planes of the early ceiling were framed with "marking-strips of waxed, soft wood" which expressed the ceiling as rising "into the roof, tent-like."[18] The tent analogy was rather consistently held. Unlike the Heurtley, Coonley, or Robie houses, there were neither skylights nor artificial lighting systems built into this ceiling. And its marking-strips were far more delicate than in any prior work; the suggestion was quite genuinely of a tent. As well as rising, however, the sense was equally of its descending, enveloping the gathering within. This was due to the location of the most dominant trim piece, the edge of the continuous dish shelf, at exactly the elevation of its exterior counterpart, the eave, and of about the same dimension. It established an emphatically intimate scale and a containment as well.

Another aspect of Taliesin also addressed containment. Wright argued on many occasions that he was trying to destroy the "box," by which he meant the self-contained wall-bounded room of traditional domestic architecture.[19] In this effort he was remarkably successful in the open plans of the Prairie houses of 1902 to 1909; and later in his career he was also notably successful in this regard. But not at Taliesin. In spite of the fluid disposition of its rooms, it was in no sense an open plan. Each room was an utterly self-contained box—rich and complex but a box nevertheless (fig. 4.8). Dining was included within the living space, but unlike the entire family of houses from 1902 to 1909, this living space did not open through articulating devices to any contiguous space, nor did any other rooms do so. This condition also obtained in the few other houses and projects of this time, the Angster house of 1911 in Lake Bluff, Illinois, for example, or the Vosburgh house of 1916 at Grand Beach, Michigan.[20] The well-known Francis Little house of 1913 in Wayzata, Minnesota, now de-

4.12 Taliesin. Living room looking north. The range of windows, only a part of which is visible in this photo, provided a sweeping panorama of the valley and the hills beyond; see fig. 4.9.

molished, also shared this condition of self-contained rooms, though the condition was less apparent because of the enormous size of the living room and its exposure to views on both flanks. Even the elaborate Sherman Booth project of 1911 for Glencoe had no rooms actually open to one another. The effect was that interior prospect, so skillfully developed at Cheney and so elaborately at Coonley, did not occur at all in these buildings, nor at Taliesin. This was appropriate at Taliesin, at least, where containment was deliberately sought and consistently developed in so many other ways.

The seating promontory and fireplace conjunction as used at Taliesin had by this time become a repetitive feature with Wright. It implies a diagonal axis from the fire, and at Taliesin this implication was realized. The room opened diagonally: the center of panorama was at the opposite corner of the living room. The view was similar to that obtained from the stone terrace before entering, a panorama north and east across the valley.

The terrace did not extend from either range of the windows that released this view. It lay rather behind the scenes, south, not east, of the fire (figs. 4.8, 4.9, 4.11). To reach it one passed under the dish shelf and an adjacent bit of very low flat ceiling, then out under an equally low roof soffit—a wing of roof projecting outward from the house for this purpose—and then to the release of the sky and the prospect across the valley, again seen through the trees. Why was the pattern modified to place the terrace as a removed lateral extension of the plan, rather than as a straightforward extension of the interior prospect condition? Had the terrace been done in the typical way, it would have required (almost certainly) a cantilever, as the hill falls away at that point and a perimeter foundation would be awkward. But Wright was no stranger to cantilevers even at this date. More probably the issue was the provision of view downward to the valley from the living room. This view would have been frustrated by a terrace, especially by one with a solid plastered rail, the usual below-sill condition at Taliesin. So the terrace was displaced as in the Glasner and McCormick schemes (see figs. 3.26, 3.27, 3.29).

The valley to which the Taliesin view was released, as Walter Creese has eloquently observed, was then bounded at its distant edges by hills comparable in height to that under which the house nestled (fig. 4.1, 4.4). (The post-1925 remodeling raised the roof of the main body of the house, compromising its original pervasive subservience to the hill.) Here too the choice of the hillside siting enhanced the sense of refuge, allowing Taliesin to be contained within the valley's boundaries rather than transcending them; its world was a finite one, the valley which Wright called "the beloved ancestral valley . . . my Grandfather's ground."[21]

Thus in 1910 Wright created in Taliesin a particularly firm but gentle refuge. Four years later he would need it much more. On August 15, 1914, a deranged employee at Taliesin murdered Mamah Borthwick, her children, and several others, and burned the house. Wright described the tragedy in what Scully has called "some of the most restrained and moving writing ever done in America,"[22] to which Wright's son adds, "something in him died with her."[23] He rebuilt the house much as it had been before; its gentle refuge was then even more desperately appropriate.

But the model of refuge that this early Taliesin provided was a limited one, and indeed Wright found it so. In later years he remodeled it to open the plan and to give far greater emphasis to interior and exterior prospect; and when, in the late 1930s, he built Taliesin West, he developed grand prospect conditions indeed. Thus, in less threatening times, he returned to a more even balance between refuge and prospect—but with a difference. Taliesin marks a turning point. In his houses of the period from 1902 to 1909, refuge and prospect were secured without loss of communality. Most of those early houses offered the inhabitant, at his choice and control, both a refuge from and a participation in the community's space, the city or suburban street. After Taliesin, that clever and effective relationship would rarely recur.

5. The California Houses

Wright's next important houses are a distinctive group of five structures in and around Los Angeles. The first is the stuccoed tile and frame Hollyhock House of 1917–21 on Olive Hill in Los Angeles, built for theater patron Aline Barnsdall. The other four, all done from 1921 to 1924, are notable for their specially cast, square, concrete block bearing walls and piers.[1] Wright was enormously proud of the first of the concrete block series, La Miniatura, in Pasadena, for Mrs. George Madison Millard, a house that has been admired in other quarters as well. But these houses, and the concrete block ones especially, have had a bad press.[2] They do appear as formidable bastioned retreats, in part at least as a result of the sense of weight imparted by the material, which has led many critics to comment on their forbidding character. But they are an important chapter in the story of Wright's pattern. And one of them, the Charles Ennis house—paradoxically and in my view unfairly the most castigated of the lot[3]—introduces not only an unprecedented manipulation of interior prospect but also the phenomenon Stephen Kaplan calls *mystery.*

All these California houses are contemporary with the worst period of Wright's relationship with the volatile Miriam Noel, which followed the Taliesin disaster. The earlier ones are also contemporary with Wright's last travels in Japan, during which he was "exhausted and sick, weakened by the climate, and quite lonely."[4] Reyner Banham has observed,

These were the years also of his spiritual wilderness. Beginning in August 1914 . . . Wright suffered a psychological battering that would surely have unhinged lesser men. The whole incredible story—a cross between *King Lear* and *Peyton Place,* with additional dialogue by August Strindberg—was to last for all of 15 years. Throughout that decade and a half, psychological uprootings alternated with physical displacements each exacerbating the effects of the other.[5]

In *An Autobiography,* Wright could describe the earlier building of Taliesin in lucid and flowing terms. His descriptions of the California houses of the troubled times are in sharp contrast; they are turgid, confused, almost unreadable. There can be no doubt that these houses coincided with the most threatened and unstable period of Wright's entire life.[6] It is easy enough to suggest that their protective character arose not only from his interest in concrete as a material but also in part from his own embattled state.

It is also true, however, that all of these California houses except La Miniatura occupy what Appleton would call prospect-dominant sites, hilltops or hillsides that command tremendous panoramic views. If any sense of secure haven were to be had on such sites, it could only be gained by an architecture with emphatic refuge connotations.

Aline Barnsdall's Hollyhock House, in its setting on Olive Hill, is an example of this emphasis on refuge. Olive Hill towers above its environs, commanding views in all directions to dramatic distant horizons. Though Wright had said that no house should ever be "on" a hill, exclusion of any of these views was, at least on the face of it, unthinkable. So he deliberately located Hollyhock exactly on the crown; he referred to it as "in full stature on its hill," adorning "that hill crown."[7]

Therefore, Wright faced a dilemma: his preoccupation with refuge was understandably paramount, yet he was designing for a site which, unlike the Taliesin valley, offered none. Refuge could be attained only by recourse to the architecture, and he shaped Hollyhock to provide it. The gentle roof pitches of the Prairie houses and Taliesin are gone. The steep slablike faces of the roof mass—there is no other word for it—reinforce most urgently the idea of a protective cave within (fig. 5.1). In this and in some other respects as well Hollyhock House does not precisely deploy all the features of the pattern on its external façades. Heavy overhangs occur, but not on the outward-facing elevations. Windows are punched into the mass below, having nothing like the horizontal sweep of his work of 1902 to 1914.

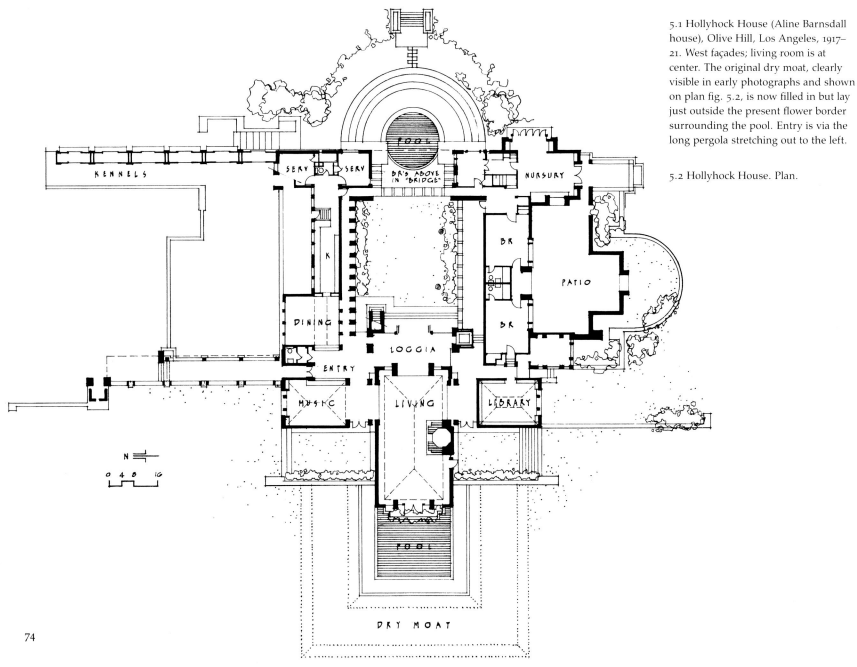

5.1 Hollyhock House (Aline Barnsdall house), Olive Hill, Los Angeles, 1917–21. West façades; living room is at center. The original dry moat, clearly visible in early photographs and shown on plan fig. 5.2, is now filled in but lay just outside the present flower border surrounding the pool. Entry is via the long pergola stretching out to the left.

5.2 Hollyhock House. Plan.

The massive walls, not the constrained windows, are in control here, holding the hill crown like a fortress bastion.[8] Unlike the Coonley house, or Taliesin, these walls are also entirely monochromatic, encouraging us to read them as a continuous thick shell. Beyond the west wall with its tiny terrace is a pool, now edged with flowers but originally surrounded by wide ditch, a dry moat. Refuge signals predominate.

Unlike Wright's typical entries, that of Hollyhock House is not particularly circuitous; length and spatial compression are made to serve the same purpose. One first passes a concrete pylon on the right, looking rather like a guard tower, then under a fantastically extended peninsula of roof. A few feet ahead, a run of steps brings one's head close to the ceiling of this extended roof; one then moves forward through three long bays of the pergola, with parapet walls to either side (fig. 5.3). At the end of this pergola the façade of the house is finally reached, but not the front doors; they lie many steps beyond, at the end of a narrow and dark corbeled tunnel. These doors—there are two of them—are low narrow valves of solid concrete. As one swings their palpable weight and moves through them, the sense is of entry into a vault.

Inside and ahead lie a profusion of pylonlike masses between which are glimpses of the major spaces. Significantly, one such glimpse reveals the fireplace of the living room, toward which one is drawn, though the path to it is indirect; one must go by way of either the loggia or the music room (figs. 5.2–5.6. The massive fireplace dominates the living room. Its hearth extends fully a third of the room's width, as did the one at Taliesin, but the hearth at Hollyhock House is otherwise quite different. An octagonal island serves as a floor for the fire; it is surrounded by a pool, the conjunction of the two conjuring up one of Wright's strongest images of a subterranean cave. And this suggestion is made by more than just the pool at the fireplace, for the water-course that feeds it begins at the circular fountain-pool at the east boundary of the garden court, moving from there in an underground stream to the fireplace, and thence, underground again, to the square pool west of the living room.[9]

5.3 Hollyhock House. Entry.

5.4 Hollyhock House. Living room, shortly after occupancy. The original seating shown here—two massive sofas contained by elaborate cabinetwork—echoed the diagonal faces of the octagonal fireplace hearth toward which they fronted.

And yet, surprisingly, aside from the fireplace, the interior sense of a contained fortress or cave is less firm by far than was suggested by the exterior. Forward of the fireplace the ceiling rises to its center (fig. 5.6). On the exterior the roof zone that contains this ceiling is ponderously weighty; the actual interior ceiling seems totally unrelated; it is light, tentlike, a descendant of the ceiling at Taliesin. The skylight over the fireplace does wonders to relieve the mass of both fireplace and ceiling. East of the fireplace, voids rather than masses are paramount: interior prospect is available to the contiguous loggia and music room (figs. 5.2–5.5), and there is a lush exterior prospect to the garden court and its distant pool. Even the west window of the living room, which had seemed so constrained from the outside, from the interior seems to encompass much of the west wall (fig. 5.6).

Nevertheless, most of the openness of Hollyhock House is to a small world, bounded, one feels, by the massive architecture of the house itself, and focused not outward but toward the interior garden. Despite the breadth of the living room's west window, there is only limited exterior prospect to the magnificent panoramas of Olive Hill; the feeling, and the fact as well, of the living room is that its orientation is eastward, to the garden court. The tiny terrace to the west can be reached through the french doors, but the terraces to north and south are blocked from the living room by solid walls, and must be reached by leaving the living room. (A small glazed door to the south terrace opens to the right of the fireplace, but it seems a minor passage, unrelated to the generous terrace accesses of Wright's work from the Cheney house onward.) Only from those north and south terraces can one really sense the prospect-dominant drama of the site, at which point one feels strangely outside the composition, entirely cut off from the major spaces of the house. Otherwise the perceived limits are the pool to the west, the garden pool and the pine/eucalyptus grove to the east, and the very solid north and south wings of the house itself. In this sense Hollyhock turns even more to its garden and less to its distant prospects than Taliesin. And only on the garden façades do the familiar deep eaves, shadowed windows, alcoves, and recesses of Wright's pattern appear in full measure (fig. 5.7). They convey from within this courtyard the penetrability that is denied by the external façades.

5.5 Hollyhock House. Interior prospect: from the living room fireplace looking toward the music room, entry, dining, and loggia.

5.6 Hollyhock House. Living room looking west.

This introversion evolved with the design. Early studies show the west condition of the house as being rather different, and its evolution to final form is illuminating. A drawing from the middle stages of the design, when the Mayan roof form was fixed but the Hollyhock ornament not yet developed,[10] showed glazed french doors from the west end of the living room opening out to a genuine and generous terrace, in east-to-west dimension about as deep as the living room itself, and extending north-to-south the full width of the main house. Though its west central boundary was marked by a planter, it had no other railing or parapet; it was edged only by broad steps to the lawn, falling away below. Such a condition was consistent with Wright's typical pattern, and would have introduced a dramatic element of prospect into the scheme. But as studies advanced, the living room seems to have been pushed forward onto this terrace, which in the process was reduced to a vestige only about 2 feet deep, while the north and south portions, cut off from view from the living room, were given solid parapet walls.

This early drawing and all subsequent ones show a range of tall and dense plantings immediately east of the house. This is typical of Wright's drawings; usually they indicate dense verdure behind the building represented, with open space to the front. Such indications intensify the prospect-refuge duality: open space, prospect, is toward the viewer; closed vegetation, refuge, is beyond. The famous drawing of the Cheney house (fig. 3.2) is one such example among many.[11] Often the vegetation seems to have been a preexisting part of the site condition, but it was not at Hollyhock.[12] Photographs of the house taken shortly after completion show new saplings to the east, and Wright himself says Aline Barnsdall planted them: "She planted pine-groves behind on the hill and great masses of the Eucalyptus to enclose the pines."[13] These plantings exactly correspond to Wright's drawings; clearly Miss Barnsdall was carrying out Wright's own intentions. These plantings to the east, together with the foreclosure of prospect conditions to the west, are the means by which Hollyhock's world was turned inward. Although there is openness within these bounds, the grand prospect-dominant site is nowhere allowed to vitiate the sense of containment.

5.7 Hollyhock House. Garden court looking toward the loggia. The living room lies beyond the dark recess under the deep eave.

La Miniatura (fig. 5.8) was done in 1921–22, in Pasadena, for Mrs. George Madison Millard, for whom Wright had done a house in 1906 in Highland Park. The site for La Miniatura is intensely refuge-dominant, a tiny ravine with lush vegetation. Significantly Wright, not Mrs. Millard, chose the site; he steered her away from one she had already purchased which was apparently prospect-dominant:

Meantime we had rejected the treeless lot originally purchased by Mrs. Millard, as my eyes had fallen upon a ravishing ravine near by, in which stood two beautiful eucalyptus trees. The ravine was reached from the rear by Circle Drive. Aristocratic Lester Avenue passed across the front.

No one would want to build down in a ravine out there. They all got out onto the top of everything or anything to build and preferably in the middle of the top. It was a habit. I considered it a bad habit . . . [although he had done just this at Hollyhock, and rejoiced in doing so].

We would head the ravine at the rear on Circle Drive with the house, thus retaining the ravine as . . . a sunken garden.[14]

Like most of Wright's houses of the Oak Park days, La Miniatura fronts directly on a city street. Unlike most of them, it directs the views of its major spaces emphatically toward the rear of the site, making of the street façade a series of richly modeled but closed surfaces (fig. 5.9).

The composition of La Miniatura's main spaces (fig. 5.10A–C) is similar to the Hardy house, from which it clearly derives (see fig. 3.24A–C). The only spatially fundamental changes are the balcony projecting from the south façade of the living room, the perforated screen over the top half of that same façade, and the flat ceiling and roof. The balcony cuts off some view to the pond in the ravine beyond; but the balcony is shallow (fig. 5.10B), therefore of minimal obstruction, and its inclusion must have seemed more irresistible in Southern California than in Wisconsin. The perforated block screen is also appropriate in the Southern California climate, serving as a light filter, softening and dappling the sunlight. The glass is carried up to the ceiling inside this screen, allowing it to act in this way.

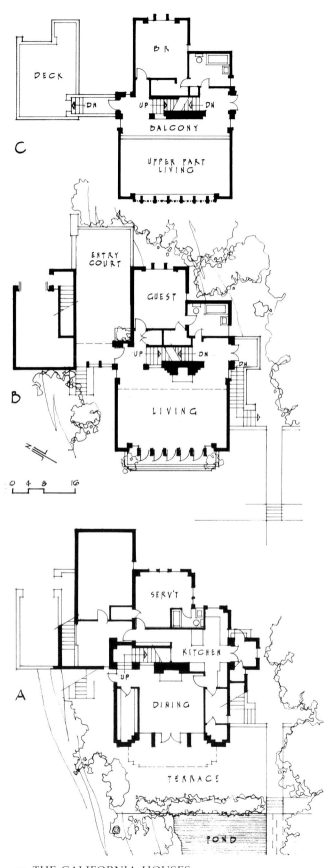

C

5.8 La Miniatura (Mrs. George Madison Millard house), Pasadena, 1922.

5.9 La Miniatura. Façades toward the street.

5.10A–C La Miniatura. Plans: A. Lower floor. B. Main floor. C. Upper floor.

5.11 La Miniatura. View from the garden.

As the Hardy house, unusually for its period, turned away from the street, so does La Miniatura, although the thick concrete walls of La Miniatura make a more forbidding barrier. But on the opposite side the Hardy house had opened to the extended prospect of its lake; La Miniatura's vista on the side opposite the street façade is short and tight. It is edged by the ravine of Wright's choice, the earth itself, all around, and above is vegetation of unusual density. At the Hardy house the living room windows turned the corners to release the view and destroy the box (fig. 3.25). At La Miniatura the corners are of fortresslike solidity, while the absence of eaves reinforces our interpretation of the building as a box (figs. 5.8, 5.11). At Hardy the living room glass extends upward to the eave; at La Miniatura the textile block occupies the upper half of the wall, and though it is pierced for dappled sunlight, it can hardly be understood as a grove, for the block has the lavalike weight of Wright's Imperial Hotel.[15] Hitchcock calls La Miniatura and its setting "marvellously beautiful,"[16] while Gill says it is "among the most beautiful houses to be found anywhere in the world."[17] Both comments are just—yet La Miniatura's beauty is that of a richly introverted megaron enfronting and tentatively peering out to the hollow of the earth, an architecture of exquisite containment.

With the next three houses, Wright's pattern began to open up once again. The John Storer house of 1923–24 presents Wright's usual circuitous entry: one wends one's way up to and across the entry court, and into the second-from-left of the range of doors ahead, then up a full flight of stairs and through five right-angle turnings—to arrive at the living room fireplace. This fireplace is the anchor of a magnificent elevated pavilion, the only room on the upper floor, with views to north and south, and terraces to both east and west (fig. 5.12 A–B). Eaves have been reintroduced as well, reinforcing the dramatic sense of outlook (fig. 5.13). Interior prospect, however, is limited to a view up to and across the balcony leading to the west terrace (fig. 5.14).

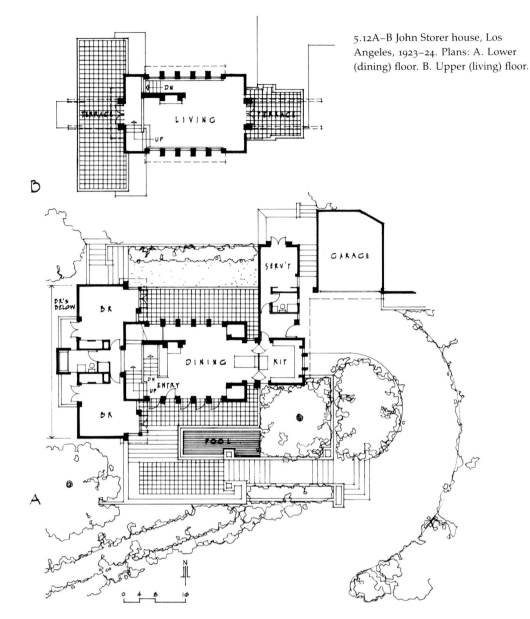

5.12A–B John Storer house, Los Angeles, 1923–24. Plans: A. Lower (dining) floor. B. Upper (living) floor.

The Samuel Freeman house of the same years also has a plan with limited interior prospect (fig. 5.15). The Freeman house is unique among the California series in having a concrete-beamed roof structure: two great north-south beams, over 1 foot wide and 4 feet deep, ponderously divide the room into three compartments. But this house also has a lot of glass, encompassing nearly half the perimeter of the living room, and for the first time Wright has made it meet at the corners without a mullion, glass butting directly to glass (figs. 5.15–5.18) to make the most box-destroying corner imaginable.[18] The balcony off the living room, with a deep overhanging eave above, is lowered by three steps (fig. 5.18) to release a stunning view south across Los Angeles. The configuration of the Freeman house is strikingly similar to that of the Cheney house, including the entry sliding into the corner of the living room next to the fireplace, the tripartite division of the major space, and the assignment of its central portion to the fireplace on the one side and the terrace access on the other (compare figs. 5.18 and 3.4).

5.13 Storer house. Exterior from the south.

5.14 Storer house. Living room, looking toward the stair to the upper western terrace. To the right of the fireplace is the stair by which this elevated pavilion is reached.

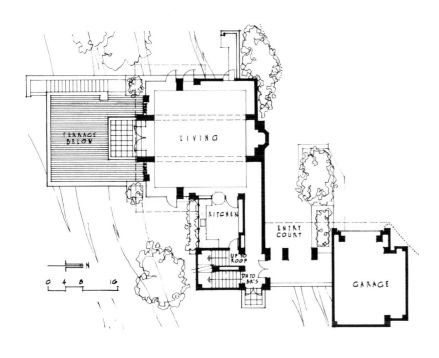

5.15 Samuel Freeman house, Los Angeles, 1923–24. Plan.

5.16 Freeman house. Interior seen from the fireplace, looking toward the butted glazing of the living room corner.

5.17 Freeman house. Exterior detail from the lower terrace, looking toward the butted glass corner

82

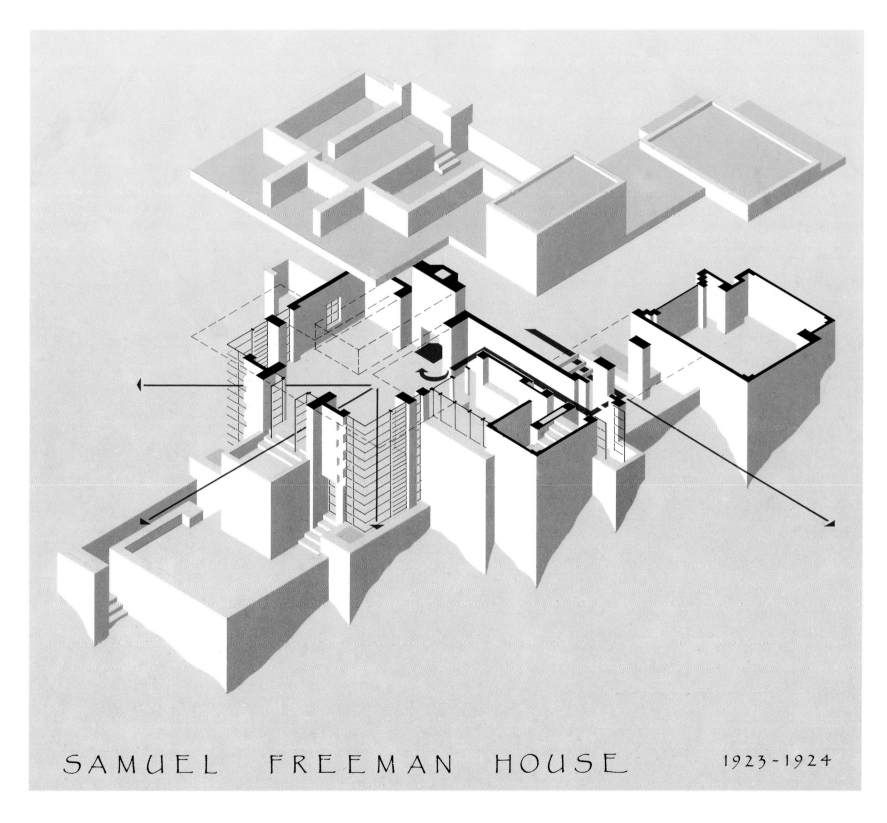

SAMUEL FREEMAN HOUSE 1923-1924

5.18 Freeman house. Diagrammatic drawing by William Hook. Compare this configuration with fig. 3.4.

5.19 Charles Ennis house, Los Angeles, 1923–24. Exterior from the south.

5.20 Ennis house. Plan.

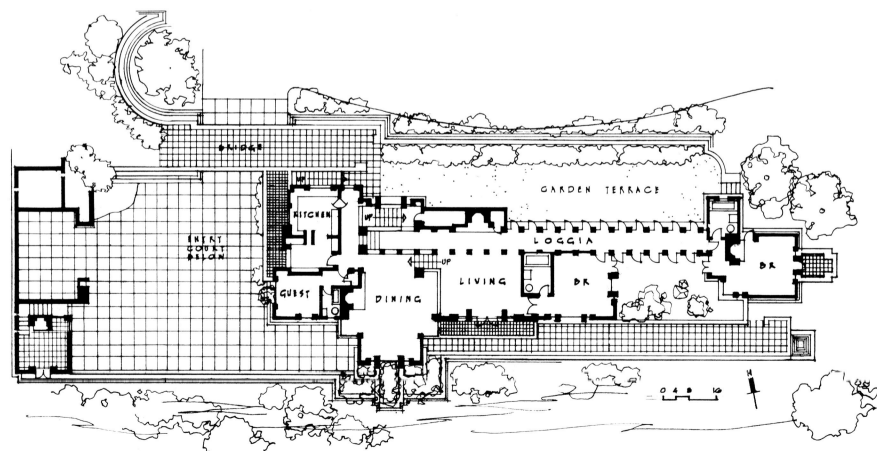

The contemporary Charles Ennis house is often considered the most overpowering of the California group. Certainly the blockwork, inside and out, is deployed with an overwhelmingly elaborate textural richness (figs. 5.19, 5.21, 5.23), while the absence of eaves, one of the strongest symbols of protective haven, leaves it devoid of that clue to domesticity. Yet the Ennis house is a building of enormous importance, one of the key buildings of Wright's career. It deserves a more detailed spatial analysis than it has yet received.

Some moves have been made to offer exterior prospect conditions: both corners of the dining room have been opened with butted glazing like that of the Freeman house; the french doors from the living room swing outward to a small balcony with a magnificent panoramic view; and the loggia, a glazed reinterpretation of that of the Martin house of 1906, is a wonderfully open phenomenon with splendid views both north and south (fig. 5.20).[19]

The manipulation of the interior, however, is the really creative aspect of the Ennis house. If we can shift our attention from the richness of the solids to the configuration of the voids—and admittedly, this is not easy—we find that this house reintroduces Wright's mastery of the open plan and interior prospect, and does so with a stunning virtuosity that includes the mature deployment of a powerful and heretofore unexplored spatial characteristic.

Typically in Wright's houses after 1904 the entry has been architecturally suppressed—hidden from immediate view, with a small, plain door opening into a low, plain vestibule. At the Ennis house the whole entry configuration is so understated that it seems out of key. One enters via a low and unimpressive door (fig. 5.21) into a low and unimpressive entry hall, only 6 feet 8 inches from floor to ceiling. This hall offers no clue to the grandiose scheme beyond it (fig. 5.22). To the left is a stair. Lacking other options, and drawn by the light above, one ascends it (fig. 5.23), turns right at the top (again for lack of options), ascends two more steps and moves forward into the main floor spaces of the Ennis interior. Brendan Gill has described the entry sequence to the Cheney house as "transforming the simple act of entering a building into a complex rite, with overtones of the sacred."[20] This is even more true of the Ennis house. The sense of sanctity is palpable, but the mood is primordial, recalling Rachel Levy's description of entries to the Aurignacian caves:

5.21 Ennis house. Entry court. The entry is at left within the dark recess; the main floor lies above.

5.22 Ennis house. Entry hall. The stair to the upper (main) floor is at left.

. . . These defenses of twisting, often very narrow, always slippery corridors, along which the intruders groped their way, clinging to curtains of stalactite, descending into chasms . . . whose dimensions their tiny lamps could never have revealed . . . and beyond these to desired recesses . . . to the painted hall with its rock-cut "throne," "a mystery desired and sought" as its discoverers describe it, "in an arcanum forbidden to the profane."[21]

The entry to the Ennis house is as close to this experience as one can come in a twentieth-century American house on a sun-drenched California hillside.

One arrives, then, at the main floor (figs. 5.24–5.26), and enters the stalactite-curtained richness of the loggia, which, as the plan reveals, is the conceptual basis of the entire scheme, the river of space and light from which the other spaces, like eddying pools, depend. To left and right the loggia extends for all of nineteen bays. So powerful is this space that one feels the need to step out of its velocity into one of those eddies; the first one available (see fig. 5.20) is the living room (figs. 5.27, 5.28).

This living room is fully 21 feet in height.[22] The moment one steps into it, the simple but enormously powerful axial prospect of the loggia is replaced by something much more complicated.

To the west the living room opens to the dining space via the wonderful transition of the stair and the screen of columns (fig. 5.29). At the southeast corner of the living room is the deep recess leading to Mrs. Ennis's bedroom suite; the upper part of the living room continues as a kind of deep minstrel gallery over the bathroom of this suite (fig. 5.28). To the north is the rich opening through the colonnade into the loggia, with its complex vistas to northeast and northwest, to sky, stairs, and the terminals of the loggia itself (fig. 5.30). The dining space shares all these vistas and looks back to and across the entry stair as well, whose fenestration mirrors and is on axis with that of the dining space (fig. 5.31). This is some of the most splendid interior prospect in Wright's career, perhaps in all architecture.

The living room fireplace, then, is not really in the living room but in the loggia, perhaps because this was the only location which could have given it a lower ceiling. (Although at its present height of 13 feet 4 inches the ceiling is hardly low by Wright's usual standards, his original drawings of this area show a very low ceiling indeed, at the height of the present loggia ceiling to east and west). Another reason for the odd fireplace location may have been to encourage an understanding of the loggia as being a part of the living room. In this

it is not very successful; the tall intervening piers keep both fireplace and loggia distinct from the living room proper. (The early drawings convey the impression that the relationship would have been more successful with the original lower ceiling, making the fireplace seem to lie within a more typically Wrightian alcove.) But the fireplace succeeds in calling attention to the importance that the loggia seems to have had in Wright's mind—for the loggia is the key to the openness of the plan, and to almost all of its vista richness. Its open relationship to the major spaces is what determines many of the vistas and a majority of the most interesting ones.

5.23 Ennis house. Ascending the stair to the main floor.

5.24 Ennis house. Diagrammatic drawing by William Hook.

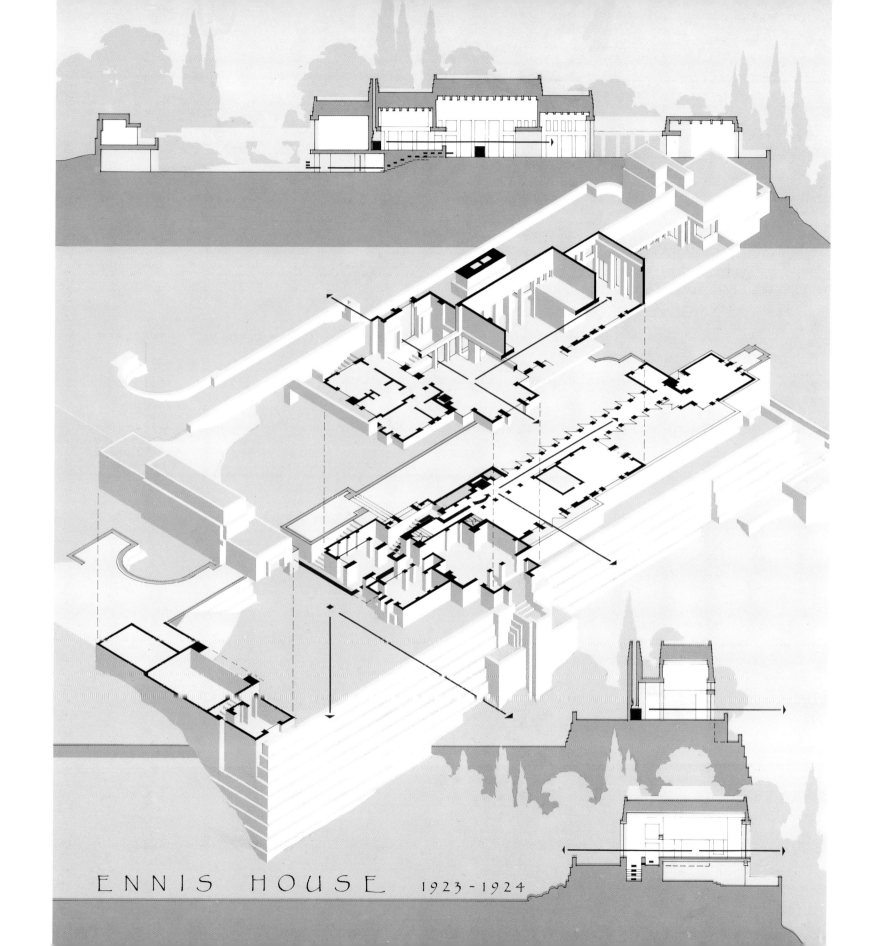

ENNIS HOUSE 1923-1924

5.25 Ennis house. Upper floor loggia. The view is back toward the entry stair. Up the short run of stairs to the left is the gallery that leads, at center, to the kitchen.

5.26 Ennis house. The loggia from the stair head; the living room opens to the right.

The loggia is also the key to a characteristic in these vista conditions that differentiates them from Wright's previous work. The plan arrangement of the Ennis house is similar to Coonley (compare figs. 5.20 and 5.24 with 3.10 and 3.11, including bedrooms, at far right in each case). The important difference is that at the Coonley house the hallway was separate from the major spaces, while at the Ennis house the hallway (loggia) and the major spaces are joined. This condition alone yields considerable spatial enrichment—but more can be said of it. Since the loggia lies to one side of the spaces it serves, views into or from it are on diagonal axes. Thus while at the Coonley house there were tentative inferences of diagonal vistas, at Ennis these diagonal vistas are paramount. They are reinforced by the elevated floor of the dining space, which yields upward and downward views rather than horizontal ones, and by the unprecedented variety of ceiling heights (figs. 5.23, 5.24, 5.29). The high glazing in the loggia north and south of the fireplace has a similar effect, as does the upward view to the "minstrel gallery" of the living room.

5.27 Ennis house. The loggia as it opens to the living room.

5.28 Ennis house. Living room, looking toward Mrs. Ennis's bedroom.

The diagonal vistas of the Ennis house also increase the characteristic of complexity, since vistas open not only in orthogonal directions but in all directions, thereby teasing our tendencies to seek further variations of experience stimuli. And this leads to a consideration of other complexities of the Ennis house: the changing floor and ceiling elevations, much more varied than is usual even for Wright; the changing textures of the blocks; and above all the ever-shifting quality of the light, from the brilliance of the loggia to the gloom of the entry stair and the kitchen hall. All this is held in control by ordering elements of enormous power. Most obvious of these is the reiterated and absolute module of the blocks themselves, which ensures modular relationships of all other surfaces. The piers of the loggia also establish a forceful rhythm, and since the loggia opens to all contiguous spaces, that rhythm informs them as well. And the exotic Mayan-Palladian window motif, a large central panel of leaded glass flanked by lower narrow panels, is repeated at five key locations: dining space, living space, entry hall, and both main floor bedrooms (see figs. 5.20, 5.24, 5.25, and 5.31). The dining and entry windows, furthermore, lie exactly on axis with one another and each is visible from the other through the open stair colonnade. These characteristics speak to our fundamental predilections for ordered complexity.

The spatial organization of the Ennis house marks another development, for it introduces yet another condition of fundamental human appeal, that of *mystery.*

In Wright's work generally, there is a sense that spaces lie beyond spaces. This is true even as early as the Heurtley house, since the entry stair and dining room are both visible through, but set off by, the screen of columns that articulates the seam between them. At the Cheney house this same phenomenon occurs through a similar instance of interior prospect: one sees spaces beyond spaces.

At the Coonley house, largely because of its horizontal extension, this characteristic is exaggerated, but is also slightly different. For there, in a modest way, the zigzags of the corridor system create a condition in which one is aware that there is a more distant space, but unlike the Heurtley and Cheney houses, one cannot precisely see into it without moving toward and into it. Thus, if more information about that sensed but unseen space is sought, it cannot be had without investigation.

5.29 Ennis house. Living room, looking back toward the loggia and the entry stair. The dining room is at left, up the broad flight of stairs.

5.30 Ennis house. Loggia fireplace.

This phenomenon of distant spaces suggested but not immediately revealed is carried very much farther at the Ennis house. From either the dining or living space, one has an extensive view into the loggia (figs. 5.28, 5.29, 5.31). But from the dining space, one cannot see the bedroom-accessing portion of the loggia, nor the spaces to which it leads (fig. 5.31), while from the living room one is conscious of that bedroom-ward extension but also cannot see it (fig. 5.28). Nor, because of the mass of the piers and the deepening light, can one grasp the limits of the loggia's extension toward the kitchen (fig. 5.29). Likewise, the beginning of the stair down to the entry is visible (fig. 5.25), but the destination is concealed. Thus, the diagonal axes of vista at the Ennis house are repeatedly accompanied by a sense that spaces exist beyond one's field of vision, and can only be understood by investigation.

This is not a trivial point. Stephen Kaplan has described an empirically validated preference for similar conditions in nature:

> The most preferred scenes tended to be of two kinds. They either contained a trail that disappeared around a bend or they depicted a brightly lit clearing partially obscured from view by intervening foliage. In both cases the scenes appeared to promise that more information could be gained by moving deeper into the depicted setting. This promise of additional information tentatively was labeled "mystery."[23]

If we replace the natural features of this description by architectural ones—textured columns for trees and foliage, brightly lit loggia for clearing—this description is close to the conditions of the Ennis house, and the condition of mystery fits as well. The appeal of such a sequence of conditions appears to have its basis once again in biology. For the behavior induced has a survival value. Either danger or delight may lurk in the suggested but unseen environment, and it is useful to the creature to find out which it is. The stimulus is the suggestion but not the immediate revelation of distant spaces. The response is exploration to seek knowledge or information about those spaces. Thus the information-seeking component of our makeup is brought into play, driven and rewarded by the pleasure we find in deploying it. The Ennis house possesses this characteristic of spatial appeal at a far more developed level than any of Wright's prior work.

5.31 Ennis house. Dining room looking toward the entry stair. The loggia fireplace is in the distance at right.

So these California houses are significant. They are, by and large, compositions within formidably closed envelopes, and they all, one way and another, deploy Wright's pattern in most of its characteristics. And yet, done at a time when Wright was under considerable stress, their inventiveness is remarkable—remarkable, in fact, by any standard. While some of them draw their direction from some previous examples by Wright—La Miniatura from the Hardy house, Freeman from Cheney, Ennis from Coonley—they are all not only significantly different from their prototypes but also radically different from one another. They mark for Wright not only growth from the Prairie house model, but development in his management of space. One instance of this is found in the Freeman house, in which Wright carved away the solid wall, and especially the corner of that solid wall, to an unprecedented degree; an even more important example is the Ennis house, in which he interwove interior spaces with a stunning and unprecedented complexity.

These developments did not immediately bear much fruit. There was very little chance for them to do so, as Wright was desperately short of commissions for many subsequent years.[24] One result, however, can be seen in changes made at Taliesin itself. Taliesin burned again in 1925, just a few months after Wright had embarked on the relationship with Olgivanna Milanoff that was to bring some stability to his life. In the rebuilding after the fire, more rooms were needed for Olgivanna's daughter from a previous marriage, and for the daughter born to her and Wright. For this reason he added a second floor of bedrooms over the central portion of the living wing, and raised the living room ceiling dramatically to interweave with this second floor hallway by way of a balcony. An adjacent clerestory was included to bring in western light (fig. 5.32). These changes, progeny of the Ennis interior, yielded a limited but exquisitely orchestrated diagonal interior prospect from Taliesin's living room to the upper hall. At the same time this living room, heretofore relatively small, was considerably expanded to the east by a large and entirely glazed alcove with a sill significantly lower than that of the early windows (fig. 5.33). These changes roughly doubled the volume of the room. Equally important is the fact that they gave it vast gains in both interior and exterior prospect. After serving as refuge for fourteen years, Taliesin after 1925 began to open both to itself and to its site.

5.32 Taliesin. Living room after 1925, looking southwest.

5.33 Taliesin. Living room after 1925, looking northeast.

6. Fallingwater

In 1936, after a decade of busywork, failed projects, and sheer inactivity, Wright designed for Edgar Kaufmann a weekend house over a waterfall, on a stream called Bear Run in rural western Pennsylvania. Wright had long since acquired the habit of naming houses; this one he called Fallingwater.

In discussing the idea of house as refuge, I noted earlier the threats against which it more or less universally protects, those of climate and of societal intrusion. Such threats have no permanent visible manifestation; one cannot normally see their presence. In this sense, this discussion of architectural examples and settings differs from Appleton's discussion of landscape painting and literature, in which he often finds such threat conditions actually portrayed as storms, cliff faces, heavy seas, or waterfalls. These portrayed threats he groups under the term *hazard*.[1] This term has seemed to me to have too much inference of apparent physical danger to be appropriate for a discussion of residential architecture as refuge. Therefore I have used the term *threat*. But Fallingwater is a house confronting a natural threat condition with dramatic visible manifestation, and a house that, furthermore, complements this with an architecture of calculated hazardous daring. The management of this complementary confrontation is, in fact, the fundamental point of the whole architectural exercise. Reference to Appleton's categorization of hazards, and use of his terms, become, in this instance, appropriate and useful.

Appleton groups hazards under three main headings: incident, impediment, and deficiency. Of these only the first two concern us here, but they concern us intensely.

Under incident hazards Appleton lists two major subheadings, animate and inanimate. Within the animate, in turn, he cites human and nonhuman hazards. The nonhuman, I think, can be ignored for our purposes. Human hazards constitute the threats of societal intrusiveness already mentioned in connection with the Illinois houses, or the more specific sense of hostility germane to Taliesin and, to a lesser extent, the California work.

Appleton's second category of incident hazards is the inanimate. This is a large group, the largest of his listings in fact, consisting of meteorological, instability, aquatic, fire, and locomotion hazards. The meteorological I have already touched on under the near-synonym of threats of climate. Instability hazards are earthquakes, landslides, and avalanches. These affected Wright's work in Tokyo dramatically, and in California more subtly, but they are not issues in Illinois, Wisconsin, or rural Pennsylvania. As for fire, it twice destroyed Taliesin, and Wright was conscious of its threat in his working out of the California houses, of whose fireproof qualities he was proud. None of these hazards, it should be noted, is for our purposes necessarily tangibly apparent.

This leaves us, under Appleton's heading of incident hazards, with aquatic hazards and those of locomotion. Both of these categories, as we will see, differ from those above in that in relation to architecture, they will always have a tangible and apparent presence. Of the aquatic Appleton says:

Even calm water can be a fatal hazard to a victim who cannot swim, but the destructive potential of water is more eloquently expressed when it is moving, and waterfalls, rapids, and storm waves figure consistently in the landscape furniture of the Sublime. Falling water can symbolize the power of the forces of nature whether in Niagara or in the absurdly genteel "cascade" of the eighteenth-century landscape gardeners.[2]

And of hazards of locomotion:

One of the most prevalent is that of falling. We all know that fatal falls can be sustained even on level surfaces, but generally serious falls are associated with high elevations, and it is these which have the power of suggesting danger and arousing fear for those who encounter them. Here again, those landscape features which display this property, "beetling cliffs," chasms, precipices of all sorts, are among the hallmarks of the Sublime.[3]

These are obviously pertinent issues with regard to the Kaufmann house, although it remains to see how Wright exploits their symbolic potential. But before leaving Appleton and turning to Wright, it is necessary to refer to Appleton's second broad category of hazards. All the above he calls incident hazards; he lists a second smaller group of impediment hazards, the most important of which, for our purposes, are natural and also tangibly apparent:

In nature dense vegetation, cliffs, ravines, etc., may impede movement, as also may waterbodies of all sorts. . . . Rivers play a particular role in this respect, because under normal conditions they continue as lines of physical separation over long distances. . . . particular significance attaches to those places where such a hazard is terminated or interrupted. A crossing-place of a river, for instance, by a bridge or a ford, focuses the attention on the opportunity which it presents for circumventing or surmounting the hazard.[4]

Why should representations of hazard in Appleton's studies, or the architectural confrontation of tangible hazard conditions, be of importance? One answer to this, surely, is that the apparent presence of such hazard conditions intensifies the emotional value of the refuge by giving an apparent evidence of the conditions against which refuge is secured. But there is a deeper reason too, for Appleton argues that survival requires sensitivity to danger signals, and this point once again invokes the pleasure-response rationale:

If we were to be interested only in those features of our environment which are suggestive of safety, cosiness and comfort, and not at all concerned with those which suggest danger, what sort of recipe for survival would that be? Seeking the assurance that we can handle danger by actually experiencing it is therefore itself a source of pleasure.[5]

Herein lies the appeal of strolls along cliff edges, or of sailing in choppy seas. More to our purposes, we all know the intensification of pleasure brought about by rain pounding on the roof while we are tucked up safe in bed, or by the storm raging outside while we are gathered around a fire. In each case we are programmed to find excitement in the presence of discomfort and even danger; we also find an intuitive pleasure in its dramatization of the value of security. The comments of Bachelard, cited in Chapter 3 in the context of the Robie house, illustrate the same point. Melville writes of a similar phenomenon in *Moby Dick*:

We felt nice and snug, the more so since it was so chilly out of doors; indeed out of bedclothes too, seeing that there was no fire in the room. The more so, I say, because truly to enjoy bodily warmth, some small part of you must be cold, for there is no quality in this world that is not what it is merely by contrast. Nothing exists in itself. If you flatter yourself that you are all over comfortable, and have been so a long time, then you cannot be said to be comfortable any more. But if, like Queequeg and me in the bed, the tip of your nose or the crown of your head be slightly chilled, why then, indeed, in the general consciousness you feel most delightfully and unmistakably warm. . . . Then there you lie like the one warm spark in the heart of an arctic crystal.[6]

6.1 Fallingwater, the Edgar Kaufmann house, Bear Run, Pennsylvania, 1936. The approach to the bridge.

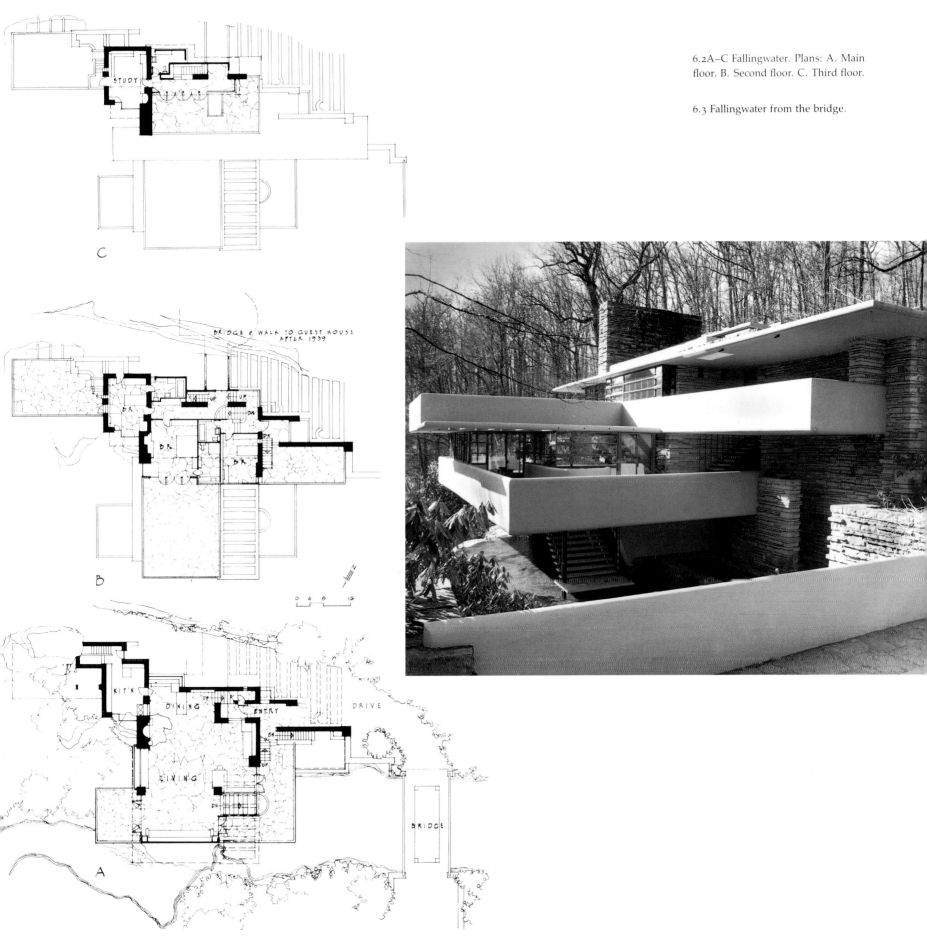

C

STUDY

B

BRIDGE & WALK TO GUEST HOUSE
AFTER 1939

BR

BR

BR

0 4 8 16

A

KIT'N

DINING

ENTRY

DRIVE

LIVING

BRIDGE

6.2A–C Fallingwater. Plans: A. Main
floor. B. Second floor. C. Third floor.

6.3 Fallingwater from the bridge.

It is time now to look at the Kaufmann house itself, to push through the dense vegetation and enter the ravine, traverse the bridge across the river, and consider the man-made beetling cliffs overhanging the rapids and the falling water. That sentence names fully six physically apparent hazard symbols; yet these are the actual conditions as they are perceived on approach to the Kaufmann house (fig. 6.1), and none of them is timidly presented. These are hazard symbols reduplicated with a vengeance. And they yield both values. They are intensely pleasurable in themselves, and they powerfully intensify the refuge and prospect symbols also present from this view. The familiar symbols are all here: deep overhanging eaves, windows, alcoves, recesses, conspicuous balconies. All are profuse. Overhanging eaves are in places so deep they mask entirely the recesses underneath; this is especially true of those portions of the house nearest the bridge (fig. 6.3). Yet in certain lights the house is all balconies. And in yet other lights, the bands of windows, more continuous and extensive than in any other of Wright's work, equally seem dominant. Alcoves and recesses likewise are everywhere. Inferences of penetrability and of protection thus are extraordinarily strong, yet almost every one of these features conveys the potential for sweeping outlook as well. Here are signals that this is the epitome of the place to see without being seen, its appeal made more intense through the dramatic confrontation of a setting against which warmth and comfort find a complementary measure. We are invited to savor danger from a haven of safety.

There is also, even in this first view, both complexity and order. Complexity reveals itself in the multiple possible interpretations mentioned above. There is also an obvious geometric complexity; probably no house since the Palace of Minos has had so complex a configuration. Twombly says that "Fallingwater seems to take flight every way at once, making it exceptionally difficult to analyze or to describe."[7] But if the eye wants resolution, that too is easily had. All the verticals are stone; from them the tan trays pinwheel, all in rectilinear shapes, all of identical vertical dimension, identical detail, and identical coloration, all separated by an identically dimensioned stratum of void.

Even from the bridge, then, the house offers an extraordinary linkage with our inherent habitational preferences. Within symbols of nature's hazard reduplicated by its own audacious precariousness, it tells us with unequaled richness of its potential for refuge and prospect, has given us a complexity inviting of further exploration, and yet has given immediate clues of order.

6.4 Fallingwater. Approach to the entry. The entry lies within the stone masses at lower left, behind the rhododendron.

Beyond the bridge, refuge symbols follow immediately. Within 20 feet of the bridge head and closing its vista is the heavily overgrown hillside (figs. 6.1, 6.2A, 6.4), its formations reminiscent of primordial refuge places, the ravine walls penetrated by early man for his cave dwellings. One turns left along this bank, which thus becomes a wall on the right flank. Within another 20 feet one is embraced by the rock pylons of the house on the left; at the same time the overhead closure of a glade is suggested through its abstraction in the concrete trellis (fig. 6.4).

One walks between two of the rock pylons to find yet another rock face ahead, and then the main entry, rock-floored and clamped between two rock masses only 4 feet apart (fig. 6.5). Immediately inside, one is in an antechamber surrounded by these rock masses, with rock still underfoot, the sense of cave reinforced still more by the depressed floor (fig. 6.6). One must climb out of this antechamber.

6.5 Fallingwater. Entry from the exterior.

6.6 Fallingwater. Entry vestibule.

And then, having done so, quite suddenly all is prospect (fig. 6.7). The single-minded emphasis on refuge so dominant at the early Taliesin and at La Miniatura has no place here. Every condition at Fallingwater is presented with a drama unique even in Wright's work. This prospect condition, suddenly come upon, is no exception. Glass is everywhere. In no earlier building, and in few subsequent ones, did Wright open panorama to this extent. The prototype of this extensive corner-turning transparency is the Freeman house, but the massive piers in this case are withdrawn from the plane of the glass; although the window mullions of Fallingwater do actually support the floor above, the impression is of a continuous panorama under a floating plane of ceiling. The verdure of the glen surrounds us. The foliate leaded glass of the prairie houses is re-placed by the actual foliage of the glen, visible through something like a 180-degree sweep occupying our entire range of peripheral vision. Diagonally opposite the entry, to the southwest, is the most extended vista, the long reach down the axis of Bear Run.

Again there is complexity and order. The route to this spot has been a complicated one, and having arrived at this point we are confronted with the usual complexities of Wrightian space. What shape is the room? Is it one room or several? But the central part is nearly square in plan and is so marked out by the stone pylons, and we are given a clear clue to this by the geometry of the ceiling pattern. The sill line is either at floor level or at the level of the terrace parapets which, seen beyond, recall the order perceived externally. The upper edge of glass is at a constant height everywhere.

6.7 Fallingwater. Living room looking south.

6.8 Fallingwater. Living room fireplace.

6.9 Fallingwater. Window seat south of the fire, looking west. The earth bank seen on entry reappears as the view through this window.

Behind to the right is the fireplace (fig. 6.8). It is a half-cylindrical void formed of the roughly coursed rock, with the same material to right and left. The void is high, going right up to the ceiling edge; it seems eroded from the rock masses of the ravine. Its hearth is the unworked surface of the living rock, two peninsulas of an undisturbed boulder which rise out of the stone-surfaced floor a foot and more.

On either side of the fire to west and north conditions occur which are a departure from the usual pattern. A seat lies to the south (fig. 6.9) and a buffet to the north (fig. 6.10)—these are predictable and canonical—but over each is glass. Normally Wright's fireplace pockets, as interior refuge, are bounded by opaque surfaces, as we have seen. Yet at Fallingwater he has been able to make the glass serve the refuge pocket because of the unique site. How so? From the window over the seat the foliage is near and dense. The hill bank rises to the right, anchored by the enormous body of rock whose eastern tip is the fireplace hearth. Downward are the cleavages of the glen's rock strata. Thus the glass looks out to a terrain of grove and cave, reduplicating the refuge character of the fire area. The glass to north over the buffet is even more effective; it looks to the cave-suggesting hillside hardly more than 10 feet away. (In this area, and in fact throughout the house, the refuge characteristics of Fallingwater are especially dependent on relationships to the foliage of the site. Thus in winter, when the deciduous foliage is absent, the house is prospect-dominant to a degree unusual in Wright's work. In that sense, it is indeed a summer house, engaged in a dialog with its site which is not only formal but temporal as well.)

The ceiling of the living room makes another departure from the pattern. Its upward extension (fig. 6.7) is modest by comparison with Wright's typical living rooms. There are habitable spaces above—the master bedroom and its terrace. This location for these spaces, as we have seen, is highly unusual in Wright's work, but is necessitated in this case by the configuration of the site. These superimposed habitable spaces prevent the usual upward expansion of the living room ceiling. Yet even had they not been there, it is hard to see how Wright could really have pushed the ceiling upward very much, given the vocabulary of flat concrete trays poised in space; the two ideas are incommensurable. That said, Wright took all the upward spatial expansion he could get by pushing the slab upward to the very underside of floor and terrace above. It is not enough; there is not here the exhilarating sense of release usual in Wright's grander high-ceilinged spaces; but it indicates Wright's determination to provide what he can of this feature, even when circumstances are against it.

6.10 Fallingwater. Buffet north of the fire; the earth bank beyond.

6.11 Fallingwater. Diagrammatic drawing by William Hook.

F A L L I N G W A T E R   1 9 3 6

The master bedroom repeats in its interior not just the pattern but its particular configuration as in the living room below (figs. 6.2A–B, 6.11). The fireplace is similarly located, and eroded from shelves of rock. The prospect, as in the living room, is the long reach of vista diagonally down the glen. The enormous terrace, however, is dramatically different. It extends toward the south, unlike the east and west terraces of the living room (figs. 6.11, 6.12). This is the most dramatic prospect-platform of the entire composition. It is the Cheney terrace, in a way, yet so much more dramatic. It reaches out to the south beyond the living room below, hovering over the falls, while its greater elevation lengthens the views and includes within them the terraces below. And from it, because of prior knowledge but also because its hovering character is recalled by the forms all around, there is the perceived hazard of falling, as there is to a lesser degree from the living room terraces. Thus, the prospect-claiming meadow with refuge behind is at the same time a precipice over space and over the reduplicating hazard symbols of rapids and falling water.

As one moves from the interior spaces outward onto the many terraces of Fallingwater, it is always by way of a transitional experience provided by a deeply overhanging eave. So far as I know, no one has ever commented on the strange eaves of Fallingwater. They play a role analogous to the one they play in all of Wright's work; therefore they are worth some discussion. And Fallingwater is the place to discuss them because here, unlike the easily built eaves of much of his other work, they were a far from easy matter, and the effort Wright put into their provision underscores their importance. Except at the south edge of the living room, they are not like the parapets; they are thin slabs cantilevered from the bottom edge of the parapet. Now this is a particularly difficult way to do an eave. Structure is not a problem, as the steel reinforcing in the slab beyond, also on the underside of the parapet, can just be continued into the eave. But making a practical roof over the eave, and especially flashing it both effectively and tidily where it meets the parapet wall—these are really hard problems. Then why is the eave done this way? The answer is complex.

The parapets generally act approximately as beams for Fallingwater's cantilevers,[8] and if they lie in the plane of the wall below, they gain a tremendous and probably essential advantage through being placed directly over the obvious line of support. (The parapet over the south edge of the living room happens to be an exception, since it is perpendicular to the direction of the cantilever and therefore acts only to stiffen the edge of the slab.) But if these parapets lie in the plane of the wall below, then obviously they cannot overhang that wall; therefore they cannot themselves become overhanging eaves. A false second parapet could have been cantilevered beyond to provide such an overhang, but it would have been heavy, and the sheer physical weight of the concrete work at Fallingwater was seen as a problem by all concerned. So the eaves more or less had to be done as they were. But if they were all this bother, why have them at all? It isn't likely that they are there—either at Fallingwater or in any other example—to protect the windows from the weather, for Wright could be appallingly casual about weather and weathering for both the architecture and its occupants. So why the eaves? They perform three interrelated roles, all explicable within a prospect and refuge interpretation.

The first, the exterior signaling of refuge and prospect, I have already mentioned in numerous examples.

The second has to do with the shading the eaves provide, and the consequent difference in light condition between interior and exterior. For eaves such as these largely prevent direct light from striking the interior.

6.12 Fallingwater. View from the second-floor terrace.

Thus the interiors of Fallingwater, like those of all of Wright's houses, are cast into shadow by the eaves, making the interior at all points darker than the exterior in daylight conditions. This is essential if the interior is to provide a clear signal of refuge, for the grove or cave to whose refuge we were primordially attracted would always have had just such a subdued light quality as one of its essential distinguishing characteristics. The eaves at Fallingwater, therefore, as elsewhere in Wright's pattern, provide an architectural replica of this contrast in light condition between sheltering grove or cave, and meadow or savannah beyond, and in so doing make available the appeal such settings have always had for us. For this condition to obtain, then, these eaves are crucial.

The eaves also modulate the transition between interior and exterior. As one moves from living room or bedroom to terrace at Fallingwater, or in any other of Wright's houses, one emerges from the darker refuge to the brighter prospect, but not abruptly; movement is through the french doors outward under the architectural bower of the eaves, and thence to the brighter light of release to the sky, as though one were gradually emerging from under the foliage of a dense forest grove into an open meadow. And for this condition also to obtain, these eaves are crucial.[9]

The sense of refuge at Fallingwater is, for some, compromised a bit by a sense of precariousness, which is not only thrilling but also occasionally disturbing. In the southern portions of the house there is a discomforting sense that it really might pitch forward into the stream. This is not all paranoid imagination. The house has not broken, as Wright said it would not, but it has bent, outward and downward.

Bending and breaking are independent considerations in engineering, based on different theory and different calculations; both have a role to play in the design of structures. A trained professional engineer will design a structure not only to prevent breaking (failure) but also to prevent excessive bending (deflection), and often it is the concern over deflection, not failure, that will drive the structural solution.[10] Wright, as an intuitive and largely self-trained engineer,[11] was often brilliant in his invention of original and failure-safe structures. But time and again he seems to have taken the issue of deflection lightly. His own account of Romeo and Juliet reveals as much. He wrote with pride about its survival against collapse. Yet he admitted that the

workmen came down from the work in high winds and said that "the tower swayed in the wind several inches."[12] This kind of problem plagued much of his work throughout his career; both the Prairie houses of his early years and the Usonians of his later life often show extreme deflection both in main spans and in cantilevers. This deflection on occasion considerably disfigures the intended elegance of the otherwise magnificent horizontals.[13]

Wright was advised at the time of Fallingwater's construction, by engineers retained by the client, that more strength was needed through adding reinforcing of the concrete trays and increased substructure. These suggestions, I surmise, were put forward out of concern for deflection as well as failure. Wright seems to have mistaken them as addressing the question of collapse, and exulted over the fact that, contrary to those views as he understood them, the building did not fall down. But it has deflected, obviously and precariously.

And yet, in studying the plan, one realizes that Wright had no real choices. The key matter is that of the withdrawn pylons under the living room and its terraces, where the deflection is most crucial and disturbing. This part of the building is responsible not only to itself, but also carries at its southern edge the entire weight of the upper floor as well. Therefore its own support condition is vital, and it is here that there are precious few options. The stair from the living room down to the rapids, most would agree, is an important element of the scheme, and its northern edge is what determines the limit of the adjacent pylon, which therefore cannot be prolonged. The others could have been, of course, but to little purpose, as a cantilever system, like a chain, is not much stronger than its weakest condition. Nor could the terrace edge be withdrawn northward, since passage to the terrace south of the stair is already more or less minimal. Nor would one want to run deep beams under the slab; these would destroy the smooth underside of the terrace at considerable aesthetic cost. So the problem was inherent in the concept, with no easy answers.

Despite his bravado about the house even Wright may have realized that he was pushing the structure very far indeed. Edgar Kaufmann Jr. recounts a moment when Wright, sick and delirious, was heard muttering "too heavy," apparently in reference to the balconies of Fallingwater.[14] Edgar Kaufmann Sr. worried about the problem for the rest of his life, with some cause.[15]

The classic view of the house is from across Bear Run and down the ravine to the southwest (fig. 6.13). Apparently this is more or less the spot where Kaufmann had originally imagined the house itself would be located.[16] It is the obvious location, since from it the waterfall of which Kaufmann was fond can be seen, as it cannot from the house as built. Almost any other architect, following Kaufmann's lead, would have chosen this as the place. Yet Wright rejected it, choosing instead the small plateau of the falls itself and the bouldered area directly above.[17] In doing so he realized several advantages.

The most obvious advantage is that the site over the falls allowed him to bring direct sunlight into the major rooms, as he could not have done downstream. This is because of the greater elevation of the chosen site, and its location on the north bank, which means that rooms looking out to the ravine, and to the slight clearing it provides, face south rather than north.

The chosen site also allowed Wright to provide his typical condition of prospect, in which the view from the living spaces is toward lower or falling terrain. The downstream site could not have offered this unless the house had looked west, away from the waterfall, in which case the whole point of that location would have been lost. Yet had the house looked toward the waterfall, and therefore toward rising terrain, the intuitive strategic advantage of a commanding elevated position would have been unavailable, and the view toward the falls above would have been overwhelming rather than stimulating; one would have felt more at the mercy of nature than in rapport with it. Thus in terms of prospect positioning, and of relationship to hazard, Wright's decision to build directly above the waterfall itself was appropriate.

Another advantage of this site has to do with the degree to which the sound of the waterfall infuses the house. It is a commonplace that the waterfall is heard throughout; it is less commonly observed that its sound is muted by the masses of concrete that intervene between the waterfall and the living spaces. Had the house been located at the spot of Kaufmann's choice, the only intervening material, presumably, would have been the glass of the overlooking windows, and glass is far less effective than concrete in dampening sound; what counts is mass, and the stone-floored concrete trays, with their concrete parapets, are ideal in providing mass, while glass is not.[18] Wright seems to have had a grasp of such issues of acoustical control from an early date; of the design of Unity Temple in 1904, he said: "The site was noisy, by the Lake Street [trolley] car-tracks. Therefore it seemed best to keep the building closed on the three front sides."[19] At Fallingwater, because he chose the site as he did, he could interpose the concrete trays between the sound source and the habitable spaces, with the consequence that the sound is heard throughout, but softly. One is continually reminded of the presence of nature's hazard while aware that one rests within a haven of security.

And yet, all these advantages could have been achieved without putting the house exactly where it is. The key is the north bank, and any other location on it would have done as well. Wright's audacious decision to put the house directly over the waterfall, however, confers a final advantage—subtle but of paramount importance—that is unique to the chosen spot: for had he chosen any other site, the house's relationship to the symbol of nature's hazards would necessarily have been passive; at any other location the house would have been, unavoidably, a composition standing apart from the waterfall rather than wedded to it. And in view of what was actually done, this can be seen as a crucial issue. For the house as built does not simply overlook nature's drama, it participates in it, and can only do so located as it is. And this helps us to understand the importance of the trays cantilevered into space over the water, for they are the essential elements on which this architectural participation depends. Their daring is obvious to anyone; echoing the overhanging rock strata of the falls in dimension, coloration, and geometry, their hovering precipices match and complement the hazard of the site. The hazard, thus reduplicated, intensifies to an unprecedented degree the refuge and prospect messages of the house itself. This is the genius of the relationship between the house and its waterfall.

A few years before Fallingwater's design John Dewey had written: "There are stirred into activity resonances of dispositions acquired in primitive relationships of the living being to its surroundings."[20] These words seem especially appropriate to this house. For at Fallingwater human habitation is configured to provide with unique intensity symbols of prospect, refuge, and hazard, and conditions of complexity and order, to which the human species is genetically attuned. Critics often regard this house as Wright's most accomplished feat. It is also quite possibly architecture's most accomplished manifestation of our fundamental choices of pleasurable setting.

6.13 Fallingwater from below along Bear Run. The view is from the area Kaufmann had had in mind for the house itself.

7. Taliesin West

In 1928 Wright, on honeymoon with Olgivanna, had gone to Arizona as a consultant on the Arizona Biltmore Hotel in Phoenix; the architect was a former employee of Oak Park days, Albert McArthur, who sought Wright's help. In January of the following year Wright returned to Arizona to work on a project for a large resort, San-Marcos-in-the-Desert, near Chandler.[1] To do the work he built a desert studio and residence nearby, which he named Ocatillo, after the flowering cactus.[2] This temporary structure, which Wright called an ephemera,[3] was an open campus of dispersed pavilions defined and joined by continuous lightweight board-and-batten walls (fig. 7.1). The pavilions and walls encircled a low mound in the desert (fig. 7.2); the entire complex, however, lay well below the elevation of the horizon and therefore was contained within the landscape's edges, suggesting a stark version of the site relationships of Taliesin on its hillside within the hill-edged Wisconsin valley. Above Ocatillo's light wood walls perched spiky triangular wooden frames, asymmetrical in their pitch; of them, Wright observed: "The one-two [30/60 degree] triangle used . . . is made by the mountain ranges themselves."[4] These frames supported tented canvas, the only roof, which both shed the rain and softened the desert sun (figs. 7.3, 7.4). "We painted the horizontal boards . . . dry rose as the color to match the light on the desert floor. . . . We will paint the canvas eccentric one-two triangles in the gables scarlet. The one-two triangles of the ocatillo bloom itself are scarlet."[5]

The wood walls that bounded the complex were only infrequently interrupted for small windows and for the entry; thus refuge from the desert's almost limitless expanse was lightly but firmly declared throughout. In the center was the camp fire, a surrogate of the fireplace at the center of Wright's more typical houses. Wright's own living room within Ocatillo (at far left on the plan, fig. 7.1) was a microcosm of the familiar pattern. Turning away from the rest of the complex, its fireplace was located within three blank walls, the fire thus becoming the focus of a refuge not only from the desert but from the remainder of the complex as well. Opposite was the largest external opening of the entire complex, leading to the predictable terrace, sheltered from the desert by the continuous wooden wall.

Wright was not always the most lighthearted of architects, yet the distinguishing and wonderfully appealing characteristic of Ocatillo was exactly its fresh lightheartedness. As Reyner Banham has observed,[6] this was true not only of the camp but of Wright's prose describing it:

A group of gigantic butterflies with scarlet wingspots, conforming gracefully to the crown of the outcropping of black splintered rock gently uprising from the desert floor. . . . A human gaiety in the desert is under way. . . . Now, when all these white canvas flaps—wings like sails, are spread, the buildings . . . will look something like ships coming down the mesa, rigged like ships well balanced in the circumstances. The little camp finished, we love it.[7]

Ocatillo turned out to be quite literally ephemeral. The stock market crash of 1929 killed the Chandler project, the camp was abandoned as a result, and some time thereafter it was dismantled by local Indians. Wright later remarked: "I have learned not to grieve long now that some work of mine has met its end; *has had its short life,* as we say."[8] But one can grieve a little about the Ocatillo camp's demise; it was one of Wright's most delightful creations.

Seven years later Wright had a severe bout of pneumonia, the cause of the delirium that revealed his worries about Fallingwater. His doctor advised him to spend no more winters in Wisconsin. Accordingly, in 1937 he went again to Arizona. But it is easy to suspect that there was more motivation for the trip than just doctor's orders, for his response to this terrain was as enthusiastic in 1937 as it seems to have been in 1929. He wandered the barren landscape to his chosen spot, "a great mesa in the mountains. On the mesa ["on," once again] just below McDowell Peak we stopped, turned and looked around. The top of the world. . . . The desert seems vast but the seeming is nothing compared to the reality."[9] Here, on land fifteen miles outside Scottsdale (then no more than a crossroads), he began the design of a new winter home and studio. It was to be a structure marrying the ephemeral character of Ocatillo with the eternity of the pyramids, for Wright would merge the idea of the

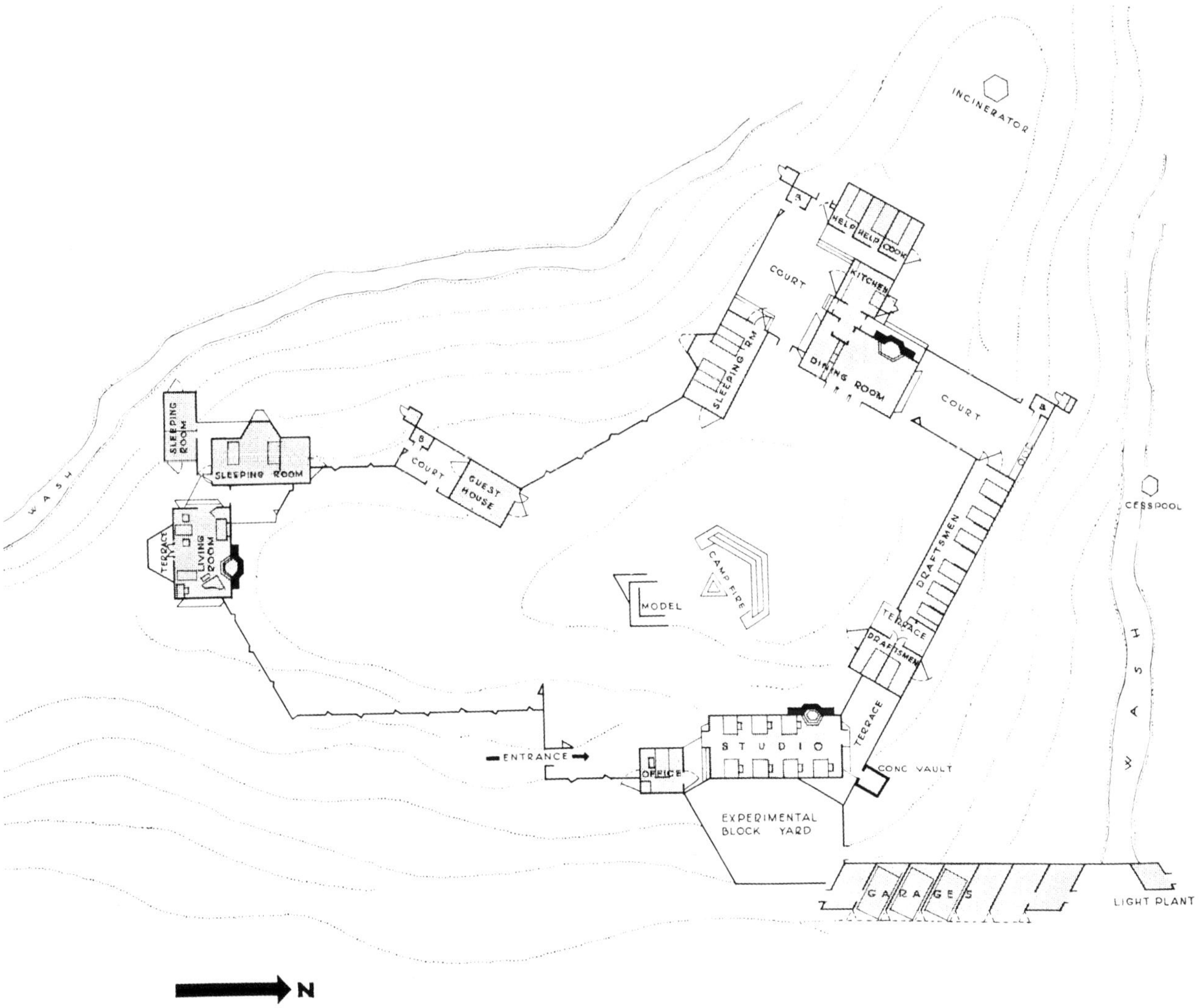
INCINERATOR
HELP
HELP
COOK
KITCHEN
COURT
SLEEPING RM
DINING ROOM
COURT
SLEEPING ROOM
SLEEPING ROOM
COURT
GUEST HOUSE
TERRACE
LIVING ROOM
WASH
CAMP FIRE
MODEL
DRAFTSMEN
TERRACE
DRAFTSMEN
CESSPOOL
WASH
ENTRANCE
OFFICE
STUDIO
TERRACE
CONC VAULT
EXPERIMENTAL BLOCK YARD
GARAGES
LIGHT PLANT
N

7.1 Ocatillo, near Chandler, Arizona, 1929. Plan.

7.2 Ocatillo. The camp on its low mound, from the west.

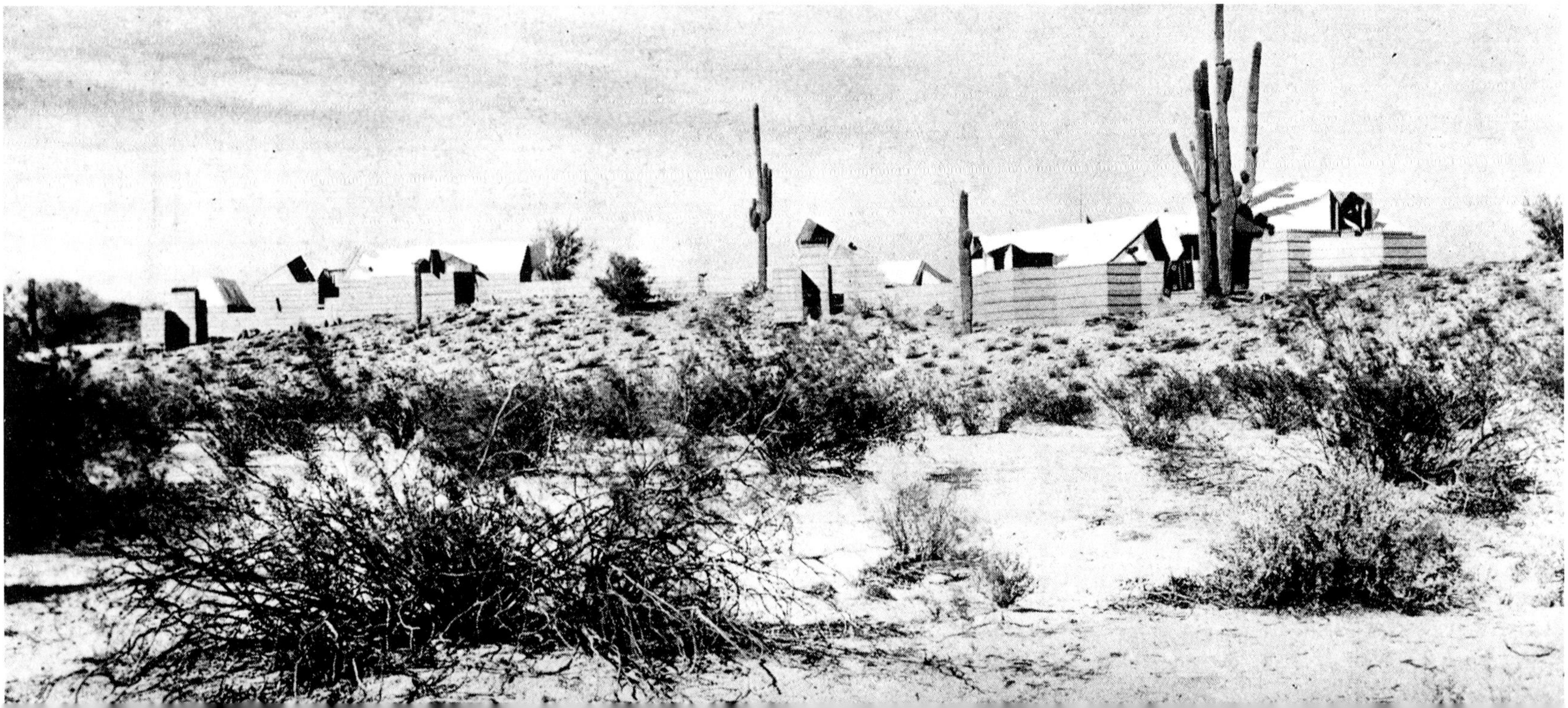

Ocatillo wood-and-canvas superstructure with a sub-structure of concrete-held boulders, a massive abstraction of the desert's geological depths. After some fumbling for a name—Aladdin and Rockledge were tried[10]—he did the obvious and named it Taliesin West.

The site (fig. 7.5) is utterly prospect-dominant. The grand sweep of desert is punctuated only by scrub growth and cactus and, the building aside, lacks any hint of refuge. The only possible inference of containment is in the distant mountain ranges, upscaled surrogates of Taliesin's hills, which are the visual horizons of the plateau. But this desert is not only prospect; in its harsh aridity it is also imbued with hazard, and is immediately and intuitively understood to be so. For in our earliest environments, the wooded edges of the savannah and later the tighter security of the cave, a part of our pleasure-driven selecting mechanisms must necessarily have been attuned to the appeal of water; had this not been so we would have perished. John Ruskin notes the presence of this feature—and of prospect and refuge as well—in the earliest literature of the Western world: "As far as I recollect, without a single exception, every Homeric landscape, intended to be beautiful, is composed of a fountain, a meadow, and a shady grove."[11] There is also sound empirical evidence to show that a pleasurable response to water is still an intact part of our makeup.[12] Furthermore, there is good reason to think that it was important to Wright throughout his life, since many of his major houses go to great lengths to include water.[13] But the Arizona desert, except for its brittle scrub growth, gives no clue to the presence of water: no trees, no rivers, no snow on the distant mountains, not even a fair-sized arroyo to record the former presence of some now-vanished watercourse.

Appleton considers this kind of landscape as one that presents a hazard of deficiency, in that characteristics crucial to survival are conspicuously absent. He quotes a passage from Ole Rolvaag's novel, *Giants in the Earth*, which describes just such a landscape:

The broad expanse stretching away endlessly in every direction, seemed almost like the ocean . . . the nearest dwelling places of men were far away. Here no warbling birds rose on the air, no buzzing of insects sounded; even the wind had died away; the waving blades of grass that trembled to the faintest breath now stood erect and quiet, as if listening, in the hush of the evening . . . the stillness had grown depressing, the farther west they journeyed. . . . Had they travelled into some nameless, abandoned region? Could no living thing exist out here, in the empty, desolate wastes? If life is to thrive and endure, it must at least have something to hide behind![14]

Why then would Wright have chosen such a site? Perhaps just for the challenge of it? For surely to the old master refuge-maker, this must have seemed a foe eminently worthy of his genius. At the age of seventy, did he perhaps envision an architectural confrontation with this dramatic desert as his last and greatest challenge? Certainly Taliesin West conveys the drama and tension that any single building, symbolizing a lone refuge, must unavoidably assume within such a site.

7.3 Ocatillo. Looking toward Wright's living quarters, from the camp fire.

7.4 Ocatillo. "Wings like sails . . ."

7.5 The desert near Taliesin West.

7.6 Taliesin West, near Scottsdale, Arizona, 1937–. Plan. The entry approach begins at far left.

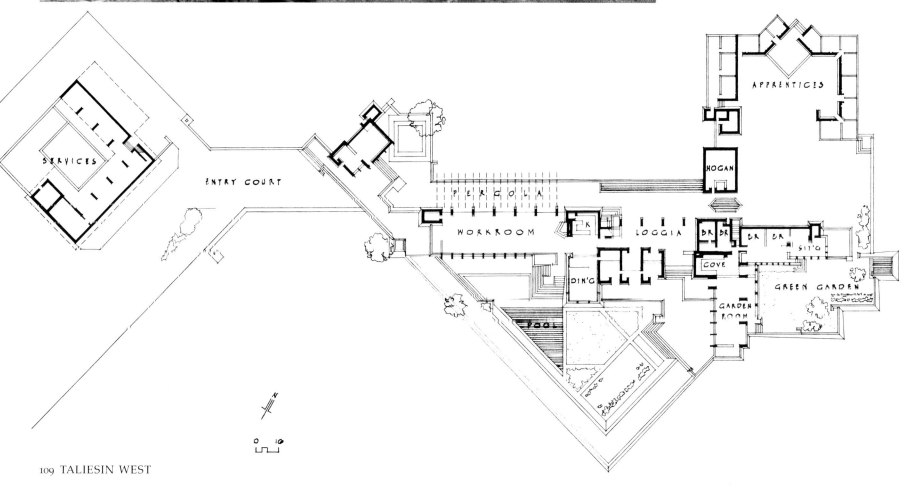

SERVICES

ENTRY COURT

PERGOLA

APPRENTICES

HOGAN

WORKROOM

LOGGIA

BR BR

DR DR

SIT'G

K

COVE

DIN'G

GREEN GARDEN

GARDEN ROOM

POOL

N

0   10

7.7 Taliesin West. Near the entry court; workroom at right.

7.8 Taliesin West. Approach to the entry court.

But there is, of course, far more to it than this. To approach and enter Taliesin West we are led (fig. 7.6), as usual, through a processional path of maximum length and complexity, to remove our consciousness, as in those prehistoric caves, far from the setting of hunter and hunted, to the secure tranquility of the special inner place. The first stage of this path takes us through the mesalike outposts of the concrete and boulder podium that is the substructure of the complex (figs. 7.7, 7.8). Wending our way through these, we approach the pergola (fig. 7.6 top center, and fig. 7.9) which, like the trellis of Fallingwater, gently suggests a tenuous refuge. As we move forward a few more steps, this sense of refuge is reinforced by the now-complete architectural containment; all views of the hazardous desert are momentarily blocked from view (fig. 7.10). Then ahead, through a slightly deflected axis, across the pool by the "hogan," the desert is allowed to appear once more in a constricted view (fig. 7.6). Controlled by human agency, its hazard is now held at bay because it is contained by the flanking masses; we peek out at it through the surrogate cave mouth, seeing without being seen. Then we turn right, into the loggia, with another contained cave mouth view to desert and mountains. Then finally, through the usual low-key entries known, or so it would seem, only to the initiate, we enter the interiors, the secret and special places. These also open to the desert—but not from areas around the fireplaces.

7.9 Taliesin West. Entry court.

7.10 Taliesin West. Pergola. The architecture now surrounds, and the desert is momentarily lost to view. It reappears ahead, after a dogleg to the right at the end of the pergola.

These fireplaces, in the workroom and Wright's own more private garden room (figs. 7.6, 7.11, 7.12), are at the ends of the spaces, and forward of these Wright has used screening devices of great cleverness to ensure that the fire-refuge is uncompromised. Masonry walls whose long dimension is at right angles to that of the room mask the exterior view from the fireplace zone (figs. 7.6, 7.13). The perception of these rooms from their fireplaces, therefore, is one of enclosure, a perception reinforced by the more conventional opaque ceilings near the fireplaces, which replace the wood and canvas ceilings/roofs typical elsewhere at Taliesin West. Then as we move forward along the axis of the room the space between the masonry pylons makes itself brilliantly, overwhelmingly evident—we look out again to that prospect and hazard from which we have been so lengthily parted, and against which refuge has been so primordially declared.

The entire lower portion of the building is a man-made mesa of terraces, steps, and retaining walls formed of concrete poured around large native boulders. This same material is carried upward to form, typically, three walls of each of the functioning spaces of the superstructure. Four fireplaces integral with the walls are cast in the same material: one in the workroom, one in the space romantically named the hogan, and two in Wright's own quarters. This entire composition of masonry, grand in extent, thick in dimension, and massive in scale, echoes the rock plateau that is the mesa. Wright noted, "Olgivanna said the whole opus looked like something we had not been building but excavating."[15] This masonry eruption from the desert floor has been shaped to create and become all the refuge spaces of Taliesin West. Thus refuge associates with the earth, as it usually does in Wright's work, but more strongly here than in any earlier example. This is especially true of the masonry cove off the garden room in Wright's own quarters (fig. 7.12). Withdrawn behind the light of the garden room proper, anchored by the enormous breadth of the dark low fireplace whose hearth merges with the floor, this is a huddling cave-refuge against the desert's barren expanse. In such an interpretation—and such an interpretation is unavoidable—the desert as hazard symbol is analogous to and as powerful as the rapids at Fallingwater, intensifying the aesthetic value of the refuge. But unlike Falling-

water, refuge at Taliesin West is entirely up to the architecture; the site has nothing whatever to offer in that category; hence these resolute masses which, quite apart from their ability to blend with the geology, are the only possible refuges strong enough to count in this refugeless expanse. At three key points the rock base enframes the water feature essential to an acceptance of the site. For pools (fig. 7.6) are provided at the end of the pergola, at the edge of Wright's "green garden," and—the largest and most dramatic—in the prow off the workroom, where it is sensed from the dining space as well.

7.11 Taliesin West. Wright's garden room. The entry is at left, with the fireplace alcove behind the wood structure at center.

7.12 Taliesin West. Wright's garden room. The alcove with its massive cave-fireplace, and seating beyond.

7.13 Taliesin West. Wright's garden room. The view from the fireplace alcove, with screening pylons at left, and canvas overhead.

Above this geological base, which holds the water-pools, is the superstructure, a vast tent of redwood and canvas (figs. 7.13, 7.14).[16]

Wright had said that he liked "the *sense of shelter* in the look of the building"[17]—both the words and the italics are his—and he did, after all, design those magnificent sense-of-shelter roofs not only of the Robie house and the Wisconsin Taliesin, but also of the later Usonians. Yet in Arizona he could say: "I found that the white luminous canvas overhead and canvas flaps used instead of window glass afforded such agreeable diffusion of light within, was so enjoyable and sympathetic to the desert, that I now felt more than ever oppressed [sic] by the thought of the opaque solid overhead of the much too heavy midwestern houses."[18] Where is the resolution to this apparent dichotomy?

In fact one could argue that Wright had been working toward the idea of such a tent above a massive earthbound base almost from the beginning. In the verdant sites of the early midwestern Prairie houses, the climate had demanded a more or less conventional roof. Yet Wright made some modification to the convention, for the roof of the Prairie house, with its echoing ceiling underneath, assumed at least something of the character of a tent within the verdure around and overhead. The roof sheltered a seemingly continuous band of windows; under this was the solid lower stratum of the house, its tie to the earth typically emphasized by an advancing wall plane just above grade, forming a weighty, anchoring plinth. The fire, associated with the earth, grew out of this grounded base, focusing and anchoring the composition at its center. Wright's own favorite work of the Prairie School period, the Coonley house, is the epitomizing example. The floating roof/ceiling, moored by the masonry core and punctuated by bowerlike skylights, carries the suggestion of a tent in a grove; it hovers over its earthbound base as an obviously thin membrane between architectural space and nature. At the early Taliesin such a tent inference became more explicit; Wright referred to that ceiling as "tent-like," and so it seems a few years later at Hol-lyhock. In Arizona, the great rock and concrete base of Taliesin West, with its integral fire-holding towers, is associated with the earth even more closely than in Wright's previous work; it seems a permutation of the desert floor itself. But what to do above? The desert offered no groves around or overhead, as most of Wright's previous sites had done; no architectural evocation of them could properly belong to this site. And yet, here was the chance to fully realize his tent-dream—and this may be the key to the appeal Arizona held for Wright—for the climate allowed an actual canvas ceiling-roof.

Thus the geologically associated earth-evoking refuge is overbowered only by the redwood beams holding the diaphanous and movable canvas; otherwise all above is sky and only sky, filtered only to the extent required for human life. And with the roof genuinely of canvas, another supportive characteristic became for the first time fully attainable. For if prospect is associated with seeing and therefore with light, then the skylit ceilings of the Heurtley, Coonley, and Hollyhock houses, the clerestories of the Freeman and Ennis houses, and the luminous panels of Fallingwater, hardly anticipate the effulgence of prospect-suggesting light that transpires through the canvas of Taliesin West.

Where does Wright's familiar pattern figure in all of this? There are bits and pieces of it—the fireplaces, the high ceilings (if we can call them that), the openings to generous contiguous terraces—but so much is missing that trying to find the pattern here is really just grasping at straws. At both Ocatillo and Taliesin West, the whole approach is so radical that the pattern just doesn't work: how can we talk about heavy overhanging eaves with a tent? or broad horizontal expanses of glass when we have movable canvas flaps? This absence of the pattern did not mark anything like a permanent shift for Wright; the Usonian houses, which began at about the same time as Taliesin West and continued as a type for the next fifteen years, exploited the pattern in all its constituent features. Thus its absence at Ocatillo and Taliesin West is a particular and not a generalizable matter.

The refuges of Taliesin West are embedded in massive rock abstractions of the desert itself; the prospects open horizontally between the masonry walls across the barren mesa to the mountain ranges, to Sidney Lanier's "vast sweet visage of space," and vertically through the redwood and canvas to the filtered qualities of the sky above—an eternal substructure plays against the most ephemeral superstructure appropriate to human shelter. Thus the drama of Taliesin West. a tension between refuge below and prospect above, each inferred through a material as extreme in character as possible. This was a bold realization, exquisitely appropriate only to the desert and not used elsewhere: "Our new desert camp belonged to the Arizona desert as though it had stood there during creation."[19] One can argue of Taliesin West whether refuge or prospect is dominant—but unlike the original Taliesin, it *is* an argument. And yet it is an argument that doesn't matter; all that is important lies in the fresh and vital tension between two powerful symbols of fundamental human appeal.

7.14 Taliesin West. The desert, the manmade mesa, the canvas, the mountains, and the sky.

8. The Usonians

From 1936 onward Wright produced a series of houses which for unknown reasons he called Usonians.[1] The Usonian house was intended as a revolutionary approach to the ultra-low-cost single-family detached dwelling, and its low cost was attempted in part by the conventional means of reduction in size. As a consequence, the Usonians typically have small kitchens and often very minimal storage; as a group, they are the smallest houses Wright ever did.

Wright's attack on cost, however, also involved a number of distinctly novel features. The first Usonian to be built, and therefore the first to demonstrate these features, was the Herbert Jacobs house, built in 1936 in Westmorland, Wisconsin, for $5,500 (figs. 8.1–8.5).[2] It was built with no basement (there is a tiny subterranean room for heating equipment) and hardly any foundations in the conventional sense; it was built on a thin concrete pad or slab placed directly on the earth.[3] Heat was delivered to living spaces by water-circulating pipes contained within the slab. This slab was inscribed with the modular grid that determined all plan dimensions of the superstructure. With this grid as a guide, and working without conventional dimensions, the upper walls were erected. Some were of brick, in particular those surrounding the kitchen (called by Wright the workspace), those flanking the carport (also so named by Wright), and those marking the ends of living and dining spaces. The remaining walls were a thin and light prefabricated composite consisting of a double layer of boards with insulation between. These were intended to be easy and inexpensive to build, although in practice they often were neither. But they saved space: in the Jacobs house they mean an additional 40 square feet of usable space as compared with conventional construction, and when one is planning on a small scale, this kind of economy counts.[4] There was no attic; the ceiling and roof were one, as in Wright's work from 1902 onward. But in the Jacobs house, as in most subsequent Usonians, the roof was flat.

For all its technical originality the Jacobs house perpetuates Wright's familiar pattern. On the exterior (figs. 8.1, 8.2) are the deep overhanging roof, the evident and generous central chimney, broad horizontal groupings of window bands, and conspicuous terraces; in all these respects this structure is the legitimate descendant of the Heurtley house.

Yet there is a difference, and it is one that will be found in most of the Usonians. For while all the typical features are found on the Jacobs exterior, the latter two, the bands of window and the terraces, are not visible on approach. From the street (fig. 8.1) one sees an almost entirely closed façade. There are reasons for this. Since the Jacobs house has its floor slab and therefore its main floor level at grade, privacy for the occupants could not have been obtained by the Cheney-Robie approach, which depended on a main floor elevated above street level. Nor would the budget allow the stained and leaded glass that contributed to a sense of privacy in the Prairie houses. Nor does the Jacobs house have the extensive site of, for example, the Coonley house, Taliesin, or Fallingwater, in which privacy was augmented by distance and vegetation. Therefore privacy had to be obtained by some other design means, and that was the closing of the street façade. Still, it is fair to note that there were instances in Wright's early career in which the lot was small and flat, and the main floor was not elevated much above street level, but in which there still was a more open relationship to community: the Roberts, Baker, and Gale houses are examples. Neither the Jacobs house nor any later Usonian explores this approach. The consequence, whether intended or not, is a loss of communality; the sense of rejection that the house conveys is almost palpable. Yet paradoxically this sense of rejection is coupled with a mysterious magnetism, due, I suspect, to the considerable drama, and therefore power, of the refuge-signaling characteristics: Appleton's "alcoves, recesses, heavy overhanging eaves," perhaps even the narrow band of window that invites us to peek over at the same time it prevents us from doing so.

8.1 Herbert Jacobs house, Westmorland, Wisconsin, 1936. From the street. Entry is through the carport at left; the living room lies behind the wall with clerestory.

8.2 Jacobs house. Garden façades.

If the Jacobs house were to follow the familiar Wrightian pattern in all other respects, it would have us reach the interior by means of a long and circuitous path. The actual entry is not quite that, but given the site limitations and the budget, it is as close a simulation as can be had (figs. 8.1, 8.3). One walks under the very low carport roof, then along the brick flank of the carport toward a blank brick wall; then a 90-degree right turn between two brick jambs, still under that very low roof. One then walks forward perhaps three feet between the brick walls, now on both flanks, at which point the front door is reached. Within is a narrow entry corridor about ten feet in length. And then the space opens out and away as view is released diagonally to the left through a great sweep of floor-to-ceiling glass in the distance, while immediately on the left is the fireplace (fig. 8.4). One always expects this sequence in a house by Wright—and yet, even expecting it, it always surprises and delights.

And so here again we are brought back to the pattern. The fire is in the heart of the building and at the internal edge of the space it serves. The living space has a relatively high ceiling which is the underside of the higher roof. There are interior views to contiguous spaces. Glass and glazed doors are located on walls distant from the fire. A generous elevated terrace lies beyond (though it is "elevated" in this case only by grading the site to lower the level of the garden). Two characteristics of the pattern are missing, however: the ceiling is not lowered over the fireplace, nor over the glazed exterior wall opposite (fig. 8.4). It seems a reasonable guess that their absence was a result of the impact of the budget on the roof structure; many later Usonians with more elastic budgets would repeat the familiar lowered conditions.

Like the Usonians that followed it, the Jacobs house has a considerable length of corridor (see plan, fig. 8.3). Like the entry it is narrow; it is also low. The walls, textured in natural wood, press in on either side; the ceiling presses down overhead. The compression engendered is a powerful device for intensifying the sense of release on arrival at the spaces the corridor serves. These spaces, then, are found on arrival to have generous floor-to-ceiling french doors opening to the vista of terrace and garden, and, in the case of the living space, there is a higher ceiling as well. Thus the tight closure of refuge in the entry and corridor complements the openness of the prospect conditions in the major rooms. This familiar principle with Wright is here employed in exaggerated form and at diminutive scale, and is especially effective for just this reason. One of the great successes of this house, as of all the later Usonians, is that it provides this intensification of spatial contrast within what is really a very small building.

The rooms themselves also contain interior refuge conditions. In the living space this is, of course, the area around the fire, although it shares with the Robie house the problem of having circulation to either side. But Wright has also provided the L-shaped brick nook at the end of the room opposite the fire (figs. 8.3, 8.4), which creates a secondary zone of refuge. In the bedrooms, the beds are all pocketed within a U-shaped configuration of solid wall.

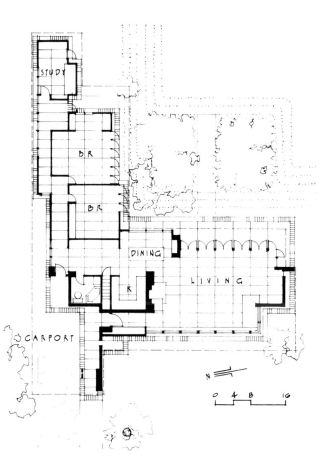

8.3 Jacobs house. Plan. Carport and entry are at upper right.

8.4 Jacobs house. Living room from the entry, with fireplace at extreme left.

Interior prospect is provided by opening living and dining space, kitchen, entry, and bedroom corridor to each other, the openings always articulated by wall returns and built-in furnishings. It bears noting that these interior prospect conditions are invariably given complexity through diagonality. In no instance is any interior prospect condition related to anything else in an axial way—always the view opens across a diagonal. This diagonality is emphasized as well by the twists of the corridor. Even more important is the displacement of the dining space so that it opens from a corner, not a side, of the living space (figs. 8.3, 8.5); it does a kind of double side-step to become an extension of diagonal rather than rectilinear spatial boundaries.[5]

The spaces of the Jacobs house are articulated by a means latent in Wright's previous work, which hereafter appears more explicitly. This means is the use of a wall plane, very much like a stage flat, projecting into the space to mark a spatial distinction; we have already seen something closely analogous to it in the pylons of Taliesin West of the year following the Jacobs house. Such projecting planes are used at the Jacobs house to define the nook at the end of the living space (figs. 8.3, 8.4); the table indicated there, though not a wall, also plays a similar role. A similar projection separates the dining room from the living space (fig. 8.5). These walls suggest another feature described by Appleton, the *coulisse*.

The *coulisse* . . . in its original usage denotes the side-pieces of scenery used on the stage. They serve a dual function in the stagecraft of the theatre. In the first place they can help to create an impression of three-dimensional space . . . they not only look nearer than objects in the distance, they *are* nearer, and they can therefore be used to accentuate the impression of perspective created by scenery on the backcloth.

The *coulisse,* however, has another function; . . . by projecting on to the stage it extends the area of concealment provided by wings into the scene of the action and, because the actors can normally pass either in front or behind, it suggests more than one place where escape from view is possible. The use of more than one *coulisse* accentuates even further the idea of refuge.[6]

Thus the coulisse, explicitly deployed for the first time in Wright's work in the Jacobs house, contributes both to an intensification of perspective and to the signaling of subordinate internal refuge conditions.

8.5 Jacobs house. Dining area, with fireplace at left.

Subsequent Usonians usually regarded as typical examples are, chronologically: the Stanley Rosenbaum house of 1939, in Florence, Alabama; the Bernard Schwartz house of 1939, in Two Rivers, Wisconsin; the Alma Goetsch and Katherine Winkler house of 1939, in Okemos, Michigan; the Lloyd Lewis house of 1940, in Libertyville, Illinois; the Clarence Pew house of 1940, in Madison, Wisconsin; and the Gregor Affleck house of 1941, in Bloomfield Hills, Michigan. As a group, these houses are more nearly alike in size, configuration, and general appearance than the Prairie houses of 1902-1910 or the California houses of the 1920s.

Of this group, the Rosenbaum house (fig. 8.6) is most similar to the Jacobs house, of which it is a refinement. The exterior is longer and seems lower, since the high central volume of the living room is well back from the street façade. The lower roof over the study (at right,

fig.8.6), makes possible a handsome reiteration of the horizontals, and brings the eye nearer the plane of the earth. The resultant proportions are especially satisfying; no street façade since the Robie house has had such a wonderful sweep of line. On the interior, the central clerestory allows greater spatial contrast, since both the book-lined wall toward the street and the glazed wall of french doors to the garden are under lowered ceilings. Otherwise the spatial and formal characteristics of the Jacobs house are generally repeated.

The Schwartz house is an extended version of a project for *Life* magazine, "A House for a Family of $5,000–6,000 Income" (Sept. 26, 1938).[7] Part of the scheme is of two stories (fig. 8.7A–B); therefore the portion of the house nearest the street does not have the dramatic horizontality of the Rosenbaum house. One enters this house at the right rear edge of the carport, and since this is the two-story part of the house, the entry path is under a very low ceiling which is the floor of the bedrooms and balcony above.

8.6 Stanley Rosenbaum house, Florence, Alabama, 1939. From the street.

Forward of this lies a spatial composition which is in some ways unique (see fig. 8.7A). The major space is noted not as the expected "living room" but as "recreation room." Wright in the mid-1930s had a fondness for renaming things; "workspace" for "kitchen" is one instance, and at the same time he was beginning to call the study a "sanctum." Renaming is a means for conceptual liberation, of course, and it probably served something of this purpose for Wright. In the case of the Schwartz "recreation room," however, the term was not a generic one; Wright's other and later houses continued to have "living rooms." The renaming in this case may have hinged on a different issue, for the space is in some key ways unlike Wright's typical living rooms. It is open to terraces on both of its long walls, for example, and both walls have glazed french doors. This is not entirely unprecedented in Wright's living rooms—that of the Francis Little house of 1913 is surely the best-known previous instance, and the condition occurs in the Storer house of 1923 in Los Angeles, and in a second house of 1927 for Darwin D. Martin at Derby, New York, whose plan configuration is roughly similar to the Schwartz house. But the condition is unusual in Wright's work. Furthermore the Schwartz recreation room fireplace occurs under a very high ceiling indeed, and seems more monumental than cozy (fig. 8.9). The consequence of these characteristics is that there is in this space no refuge condition. Would Wright have found the term "living room" impossible for just that reason? In any event the more usual Wrightian refuge conditions are found in a subspace, the "lounge," set off by the coulisse of the fireplace masonry. In this lounge (the distant dark space in fig. 8.9) are a second fireplace, with a low ceiling above, a higher ceiling beyond, and glass opposite leading to a terrace—in short, the conditions of the pattern. Why, then, not call this the living room? Because it was a subspace? Dining is provided by the side-stepped space off the recreation room, demarked by a brick coulisse.

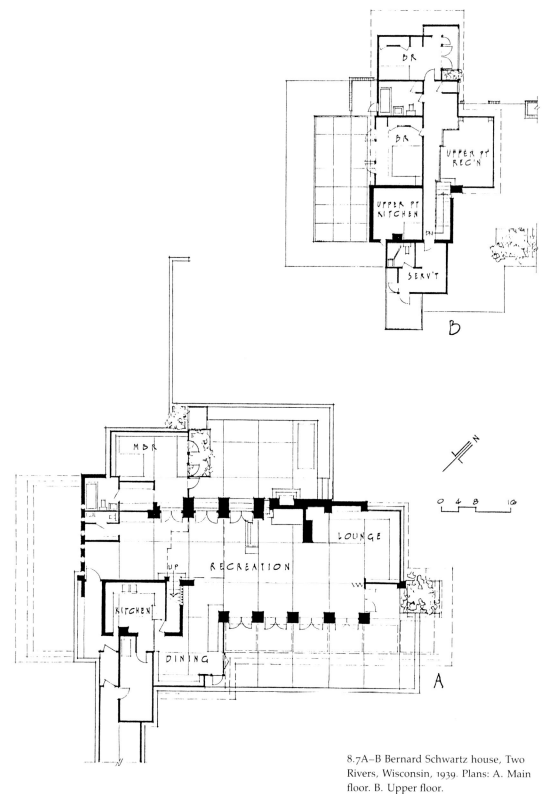

8.7A–B Bernard Schwartz house, Two Rivers, Wisconsin, 1939. Plans: A. Main floor. B. Upper floor.

8.8 Schwartz house. From the garden. The recreation room is at center; the two-story portion toward the street is in the distance.

8.9 Schwartz house. Recreation room, looking toward the lounge.

The Jacobs, Rosenbaum, and Schwartz houses also illustrate the conditions of complexity and order. Order is established in an obvious way by the modular grid easily discerned on all plans. Such a grid was no new thing to Wright, of course; it goes back at least to the Coonley house. In these Usonians, as at Coonley, the grid is evident in the actual experience of movement through the house, in the rhythms of wall locations, window and door mullions, and often in decorative details. And like Coonley, the Usonians are designed to a vertical module as well, the dimension of the horizontal board-and-batten unit used for all wood walls. This module determines all eave, ceiling, and sill heights, and all shelving (see figs. 8.4, 8.5, and 8.9). The complexity of the plan configurations, extraordinary for such small houses, teases this order. Special enrichment is provided by the pervasive diagonality of interior prospect which, as in its origins at the Ennis house, adds yet another layer of complexity, demanding from the occupant continual exploration and discovery. It also contributes to the illusion that these houses are larger than they really are, since the space in its permutations and extensions can never be wholly apprehended from any one point; movement is necessary to discovery and clarification. One owner has said that the Usonian house offers "a continuing succession of mysteries leading you on beyond what your eyes could see. The house gives you a sense of protection, but never of being closed in."[8]

The Usonians have Wright's usual coy and understated entries; in the three so far discussed, the front door is tucked away in an unassuming corner of the carport. At the Goetsch-Winkler house (figs. 8.10–8.12) one walks under the incredible length of the low cantilevered carport roof, then along at least half of the long façade toward the brick coulisse ahead, to enter through a random choice of one of the eight french doors (figs. 8.10, 8.11). This house is about the same size as the Jacobs house, and Wright has again condensed all his spatial and formal devices. A low roof, an extension of that of the carport, glides over the gallery, workspace, bedrooms, and alcove; the higher roof occurs over the living room–studio. The alcove here becomes the refuge (fig. 8.12), with low ceiling and fire, and with book shelves on the remaining two walls. The living room-studio's glazed walls are opposite, with french doors leading to the grass lanai, a surrogate for the terrace. Beyond this lanai, and beyond the glazing of the living space, the site falls away rather steeply to a wooded glade, so that, as usual, the living spaces lie well above the landscape they overlook.

8.10 Alma Goetsch and Katherine Winkler house, Okemos, Michigan, 1939. Plan.

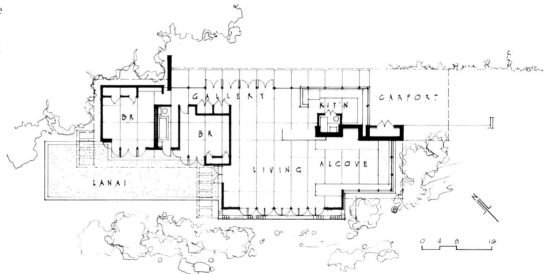

8.11 Goetsch-Winkler house. Exterior.

8.12 Goetsch-Winkler house. Living room and fireplace, from the alcove.

The Lloyd Lewis house (figs. 8.13–8.19) is again a two-story scheme, but one which, unlike the Schwartz house, elevates the main floor; "I knew it was so damp and hot out there on the prairie by the Des Plaines River where he wanted to build that I set Lloyd well up off the ground to keep him high and dry in Spring, Fall and Summer."[9] So again, the approach façade is tall. And the circuitous entrance has returned with a vengeance: one has to move through the full depth of the carport (figs. 8.13A, 8.17), then traverse the length of a dark and rather dank loggia (fig. 8.14) to enter the low and dark vestibule whose flanking stair, like that of the Ennis house, leads we know not where (compare fig. 8.17 with fig. 5.24). The Lewis entry, like the Ennis one, recalls those primordial cave entries of dark, lengthy corridors meandering through their mystical courses to the special place.

Yet once beyond the entry, circulation through the Lewis house evokes another and quite different image. The paths through the Coonley house were earlier considered as analogous to forest paths leading from glade to glade, the effect reinforced by the dappled light of the skylights. Such an effect was also latent in the Usonians from the beginning, in the usual long, low, and narrow corridors. At the Lewis house, this effect has been realized and emphasized by opening the upper parts of corridor and entry walls to a similar phenomenon of dappled light, filtered through a fretwork pattern visible in figure 8.19.[10] Thus, as at the Coonley house, one ascends from darkness to light, from closure to expanse; and as at Coonley, one arrives at the broad masonry fireplace contained within its pocket of sanctum wall and seating peninsula. Forward of the fireplace the ceiling ascends—or seems to: in fact the impression of a hipped Coonley-like ceiling is an illusion, although a powerful one, created by the lapped boards of which the Lewis ceiling is made. Opposite the fireplace, at the seemingly lower distant ceiling edge, are the glazed walls and terrace of the elevated pavilion, within the forest by the riverside (fig. 8.15, 8.16; compare with figs. 3.15, 3.16).

In another respect, too, the Lewis house is a descendant of the Coonley house. One exits the living room to go to the bedroom wing by moving to the right of the fireplace, then down that long, low, light-dappled forest path to reach, finally, the glade, a master bedroom, that is an elegant microcosm of the pattern (figs. 8.13B, 8.17, 8.18). For here is the fireplace refuge yet again, pocketed by a brick wall of four enclosing planes, one side of which contains the familiar half-inglenook seat. Opposite are the french doors opening to the balcony, and the prospect of the river beyond.

8.13A–B Lloyd Lewis house, Libertyville, Illinois, 1940. Plans: A. Ground floor. B. Main floor.

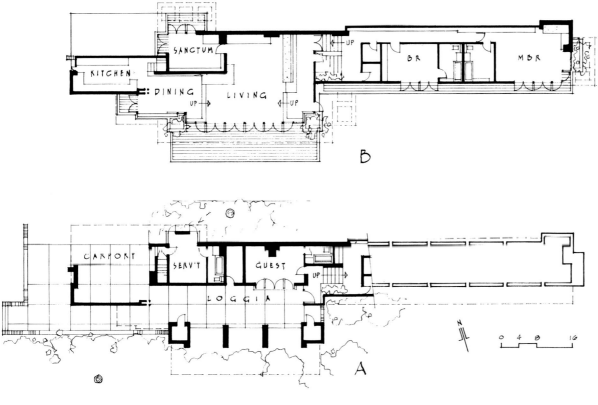

8.14 Lewis house. View along the loggia; dining above, entry ahead.

8.15 Lewis house. Living room, looking toward the fire.

8.16 Lewis house. Living room, looking toward the terrace; compare with figs. 3.15, 3.16.

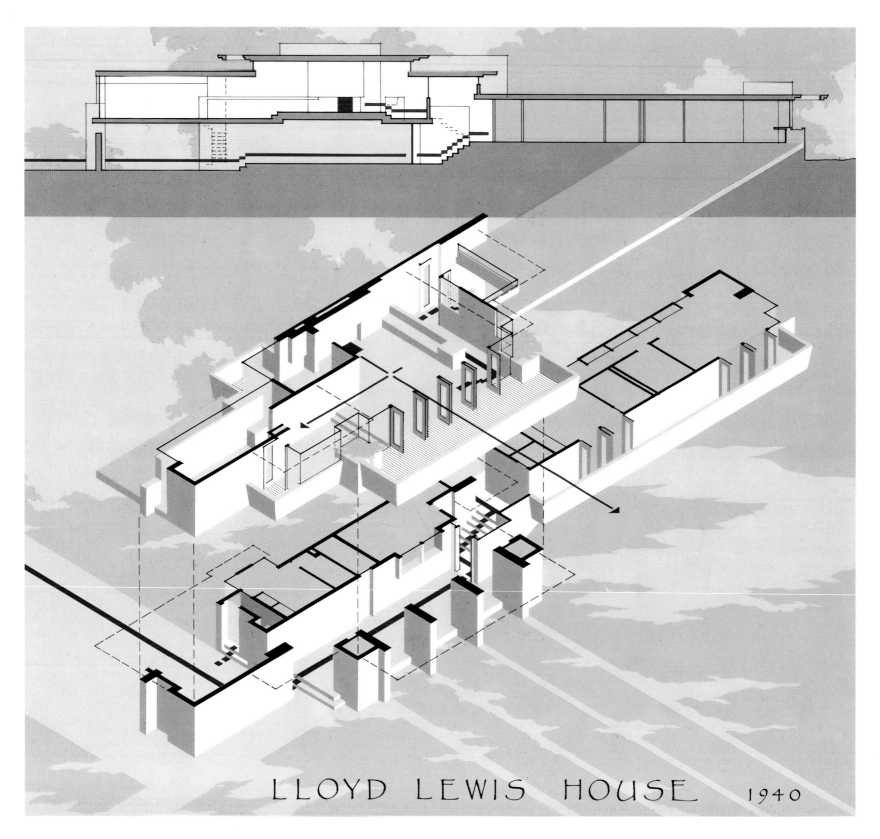

LLOYD LEWIS HOUSE 1940

8.17 Lewis house. Diagrammatic
drawing by William Hook.

8.18 Lewis house. Master bedroom from the exterior.

8.19 Lewis house. Exterior as seen from the gardens and the river.

Wright seems to have been especially fond of both the Coonley and the Lewis houses.[11] Both presented him with congenial client relationships. The Coonleys were open and uncritical admirers with a lot of money; Lewis was a long-standing personal friend; and perhaps this congeniality brought out the best in Wright, or at the least supplied the best memories. He created for them two of his best houses, the one a later and far more economical version of the other, and each within its type and time especially rich in its evocation of prospect and refuge.

The Lewis house uniquely among the Usonians makes a tentative gesture toward opening up the approach façade by facing the sanctum and its balcony in that direction (figs. 8.13, 8.17). In this instance Wright deployed his old parapets-and-sight-lines devices: there is on record correspondence between Wright and Lewis in which, Lewis having complained about high balcony parapets, Wright responded "I lifted the parapets to give you privacy from the road." But Wright's justification applies only to the sanctum. The other spaces open only to the opposite side, away from road and entry; and, oddly, these spaces also have the same high parapets as the sanctum though the justification no longer applies; in fact as Lewis forcefully pointed out they deny the occupant a view of the river. (Wright offered to Lewis the additional argument that it was all a matter of proportion, and this seems to have carried the day, though in looking at the house in actuality the justification is unconvincing).[12]

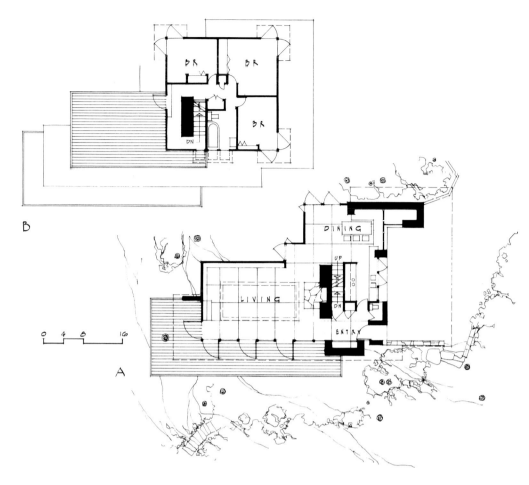

8.20A–B Clarence Pew house, Madison, Wisconsin, 1940. Plans: A. Lower floor. B. Upper floor.

8.21 Pew house. Exterior. Carport; the entry is at the far side.

If the Lewis house is a descendant of Coonley, the Clarence Pew house of 1940, in Madison, has a different ancestry. To enter the Pew house (figs. 8.20A–8.23), one has to wander to the far side of the carport, then around the corner and under the deep roof overhang, to find the doorway to the stone-flagged hall. The sequence suggests a mirror-image of the entry to Fallingwater.

Nor is this the only parallel, for the roofs and terraces of the Pew house cantilever over the hillside in a similar fashion (fig. 8.22) and even manage to suggest through their height a modest sense of hazard. There is also a genuine second floor which, like that of Fallingwater, is perched over the uphill portion of the house, and opens to a grand terrace which is, again, the living room roof. But this is as far as the analogy can be stretched; beyond this, the Pew house is a Usonian, and the smallest of those discussed here.[13] Perhaps because of its small size its allegiance to a module, both horizontal and vertical, is even more evident than in other Usonians. Its dining space not only side-steps but does so twice; and the preoccupation with diagonality extends even to locating the fireplace off the axis of the living room, whose grand ceiling coffer emphasizes the eccentricity (figs. 8.20, 8.23).

8.22 Pew house. Exterior. The carport and entry are at right, the living room and its balcony/terrace to the left.

8.23 Pew house. Living room toward the fire. Entry is at right; the dining space is seen diagonally at left in the distance, suggesting and inviting exploration.

The Gregor Affleck house of 1941 in Bloomfield Hills, Michigan (figs. 8.24–8.28), is another example of a house built with a congenial client relationship. Affleck had also spent his boyhood in Spring Green, Wisconsin, and although this was just after Wright's departure for Chicago, Affleck seems to have held Wright as a hero-figure from those early days. On the face of it, the Affleck house is a two-story scheme, but the lower level in fact has little to do with family living spaces; under the guise of utilities and servant accommodation, it really is a pylon to perch the house over the steep wooded hillside site. The organization of exterior and interior conforms to Wright's pattern in all respects except that the fireplace is within the zone of the high ceiling. The Affleck house shares with the Lewis house an in-line arrangement of living and dining spaces rather than the usual Usonian double-side-stepped relationship.

In the Affleck house, however, prospect and refuge are augmented by a number of highly effective means. The range of french doors to east and south turns the corner more emphatically than in other Usonians (fig. 8.24), opening to a terrace which, like that of the Pew house, also turns the corner (fig. 8.25); both door and terrace configurations thereby enlarge the sweep of prospect. At the opposite end of the space, Wright's old habit of built-in seating is used to create a giant inglenook opposite the fire (figs. 8.24, 8.27). This seating, which also serves dining, turns the corner as do the french doors opposite, but since the walls are solid the effect here is to create the embracing enclosure of refuge. This emphasis on corners reinforces the sense of diagonal orientation common to the Usonians, although that characteristic is less evident in the Affleck house than in other examples. A vertical diagonality is also introduced by the various floor levels, to which is added the enrichment of a more dramatic vertical dimension: at the center of the house the living room, entry, and guest room merge into a higher atriumlike space opening to the sky above, and to a sunken garden with pool below (fig. 8.28).

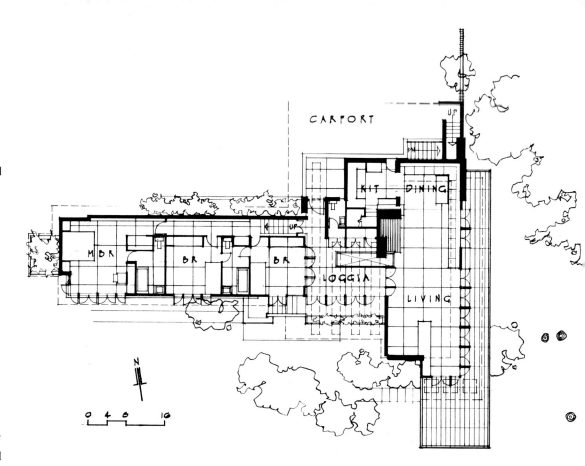

8.24 Gregor Affleck house, Bloomfield Hills, Michigan, 1941. Plan.

8.25 Affleck house. Exterior from the south. The living room terrace is prominent in the foreground.

8.26 Affleck house. Exterior from the west.

Here perhaps a word or two should be said about dining spaces. In the Usonians, they are never an afterthought. In all the examples so far discussed, and in all other Usonians as well, dining has been given a space architecturally articulated and dedicated specifically to this function. The furniture appropriate to it was indicated by Wright on the plan and is closely integrated with the architectural provision. With the exception only of the Goetsch-Winkler house, an elegant outlook has also been developed for dining that is at least equal to that of any other space in the house: in the Lewis house, for example, the dining space is the only one from which the river can be seen while one is seated. This ceremonial treatment of the dining space, of course, is a very old habit with Wright; in his entire career, there is hardly a house in which it is not treated in a similarly considered way (with two surprising exceptions, Taliesin and Fallingwater). The Usonians raise the point in a special way, however. While Wright's houses before 1935 emphasized dining, so did most houses of the time and of comparable cost.

But the Usonians were small, inexpensive houses, and by their time, that is the mid to late 1930s, small low-budget houses typically either offered no separate dining space, or provided it through an undistinguished extrusion of the living room. By comparison the dining space in the Usonians is always a clearly defined space handled with emphasis, and even ceremony.

Like prospect and refuge, complexity and order, the significance of this emphasis on dining as ritual goes back very far. Clearly there is strong precedent in the western world—not only architectural precedent in such spaces as the British great hall, but precedent in the practices of human life. Even today, almost all social interaction includes the sharing of food and drink, and this was true even at the threshold of western consciousness; every important social encounter in Homer, for example, is accompanied by feasting. Nor is this only a western issue: in Japan, whose image certainly loomed large with Wright, even the most casual encounter is accompanied by tea, at least, without fail.

These customs, too, may have a biological basis. Chromosomally we are differentiated from the great apes most significantly by our protracted adolescence; we take a long time, in terms of the animal world, to mature. During this protracted adolescence, the crucial thing is that we be fed not by our own efforts but by the efforts of our parents; we are the only species in which the parents feed the offspring for ten to twenty years. This, of course, is what has allowed us to develop tools, language, and all that follows therefrom. And this activity, this sharing of food, like prospect and refuge, complexity and order, cannot logically have been a behavior chosen out of conscious recognition of its species value. Like those other characteristics, it must have been something in which we found enjoyment from the beginning. Wright's emphasis on the specialness of dining, then, represents another instance of his intuitive sensitivity to a fundamentally human predilection, and one of such pervasive importance to him that he would not relinquish it even in these small houses where space was at a premium.

The Usonians command attention. This is their joy, and sometimes their problem. For buildings of such small size, Wright has provided an extraordinary complexity, which is relentlessly enriching, relentlessly tantalizing. It in turn requires an extraordinary order, which Wright has also provided, and which is relentlessly cohering, relentlessly controlling. It is exhilarating to contemplate the relationship between such a forceful order and such a rich complexity, but often there is little opportunity for the occupant's intervention. And yet the experience is magnetic and mesmerizing: there is always the sense of being in a building which is, in the end, quite small but quite irresistible in both the good and bad senses of the term, charged with vigor, presence, warmth, and above all an absolutely indomitable will.

Questions of craftsmanship, maintenance, and durability, often issues in Wright's work, also loom large in the case of the Usonians. They attempted a lot for a little. There are those who would defend them as finely constructed buildings, and in some cases this may well be true. But tight budgets and tricky site conditions, in conjunction with the novel features of innovative and lightweight construction, nonvertical walls, extravagant cantilevers, and radiant heat—all described to the builder through meagre and undimensioned working drawings, with inexperienced apprentices supervising—these are formidable challenges to craftsmanship. Most of the Usonians bear at least some witness to the effects of these challenges.[14]

8.28 Affleck house. Loggia, with the living room beyond.

The rectilinear plan configurations represented in these examples were not the only configurations explored by Wright within the Usonian type. In 1936, the year of the Jacobs house, Wright also did a house for Paul R. and Jean S. Hanna, to be built in Palo Alto, California, the plan for which is generated by a hexagonal module.[15] The Hanna house is usually considered a Usonian, as it utilizes the heated slab on grade, the absolutely modular plan and elevation, and prefabricated sandwich walls. Its ambience, however, is quite different. Though originally intended to have been built on a budget of $15,000, it cost in the end well over twice that, and thus, although contemporary with the Jacobs house, was seven times more costly.[16] The expense is evident in the far greater size of the Hanna house,[17] its pitched roof and the resultant more complex ceiling planes underneath, the extensive brick-parapeted terraces, and above all the hexagonal module, for the Hanna house is the first, although by no means the last, of Wright's houses to use such a module to generate the entire plan configuration in all its details (fig. 8.29).

Nevertheless the pattern remains. On the exterior are the familiar features: the deep overhanging eaves, alcoves, recesses, broad expanses of glass, and large conspicuous terraces (fig. 8.30). Inside is the central fireplace at the inner edge of the living room, under a low ceiling (although a token one) and flanked by a seating promontory; beyond this the ceiling rises, echoing the roof's form, then returns to a low outer edge (figs. 8.31, 8.32). Interior vistas open in profusion. At the low outer edge of the ceiling are extensive glass and glazed french doors opening to the broad terraces and to landscape prospect beyond. Exactly similar conditions are found in the sanctum (in fig. 8.29, the space above the entry). This is the classic Wright pattern in its entirety, the repetitive configuration that allies this house with the Heurtley, Cheney, and Coonley houses, Taliesin, and Fallingwater.

The interior, like those of the other Usonians, is impossible to apprehend in its entirety from any single viewpoint; one must experience it through motion, each change of viewpoint yielding different spatial understandings. The greater size of the Hanna house, however, and especially its hexagonal grid, offer a special enrichment to this phenomenon, in making the interior prospect conditions extraordinarily fluid. One is continually led on to further exploration of more distant spaces through the promise of additional experiences,

the promise that Stephen Kaplan has called mystery, and which Wright had previously deployed with unprecedented richness in the Ennis house.[18] At the Hanna house, this promise is even more richly suggested, and yet more gently too. For following the obtuse angle of the module, the vistas of the Hanna house are comprised of grand but gentle sweeps of bending space sometimes leading to light, sometimes to darkness, always accompanied on the flank by the dappled light from the glazed walls (figs. 8.31, 8.32). Because of the diagonal component of the module, these glazed walls, and the solid surfaces too, for that matter, have the magical characteristic of deflecting these grand sweeps of space without terminating them. This is the particular quality which accounts for the special appeal of the Hanna house, surely one of Wright's loveliest and most intriguing creations. The diagonal vistas of the Ennis house have here become the entire spatial concept.

The plan has been bent to follow roughly the contour of the hill. In this feature, the plan is analogous to that of Taliesin. In each case, the fireplace is located at what one might call the hinge of the bend. Within the Hanna house configuration, this has a not entirely fortunate consequence. It means that the fireplace occupies the external corner of its chimney mass (figs. 8.29, 8.31, 8.32) and forms the hinge between the two wings of the main space, each of which seems to retreat from it. Therefore the fireplace focuses on neither. Consequently, furniture groupings around it also seem to be in neither wing, while at the same time, the fireplace seems to turn its back on the seating promontory that flanks it.

The siting condition of the Hanna house, and Wright's management of it, are unusual in his late career. The land slopes toward the street rather than away from it. It is also a site that was not chosen by Wright. He has opened the main spaces toward the fall of land, as he had to do if they were to overlook falling terrain (fig. 8.33). But this also means that they open toward the street; he has therefore buffered the street exposure by masonry terraces that recall such early examples as the Cheney house. They are much shallower front to back, and so do not generate the privacy that was ensured by the Cheney configuration—but then they do not need to, for this idyllic extensive site in hilly Palo Alto is in no way like the communal coziness of Oak Park, and privacy is easily provided by distance and vegetation.

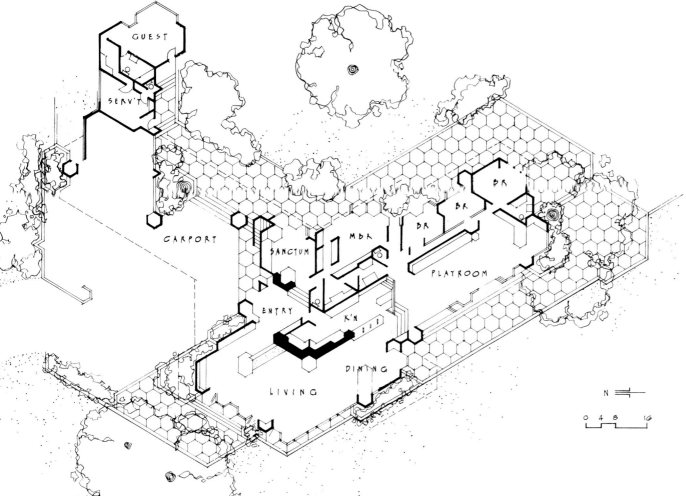

Labels on plan: GUEST, SERV'T, CARPORT, SANCTUM, MBR, BR, BR, BR, PLATROOM, ENTRY, K'N, DINING, LIVING

N

0 4 8 16

8.29 Paul R. Hanna house, Palo Alto, California, 1936–37. Plan.

8.30 Hanna house. Exterior from the drive; living room at center.

8.31 Hanna house. Living room looking toward the half-inglenook seating.

8.32 Hanna house. Fireplace from the lounge.

In 1943 Wright began the design of a second house (the third, actually, a second scheme having gone unbuilt) for the clients of the first Usonian, Mr. and Mrs. Herbert Jacobs; this was built, after nearly four years' delay, at a site in rural Wisconsin near Madison. This house is hardly a Usonian by any stretch of the term. Its plan (fig. 8.34A–B) is a hemicycle, the outer arc of which is of stonework buried to half its height in a berm of earth. This masonry arc contains utilities and, of course, a sizeable fireplace, and embraces two stories of space—living-dining-workspace below, bedrooms above. But Wright did not relinquish the idea of the major spaces lying right under the roof, because the suspended bedroom floor is in fact a balcony whose edge is an arc concentric with the masonry hemicycle. Forward of this is a two-story portion, the edge of the major ground-floor spaces whose ceiling in that zone

is, of course, the underside of the roof (fig. 8.35). The exterior wall of glass, two stories high, is also an arc; beyond it lies a narrow concentric stone terrace, then a sharp slope downward to a lower circular garden (fig. 8.36). In short, all the familiar features are here, too, in a house that seems radically different from anything Wright had done before. The almost unrelieved stone wall, the fire burning deep within it below the grade of the earth berm outside, and the ceiling under the second floor area, low even for Wright, give the second Jacobs house a mood more palpably cavelike than any other of his work. And yet, as always, opposite is the grand elevated prospect of the expansive meadow, seen through the unusually high and continuous sweep of glass that complements the otherwise claustrophobic refuge by the fire.

8.33 Hanna house. Exterior from the road.

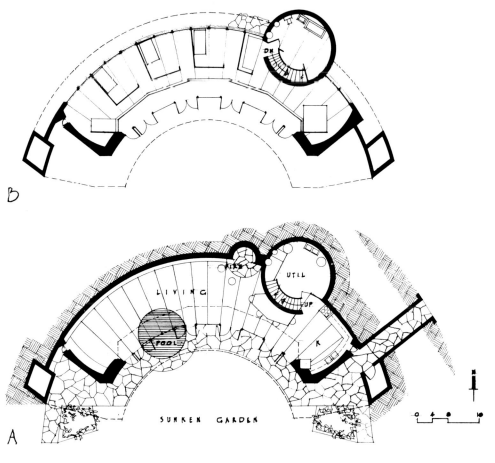

B

A

LIVING

POOL

UTIL

UP

SUNKEN GARDEN

8.34A–B Second Herbert Jacobs house
near Madison, Wisconsin, 1943–47.
Plans: A. Lower floor. B. Upper floor.

8.35 Second Jacobs house. Living area.
The fireplace is at center; at right the
wall of glass rises past the balcony edge
to the underside of the roof.

8.36 Second Jacobs house. Exterior. The glazed arc of the garden façade, sweeping around the terrace and the sunken garden.

8.37 William and Mary Palmer house, Ann Arbor, Michigan, 1950–51. Exterior from the road.

The pattern continued to inform the work of Wright's late years. A particularly elegant example of those years is the William and Mary Palmer house of 1950–51, in Ann Arbor, Michigan (fig. 8.37), in which Wright's personal involvement is known to have been central and extensive. This is sometimes considered to be a Usonian,[19] and it does have the slab-on-grade feature, although in other respects it is quite different. Most of the exterior walls are of a particularly beautiful soft tan brickwork; interspersed are strata of specially cast ceramic elements of identical coloration, which have glazed openings to admit light to the kitchen (fig. 8.38) and the bedroom corridor. The exterior is marked by deeply overhanging eaves, an evident central chimney, broad horizontal groupings of window bands, and conspicuous terrace-like projections. The roof is hipped. The plan (fig. 8.39) derives from a module of equilateral triangles.

Entry to the Palmer house is by way of a flight of steps along the flank of one of the brick and pierced ceramic walls; ascending these steps, with the earth of the hill-mound on the right, one is brought ever closer to the low eave overhead (figs. 8.37, 8.40). Moving fully under it for a distance of perhaps fifteen feet, and ascending another short flight of steps that tuck one firmly and tightly under that eave, there is a turn through a slight angle, and then one enters the body of the house. To the right lies the corridor to the bed rooms: ascending a few steps past a coulisse, one encounters a complex dogleg jog to the right, then moves along the corridor, the forest path, with dappled light entering through the pierced ceramic units (fig. 8.41). After a while this path widens, then, finally, opens to the glades that are the bedrooms (figs. 8.42, 8.43), whose glazing in turn reveals and frames the prospect of the falling landscape beyond.

Retracing one's steps back toward the major spaces, one finds, at the end of the corridor sequence, a vista toward the terrace. Turning 120 degrees back to the right, around the coulisse of the seating promontory, one finally faces the fireplace; the heart of the secret and special place has been reached (figs. 8.40, 8.44).

The fireplace is pocketed in the contained and withdrawn far corner of the living room, at the distant low edge of the ceiling. The living room opens to contiguous spaces set off by articulating architectural features: the dining table, the old familiar seating promontory, and the half-hexagonal coulisses of the hall and kitchen end walls (fig. 8.39). By these means, and within a quite small house, extraordinarily complex vistas of interior prospect are made available; bending as they do at the Hanna house, they hold the mystery of distant spaces suggested but not revealed without exploration. Forward of the fireplace, toward the center of the living room, the ceiling rises following the planes of the roof above, then descends, at its edges, to the above-fireplace height. The low circumferential ceiling edge occurs at exactly the height of the exterior eave and is detailed similarly. At this edge are the windows and french doors which open to the terrace (fig. 8.45), elevated above and surveying the rolling landscape beyond, commanding its prospect from a strategically advantageous height.

The spatial description could be that of the Heurtley or the Cheney house. The Palmer house is a beautifully crafted encapsulation of a half-century of Wright's pattern; it brings us full circle.

8.38 Palmer house. Kitchen. The glazed ceramic units seen at center in fig. 8.37 serve as light sources above and below the cabinets.

8.39 Palmer house. Plan.

8.40 Palmer house. Diagrammatic drawing by William Hook.

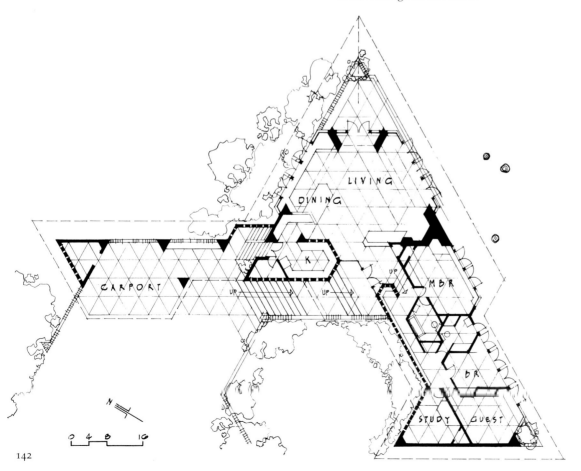

PALMER HOUSE 1950 - 1951

8.41 Palmer house. Bedroom corridor. The dogleg that is the corridor's beginning is in the distance; at upper left are the glazed ceramic units.

8.42 Palmer house. Study and bedroom at the end of the corridor.

8.43 Palmer house. Master bedroom.

8.44 Palmer house. Living room looking toward the fireplace.

8.45 Palmer house. Living room looking toward the dining area and the terrace. The prospect is across a sharply falling hillside to wooded hills beyond.

9. Some Conclusions

Wright's houses hypnotize. Though beset with problems, irritations, willfulnesses, and eccentricities, whether pristine or shabby, and whether we wish it or not, they bring us under their spell. I have suggested that their effect is more than an esoteric phenomenon, that it has to do with some fundamental human attractions to characteristics of prospect and refuge, complexity and order. Wright had an intuitive but uniquely firm grasp of the shaping of habitation as an interweaving of these characteristics. From 1902 onward this was embodied in his particular and repetitive way of configuring space that I have called his pattern. Taliesin West and its precursor, the Ocatillo camp, are exceptions, although by other more radical and specialized means they, too, achieve similar purposes. But among major houses by Wright's hand from 1902 through the early 1950s, they are the only exceptions; otherwise his work pervasively shows the familiar pattern, which in turn yields its repetitive characteristics.

In the last years of Wright's life, from the early 1950s to his death in 1959, the pattern is much less consistently found, and this is also the period in which increasing numbers of the houses are designs of exotic and even bizarre fantasy. There are at least two possible reasons for this, and they are not mutually exclusive; indeed they may be closely intertwined. The first, of course, has to do with Wright's extreme age. In 1950 he was eighty-three; he must have known that he had little time left to him. It should not be surprising that he felt driven to attempt grand last gestures. And it may also be realistic to suggest that there was a diminution in his control of these late gestures. It is also likely, however, that the energy he could contribute in these last years was also sharply diminished—how could it be otherwise? Thus, increasingly, the work must have fallen to what one client has called "the busy pencils of Taliesin,"[1] with a consequent distancing of each design from Wright's own involvement. I have already noted, and will note again later in this chapter, that there is no evidence that Wright ever brought his deployment of the pattern to a conscious level. Therefore he can

hardly have explained it to those "busy pencils" to whom the work increasingly fell. Lacking Wright's intuitive grasp of the power of this configuration, they carried on the work as best they could in the late 1950s by emulating other of his characteristic devices—but they could neither perceive nor reinvent the configuration that was the real key to his architectural power. Thus, the pattern seems to hold in Wright's houses with some consistency until the very early 1950s, but much less so thereafter.

The Palmer house serves as an appropriate concluding example of Wright's pattern and of the characteristics of psychobiological appeal that that pattern provides. At this point it might be useful to attempt to clarify and perhaps even to quantify some general aspects of those characteristics.

Some terms used to describe architectural form and space, such as low and tall, or closed and open, represent mutually exclusive conditions. But the terms that have dominated this discussion of Wright's houses are not of that sort. An increase in complexity need not mean a decrease in order, nor does an increase in prospect have to be accompanied by a decrease in refuge. As we have seen, those houses possess a great deal of both complexity and order, and numerous and rich reduplications of both prospect and refuge. If one is to compare Wright's houses with other domestic architectures, or to evolve a general view toward the inclusion of these characteristics in design, it is good to keep in mind that there are considerations of degree but not of trade-off. Thus, degree is a key issue. It is evident, and has been pointed out, that the familiar characteristics of prospect and refuge, complexity and order, can be found in quite elemental domestic architectures, and certainly to some greater degree in all sophisticated ones. But the thesis here is that the degree to which they are present in Wright's work appears to be unique. If Wright has a claim, and there is wide agreement that he does, to a quite extraordinary significance in architectural history and especially that of the dwelling, this seems to me to be an essential part of its foundation.

But here we open important questions which lead to further useful observations. For given the above paragraph, it is fair to ask: how much of each condition is enough—and how much is too little, and how much is too much? The answers to such questions will vary depending on the predilections of the person making the judgement. For in spite of what seems to me to be the fact that these conditions are present in Wright's houses to a unique degree, not all will agree that his houses represent an ideal of the dwelling. A little more discussion of this issue may prove rewarding.

In the introduction I spoke of the "sheer power" of some of Wright's spaces, that can "intimidate the more varied and spontaneous acts of ordinary daily life." Vincent Scully once made a similar point with regard to the Coonley house: "It was a kind of freedom and there being, as it were, no end to it, it was also a kind of death; underneath everything, how great and terrible an architecture it was. We ask ourselves about the clients. Did they know what they had, or what had swallowed them?"[2] And I have revealed some of my own quite personal reactions in saying of the Usonians that there is a lot going on in them and not much ground left over for the occupant. Is there more to be said on this point?

The complexity-order and prospect-refuge model of analysis put forward here may be of help in understanding such negative reactions. For I suggest that such reactions probably arise from an overload of the first of the two pairs of conditions. There is little doubt that the high levels of complexity and order that these houses exhibit make them extraordinarily intriguing as works of art. But these same high levels of complexity and order can also make these houses inhospitable to the various incursions of individual lives, whose differing and more personal complexities and orders have little chance against the already rich conditions of the architecture. And typically in Wright's houses, there is no real way to modify one's exposure; complexity and order are not only typically strong, they are also typically pervasive. One can neither escape them nor mute their intensity.

But if we turn from conditions of complexity and order to those of prospect and refuge, we find that the analytical model used here leads to a helpful distinction. Although the occupant must confront high levels of both complexity and order in whatever part of the space he occupies, on the other hand movement to various positions within the space clearly yields a wide range of choice between various degrees of prospect or refuge. Thus the degree of refuge or of prospect is subject to infinite variety and can be manipulated by the occupant at will simply by moving to the condition he wishes to enjoy at any moment. We move around, we take our pick, we suit our mood. And when our mood changes we know there are other spaces in the house that can suit the new mood too. That Wright was able to provide not only a rich array of these conditions, but also a range of choice with regard to them, is an extraordinarily important legacy of his work. It is exactly this issue of choice that makes all the difference between a dictatorial surrounding and a malleable one.

Many persons who have, or have once had, an unequivocal love affair with Wright's work also possess, I suspect, a high tolerance for, or a deep attraction to, rich portions of both dualities of conditions. But the many whose responses to his work are more complex may be repelled by the compulsive grip of an inescapable and titanic complexity and order, yet at the same time feel the much more supple but equally powerful appeal of the prospect and refuge choices.

Is it possible to describe more closely the manipulations of architectural material by which Wright achieved his particularly effective prospect-refuge juxtapositions?

Refuge conditions are fundamentally created by generating a sense of containment. This can be done by using wall planes to create or infer pockets of space of relatively small dimension, such as the fireplace zones of the Cheney and Goetsch-Winkler houses, or the typical narrow Wrightian corridor. Wright's typical built-in seating, often treated as an embracing promontory next to the fire, is also wonderfully effective in reinforcing a sense of containment. But of even greater importance is the height of the ceiling plane in such areas, as Thiel et al. have shown.[3] In the refuge areas of his houses Wright generally used either a low ceiling or a low ceiling edge, and he admitted that he derived its height from his own. Now the dimension from top of head to ceiling is a sensitive one. Wright was about 5 feet 8 inches tall[4] and on occasion used floor-to-ceiling heights as low as 6 feet 1 inch, which for him would have meant about a 5-inch head clearance. Obviously, increasing the floor-to-ceiling dimension by just 5 inches would double the clearance for anyone of Wright's stature, though for the person who stands 6 feet 6 inches there will be no headroom at all even at this more "generous" dimension. Therefore this dimension more than any other must be tailored to the individual client if one wants to manipulate with maximum effectiveness the sense of containment engendered by it. Wright generally did not do this; instead he tailored this dimension to his own stature, no matter how tall the client.[5] Nevertheless, perhaps a general observation can be made, which is simply that the achievement of a sense of containment as powerful as Wright's depends at least in part upon lowering the ceiling plane to a level something less than a foot from the top of the subject's head. Most modern residential codes in fact do not allow ceiling heights of less than 7 feet 6 inches; Wright's work suggests that such codes might benefit from a finer tuning.[6]

Prospect conditions are essentially conditions of release, demanding, and in Wright's case receiving, higher ceilings. The head-to-ceiling dimension is of itself less important, there being automatically a far greater and therefore less critical distance; what counts is the contrast between low and high. One of the major watersheds of Wright's career, as we have seen, was to ensure opportunity for dramatic contrast between low and high spaces by locating the major spaces directly under the roof, a characteristic that began with the Heurtley house of 1902 and was used almost without exception thereafter. Here, too, it is hard to find a precise conclusion about how much contrast is enough—but it may be possible to delineate some kind of approximate range of conditions that Wright used. In his major houses, with one exception, the ratio between the height of the low ceiling and that of the high one (taken at its highest point) never seems to be less than about 1:1.25; this is true, for example, in the living rooms of the Robie and Affleck houses and the first Jacobs house. The ratio at the Cheney house is about 1:1.3, and this figure is a common one, occurring in many of the Prairie houses and the Hanna and Goetsch-Winkler houses. At Coonley, the first Taliesin, and Hollyhock, the ratio is about 1:1.7—while at the post-1925 Taliesin it is in the order of 1:2. That ratio, or a little more, is also found at the Hardy and Roberts houses, La Miniatura, and the second Jacobs house, for the obvious reason that each has a living room that interlocks with two floors of contiguous space.[7] Thus we might be led to a tentative conclusion: Wright's work suggests that ratios between low and high spaces lying in the range from 1:1.25 to 1:2 or more are effective in developing a contrast between a sense of containment and one of release.

Fallingwater is the notable exception; its low and high ceiling dimensions are in a ratio of about 1:1.15. In my view, this figure is inadequate, and although the building presents unequaled drama in other ways, many who experience Fallingwater's spaces are far less conscious of contrast between low and high than in Wright's other buildings—although I recognize that this issue is subject to individual judgment and needs much more empirical work to justify a norm. In any event, Fallingwater is the lone major exception to the higher figures.

Another key element in the provision of the prospect condition is, of course, the terrace as the external prospect-claiming platform. I have characterized Wright's terraces as being generous. How large is "generous"? In many of the houses, a firm figure is hard to come by. At the Jacobs, Goetsch-Winkler, and Palmer houses, for example, the lawn beyond the paved surface is clearly a part of the prospect-claiming expanse. Some examples, again, defy a crisp figure for other reasons: many have multiple terraces—a point that needs separate attention—and what, exactly, one should count at houses such as Robie or Ennis is unclear. To make the matter still more complex, both Fallingwater and the Pew house have terraces off the bedrooms rivaling or exceeding in size those from the main spaces.

Nevertheless a few generalities emerge. Wright's terraces are usually at least one-third the square footage of the space they serve, and this is true whether they serve major spaces or bedrooms. In many instances, as for example Cheney, Hollyhock, La Miniatura, Fallingwater (main floor), Pew (main floor), Affleck, and Hanna, the size of the terrace is about equal to that of the space served. In at least two dramatic instances, the second floors of the Pew house and Fallingwater, the terraces are actually much larger than the spaces from which they open. And in many cases—for example the Cheney, Coonley, Robie, Lewis, Hanna, and second Jacobs houses, the terrace extends across an entire façade of the space from which it opens. Wright's terraces are also generous in number. In these chapters, plans of the Willits, Heurtley, Cheney, Coonley, Robie, Hardy (counting the lanais off the bedrooms), Glasner, McCormick, Taliesin, Hollyhock, La Miniatura, Storer, Freeman, Ennis, Fallingwater, Taliesin West, Schwartz, Lewis, Pew, and Affleck houses illustrate this. Among these twenty houses I count sixty-one terraces; in fact, among Wright's houses, examples having only one terrace are more the exception than the rule. I have also pointed out that from the Cheney house onward Wright's terraces are partly covered by roof, partly open to the sky. How much is covered? If we ignore the Cheney house as the first instance, and Hollyhock and Ennis because they have no eaves, the answer is typically between 20 and 33 percent. (La Miniatura is also eaveless, but its living room balcony, covering 31 percent of the terrace below, nicely brings it into the typical group).

Therefore of Wright's ubiquitous and "generous" terraces we can say that they are usually at least a third the size of the space they serve and often much more than that; from one-fifth to one-third of their area is under a roof, and a majority of the houses include several of them. Such quantifications are inexact and will have to remain so; they depend on what one counts and the examples one picks. What seems undeniable is that Wright consistently enriched his houses with prospect-claiming extensions of significant area and unusual profusion.

These quantifications only attempt to describe more closely characteristics that have had an unequaled appeal to both a lay and a professional audience over a long period of time, an appeal explicable in terms of a theoretical foundation of which it seems to be an extraordinarily rich manifestation.

Throughout this book I have maintained that this degree of manifestation is particular to Wright. That point now surely needs some substantiation. For if the characteristics attributed to Wright's houses are found in houses generally, or even on a widespread basis, then no discriminating purpose has been served. But I think this is not the case. Let us make a few of the more obvious comparisons.

The well-known Scottish architect Charles Rennie Mackintosh was an almost exact contemporary of Wright. Though Mackintosh did far fewer houses, they comprised an important part of his practice; and like Wright he sought to design the totality of these houses including glazing and furnishings (indeed, unlike Wright, a measure of Mackintosh's reputation is based on his furnishings per se). But none of his houses develops interior prospect through manipulation of an articulated open plan. Nor is there a significant manipulation of the ceiling plane to reinforce interior prospect, because the major spaces do not lie immediately under the roof.[8] Nor do generously proportioned terraces open from extensive glazed walls opposite a fire-focused refuge. Therefore Mackintosh's houses do not present the range of prospect-and-refuge characteristics of Wright's typical work, nor the powerful magnetism that such characteristics hold.

Similar observations might also be made about the work of two American contemporaries of Wright, the California architects Henry Mather and Charles Sumner Greene. Their work may have a special claim to discussion in this context, because while possessing a richness equal to Wright's and an unequaled quality of craftsmanship, it also comes close to the power of Wright's spatial model. The inglenook-contained fireplace areas have all the refuge appeal of Wright's and, because of the magically tactile qualities of the details, sometimes more so. From the exterior, the recesses, the deep eaves, and the conspicuous balconies carry the familiar messages. And although the entries to the houses of Greene and Greene are usually straightforward, the passage into the depths of the dark interior can be nearly as effective in conveying the sense of entry into the protective refuge, removed from the world of the chase. But Wright's early use of strongly modeled ceilings rising into the contiguous roof, the invariable opening of rooms to adjacent rooms, and the elevation of main floor and terrace substantially above the level of the surrounding terrain—all these devices give Wright's houses a richer and more complex sequence of prospect features than those of Greene and Greene, and therefore a more powerful complementary juxtaposition with the refuge features.

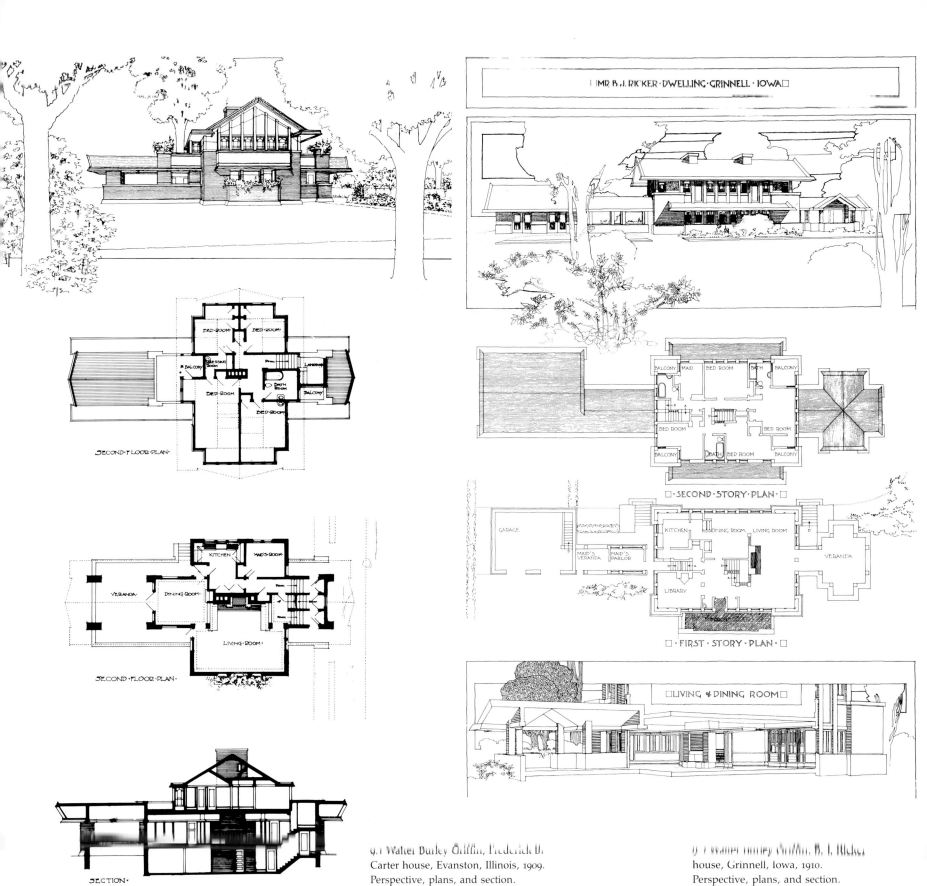

SECOND·FLOOR·PLAN·

SECOND·FLOOR·PLAN·

SECTION·

□ IMR·B·J·RICKER·DWELLING·GRINNELL·IOWA□

□ SECOND·STORY·PLAN· □

□ FIRST·STORY·PLAN· □

□LIVING ᵥ DINING ROOM□

9. Walter Burley Griffin, Frederick B.
Carter house, Evanston, Illinois, 1909.
Perspective, plans, and section.

b. Walter Burley Griffin, B. J. Ricker
house, Grinnell, Iowa, 1910.
Perspective, plans, and section.

That this richness of manifestation is particular to Wright can also be illustrated by comparison to the most obvious body of work of all, that of Wright's early colleagues, the architects of the Prairie School.[9]

The Prairie School comprised a group of architects who found their inspiration and focus in Wright and whose own independent work is marked by obvious similarities to his. Their practices were most productive in the early decades of the century, and especially in those years just after Wright's departure for Europe in 1909. The major architects were Walter Burley Griffin, Marion Mahony, Barry Byrne, William Purcell, George Elmslie, William Drummond, John S. van Bergen, and perhaps Andrew Willatsen.[10] All except Purcell and Elmslie[11] had worked with Wright at the Oak Park Studio for varying lengths of time between 1900 and 1909, the crucial period for the emergence of Wright's own pattern of spatial organization. All of them drew on many characteristics of Wright's manner: broad window bands, deep eaves, prominent fireplaces, dark trim, and absence of historically derived ornament; and many drew on Wright's devices for allowing spaces to flow into each other. But in the entire corpus of their work there are, so far as I am able to discover, no examples that deploy Wright's spatial pattern in its totality.

Walter Burley Griffin's work might perhaps be taken as representative.[12] Griffin's Frederick B. Carter house of 1909, in Evanston, Illinois, locates the bedrooms on the upper floor, and one of these bedrooms partakes of the roof's volume for its ceiling, but the living room is on the lower floor with a flat ceiling (fig. 9.1; note that the lower floor is mislabeled as second floor). His next work, the B. J. Ricker house in Grinnell, Iowa, also has living and dining rooms with flat ceilings that are the undersurface of an upper bedroom floor (fig. 9.2). Of that upper floor H. Allen Brooks says, "The double-pitch ceilings (like the underside of a gable roof) of the bedrooms give an amazing sense of spaciousness—weightless like a tent and high above the head,"[13] which is true, but is exactly the spatial characteristic that Wright was able to provide, not only in bedrooms, but far more importantly in the major spaces of the house. Griffin's "Solid Rock" house of 1911 (fig. 9.3) does, at last, have the living and dining spaces under the roof, nine years after Wright had done this at the Heurtley house, but Griffin takes no advantage of this whatever: the ceilings of those spaces are as low and flat as though there were a superimposed floor.

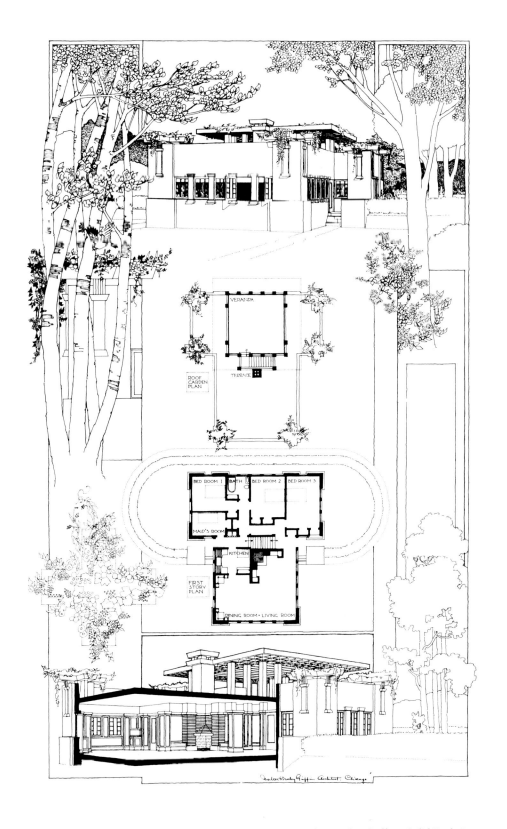

9.3 Walter Burley Griffin, "Solid Rock," Kenilworth, Illinois, 1911. Perspective, plans, and section.

Thus Griffin's work forgoes the opportunity for spatial contrast that marks Wright's work, and also forgoes the reinforcement that that contrast would give to conditions of interior refuge and prospect. Nor do Griffin's houses consistently provide an exterior prospect feature as effective as Wright's. The Carter house has a veranda, closed to the sky, off the dining room, but none from the living room. The Ricker house has a veranda off the living room, also entirely closed to the sky. Thus, both examples provide for exterior prospect from a major space, but neither uses sky exposure to develop contrast between light and dark which would intensify the juxtaposition of refuge and prospect as Wright had done from the Cheney house onward. Solid Rock, furthermore, has no veranda or terrace that is linked to any major space. Of all of Griffin's work, his projected house of 1912, in Winnetka, Illinois (fig. 9.4), for himself and his bride Marion Mahony, comes closest to realizing the pattern. The ceiling of the one and one-half story living room echoes the roof planes; the fireplace is withdrawn to the far corner; the entry has the ambiguity of that of the Cheney house. And yet even here important elements are unrealized: the fireplace is located under a very high ceiling edge, and there is no orchestration of exterior prospect conditions at all: no french doors, no terrace, no external balcony.

Similar comparisons can be made regarding issues of complexity and order, using the same examples. Typically with Griffin, a major space will open to one other major space (figs. 9.2, 9.3, 9.4, where the living room opens to the balcony), though even this is not really true of the Carter house. But neither the Carter nor Ricker houses, Solid Rock, nor Griffin's own house present the opportunities for multiple spatial interpretations that can be found in the Cheney or Coonley houses, for example. Therefore the degree of spatial complexity in Griffin's work is considerably less than in Wright's. Furthermore, in Griffin's work the linkages between joined spaces lack the refinement of, say, Wright's Cheney house, in which connections from the living room to two contiguous spaces, not one, are clarified by the organizing architectural features, the dark columns and the horizontal trim above (as in figs. 3.6 and 3.7).

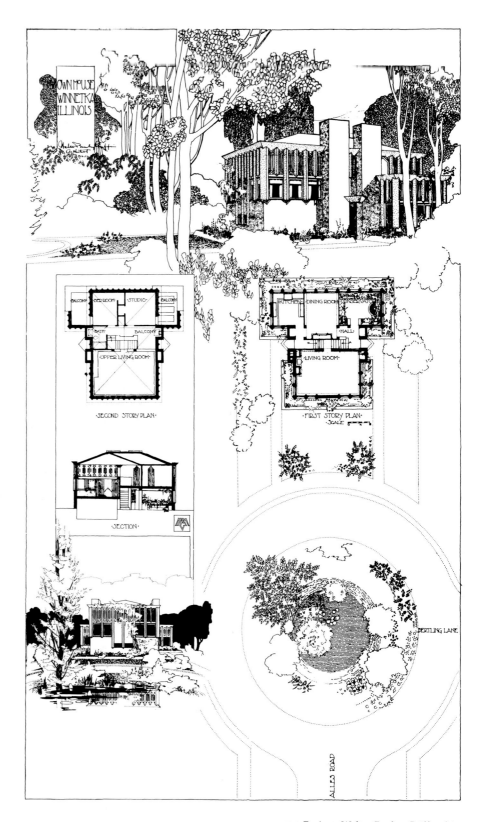

9.4 Project, Walter Burley Griffin his own house, Winnetka, Illinois, 1912. Perspective, plans, section, and elevation.

9.5 Carter house. Living room, toward the fireplace.

This observation introduces the issue of order. For just as Griffin's houses are less complex, their order is also less firm. Wright's Cheney house uses an absolutely continuous ceiling edge trim, located at the same height as the exterior eave and of similar dimension, to cohere the complex interior and to relate it to the exterior; and this device is used in many of his other houses, as we have seen. Griffin uses a similar horizontal interior trim, as for example in the Carter house (fig. 9.5), but since the ceiling is flat, the trim does not edge it. This trim correlates with the exterior trim of the veranda eave, but it is not continuous: it is interrupted by the rising masonry of the fireplace, which robs the fireplace of a refuge reinforcement and robs the trim of its ordering value. At Solid Rock (fig. 9.3) a similar trim line is continuous but is not related to an external eave because there isn't one.

Similar points could be made in equal detail of the work of Mahony, Byrne, Purcell, Elmslie, Drummond, van Bergen,[14] and Willatsen, though separate mention should be made of Purcell, Feick, and Elmslie's magnificent Bradley bungalow of 1911–12 at Woods Hole, Massachusetts. It has many features of considerable interest to a prospect-and-refuge interpretation: a fireplace at the heart of the house and at the interior edge of the living space, under a low ceiling; a ceiling forward of it rising into the roof; a wonderfully broad sweep of windows opposite overlooking falling terrain and a magnificent view. But one cannot move from the living room onto a terrace: the windows toward the view are simply windows, while the actual terraces are small, are at a considerable remove from the living space, and are not visible from it. Nor is there any but a modest development of interior prospect; interior views open only to the hall, and that lies behind the fireplace.

None of this is meant to suggest that the work of any of these other architects was of poor quality. By many measures they were in fact superb architects, architects of talent and dedication, many of whom have garnered their own particular fame—and I have the sense that in many respects they may well have served their clients far better than Wright served his. The point is that in spite of evident similarities, and even superiorities to Wright's work, they did not organize space in his way, and in the end this is the crucial matter. Wright's way has had the stronger and more enduring value. In viewing work of the Prairie School, after even a little experience one knows instinctively whether the work is by Wright or one of the others. It is a question of whether we sense, intuitively and immediately, that the building draws us in; that having been drawn in, we perceive that there are warmly containing spaces juxtaposed with a grandeur of release; whether we feel that we hold the option of seeing without being seen, whether we enjoy the choice of prospect and refuge; whether we are led to explore inexhaustible complexities because we see them as variations within an evident and pervasive order. It is the uniquely rich and pervasive presence of these characteristics that sets Wright's work above that of his Prairie School colleagues.

In later years Wright continued to have colleagues, employees, and, increasingly, students. In the 1920s they included Rudolph Schindler, Richard Neutra, and Wright's son Lloyd Wright, all of whom developed careers of importance. Within those later careers the story is similar to that of the Prairie School; Wright's pattern, and with it the characteristics that constitute its value, rarely appear. The best known work of any of the three is Neutra's magnificent Philip Lovell house in Los Angeles of 1927–29 (figs. 9.6, 9.7). Here Neutra pursued a direction of his own which eventually yielded its own progeny, and for which Wright's pattern could only be incidental; was in fact set

9.6 Richard Neutra, Philip Lovell house, Los Angeles, 1927–29. Exterior from the southwest.

aside in almost all respects.[15] The overhanging eaves are gone, the fireplace is at the edge of the house rather than in its center, the main spaces are on the middle floor with bedrooms generally above, and terraces from major spaces are tiny. As a consequence of the absence of overhangs, the thin steel mullions of the windows, and the extent of glass area (far greater than Wright had dared to this date), emphasis is all on prospect. There is little to distract the eye as it glides along the sleek surfaces and out to stunning views beyond, in which it is unimpeded by deep terraces. The absence of eaves also admits a far greater quantity of light into the house than is at all common in Wright's work. In all these characteristics, Neutra's Lovell house is similar to Le Corbusier's slightly later Villa Savoye at Poissy-sur-Seine. Each house creates a breathtakingly liberating prospect-claiming setting, but to do so, each sets aside many of the symbols and provisions of refuge. This alternative pattern, if we can consider it to be that, yields prospect characteristics of extraordinary strength at the expense of a more catholic range of experiential possibilities.[16]

W right's followers, then, more or less consistently did not adopt his way of composing spatial experiences, although they might or might not adopt other characteristics of his manner. It follows that his way of composing those spatial experiences is to some extent independent of the other characteristics of his manner. Can cases be cited which illustrate an opposite situation, that is, a situation in which his other characteristics do not appear, but which demonstrate the adoption or independent discovery of like ways of composing spatial experiences? The question is an important one. For the other characteristics of Wright's manner are by no means appropriate to all tastes, and are as much a part of history as those of Brunelleschi or Michelangelo or Soane, while his larger compositional values may well be universal and timeless. Can these values of his work be drawn upon without simply cloning?

9.7 Lovell house. Interior.

No doubt there are many answers to this; one lies in the work of the Seattle architect Wendell Lovett. Lovett, even more than Wright, has been an architect of houses, and also commands a dedicated and enthusiastic clientele. Typical of his best work is the Max Scofield house of 1980, on Mercer Island, Washington. Lovett is not an architect who sees Wright as one of his heroes; therefore it is not surprising that the Scofield house is not Wrightian in any obvious way. Few, looking at it, would see any connection whatever. Its external configuration is complex, with many recesses and alcoves, but like Neutra's Lovell house half a century earlier, the Scofield house has no heavy overhanging eaves (fig. 9.8); the entry sequence, furthermore, is in its exterior portion fairly straightforward. What makes the house of interest in this context, and differentiates it from Neutra's Lovell house, is that the interior repeats many of the characteristics of Wright's pattern, and does so with conscious intention on Lovett's part to create juxtapositions of prospect and refuge or, as Lovett would put it, cave and meadow. For once inside the house, the path to the living room has a Wrightian circuitousness, which takes one through several turns, a considerable horizontal distance, and a vertical change of one full floor (figs. 9.9, 9.10). Having reached the living room we are, as so often in Wright's pattern, on axis with the fire, in view straight ahead (fig. 9.11). The fireplace, a ubiquitous feature with Lovett as with Wright, is located under a low ceiling (fig. 9.12). Forward of it the ceiling rises and in doing so becomes the undersurface of the roof. Opposite the fireplace, expanses of glass (fig. 9.9) lead to the deck, which is partly roofed, partly open to the sky. This deck, analogous to Wright's elevated terraces and, like them, distant from the entry, in turn commands an extensive prospect, the wooded hillsides of Mercer Island, with the expanse of Lake Washington beyond.

9.8 Wendell Lovett, Max Scofield house, Mercer Island, Washington, 1980. Exterior from the street; entry at left.

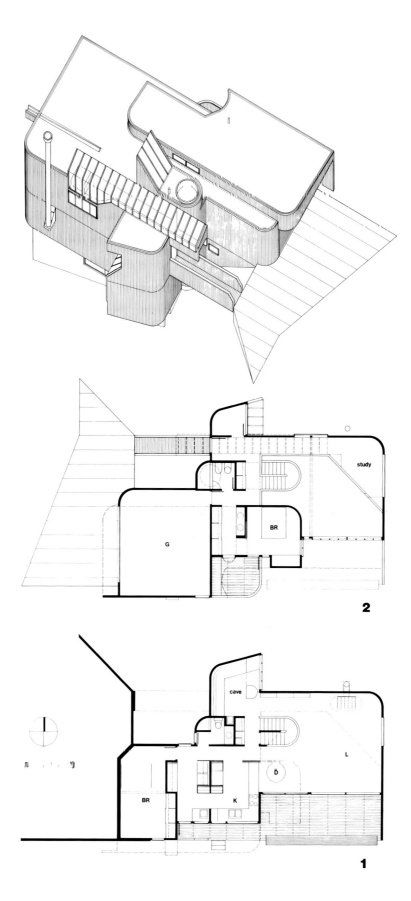

9.9 Scofield house. Plans: upper floor, above; lower (main) floor, below. Entry is at upper left of the upper floor; one then descends the stair at center; at bottom one turns 180 degrees to the right and moves toward the fireplace. The terrace is at lower right of the main floor plan.

2

1

9.10 Scofield house. Upper hall looking down into the living space. The fireplace is at far left; the dining space is under the lower ceiling at right.

9.11 Scofield house. Lower hall; the fireplace is straight ahead.

The Swiss architect Mario Botta in recent years has attained a fame comparable to that of Wright in his Oak Park period. Like Wright, Botta has done a large number of houses on which much of his fame rests. These houses also do not in any immediately obvious way resemble Wright's work. So far as I know no critic has ever linked the two, nor does Botta claim Wright as model or influence; his inspirations are, on the face of it, Le Corbusier, Palladio, and most of all Louis I. Kahn, for whom Botta once worked. It is all the more surprising, then, that the way he composes the features of his domestic spaces is similar to Wright's. In recent years Botta seems to have discovered, quite independently, a pattern of domestic composition which in almost all its characteristics is describable in the same terms, and is equally hospitable to a prospect and refuge interpretation.

Like Wright, Botta spent a number of years trying different themes. His counterpart to Wright's Heurtley house is the round house or rotunda of 1980–81 at Stabio, Switzerland,[17] in which his mature pattern appears in all its constituent characteristics for the first time (figs. 9.13–9.16). What is that pattern? On the exterior (fig. 9.13) there are alcoves, recesses, and conspicuous bands of windows. There are no deep overhanging eaves in the usual sense, but the window areas are cut so deeply into the volume of the building that the effect is the same: shelter is inferred in the deeply pocketed voids within which the glass resides, while the overhanging brows also communicate that, from inside, there is abundant opportunity for panoramic outlook. Thus the house forcefully conveys that, within its accessible refuge, one can see without being seen.

From the ground floor vestibule, one doubles back and up the dramatically towered stair—whose configuration and fenestration suggest a castle—to arrive on the elevated first or main floor near the fireplace, under a low ceiling (figs. 9.14, 9.15). Beyond is the curved wall that is part of the cylindrical masonry shell of the house; this adeptly creates a partial pocket of space of which the fireplace is the focus. In the center of the house the ceiling rises, opening through the glass to the sky above. Opposite the fireplace is an extensive area of window, with a generous elevated terrace beyond looking out over a gentle fall of land to a meadow and a distant rising horizon (fig. 9.16). The forms and spaces of Botta's house of 1982 at Viganello, Switzerland, can be described in almost exactly the same way, except only that a pair of orthogonal walls are substituted for the curved wall of the Stabio house.

9.12 Scofield house. Living room toward the fireplace. The entry is at upper left, the stair at center left. Glazing and the terrace are behind the camera.

9.13 Mario Botta, house at Stabio, Switzerland, 1980–81. Exterior from the south. Living spaces and terrace are at center.

9.14 House at Stabio. Isometrics, clockwise from bottom: lower entry floor; main living floor; upper bedroom floor. At right, a composite isometric of all levels.

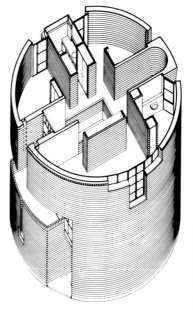

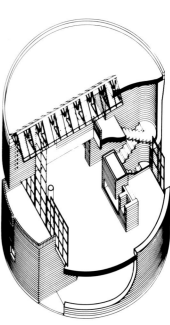

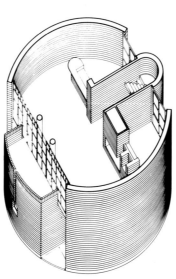

9.15 House at Stabio. Central atrium looking toward the stair. The fireplace is at right, under the low ceiling; the dining space is at left.

9.16 House at Stabio. Central atrium looking toward the terrace. The living room is at left; the fireplace is behind the camera at left.

The pattern is epitomized in Botta's work in an unbuilt project of 1984 for Bellinzona, Switzerland (figs. 9.17, 9.18). The project is for a steep hillside. One approaches by a long sequence of steps, and penetrates the entire depth of the house to a cylindrically walled stair at the back, a stair literally buried in the hill. One twists up this dark shaft to arrive at the first floor, on the flank of the fireplace, also buried in the hill, its back to the wall as were Wright's fireplaces at Taliesin. And as at the second Jacobs house, this recessing of the fireplace in the earth, even more literal and more extreme with Botta than with Wright, is appropriate to the role of the fire as the focus of the cave-refuge. Beyond is the living space, at the opposite side of which is a wall of glass leading to the terminal experience of the spatial sequence, the two elevated terraces that look out over falling land to the valley beyond. Only two aspects of these descriptions differ from those that describe Wright's pattern: Botta's main spaces typically have a bedroom floor above; and, for that reason, there is a very considerable expanse of low, flat ceiling forward of the fireplace, much greater than in Wright's houses.[18]

Botta's houses are of special interest in this discussion because on the surface they seem so different from Wright's work, yet at the same time they are so similarly organized. They are also of interest because Botta has come so close to describing his goals for these houses in prospect and refuge terms. He has said: "I believe that the primary need of the house is one of protection, but I also believe that the need exists, inside the house, to project outward. This is perhaps why, in my work, the two things coexist—that is, the need to enclose and the need to thrust outward."[19] And Christian Norberg-Schulz also comes tantalizingly close to the issue when he says, "The importance of the houses of Mario Botta resides in their having revived archetypal forms of the human dwelling. Thus they represent reinterpretations of the original cave-like enclosure, the interior 'hall' as well as the extrovert 'veranda.' A spontaneous feeling of coming close to the essence of house is thus created."[20]

In these houses by Lovett and Botta, the major spaces are elevated well above the terrain they overlook. The fireplace, withdrawn into the house, is at the internal edge of the space it serves. Above it is a low ceiling. Forward of the fireplace zone the ceiling rises (although in Botta's work this happens at some remove), at the same time becoming the undersurface of the roof. Interior views are developed between contiguous spaces. Glass and glazed doors comprise walls distant from the fire; these glazed surfaces open to a generous elevated terrace. The exterior has deep overhangs casting the broad expanses of glass in deep shadow (more strongly in Botta's case than in Lovett's). The path from the exterior to the major interior spaces is relatively lengthy and convoluted. The only elements from Wright's pattern that are absent are the externally conspicuous chimney and the lowering of the window head toward the terrace. Thus the work of these two architects demonstrates that the pattern vital to Wright's work can have a larger creative application.

This inquiry into the meaning of architectural configuration has emphasized the single-family detached dwelling, since this is the obvious building type in which to expect habitat choices to have importance.[21] This building type was also the one most frequently addressed by Wright in his professional career. Within that body of work, I have discussed all those examples commonly thought to comprise his major houses, those on which his significance fundamentally rests. All of them except only Ocatillo and Taliesin West share the repetitive spatial and formal configuration that I have called his pattern. Perhaps at this point it might also be fair to put the case in the opposite way—to say that those of his houses that embody the pattern in its strongest, clearest manifestations are exactly the ones that have come to be regarded as his most significant works.[22]

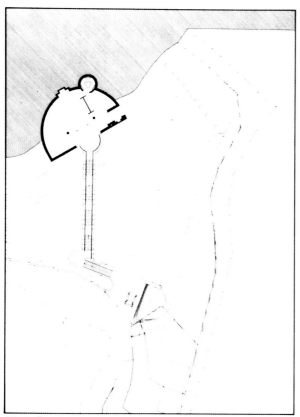

First floor

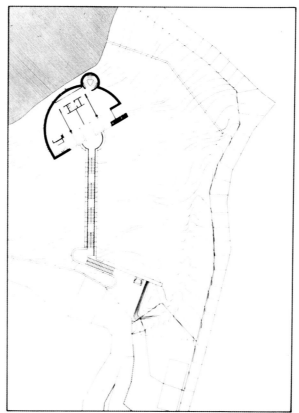

Second floor

9.17 Project: Mario Botta, house at Bellinzona, Switzerland, 1984. Plans. The stair is the small cylinder at the upper edge of the plans; the fireplace is the rectilinear projection next to the stair on the first floor. Both the stair and the fireplace are buried in the earth of the hill.

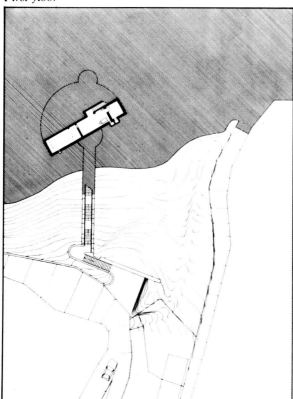

Basement

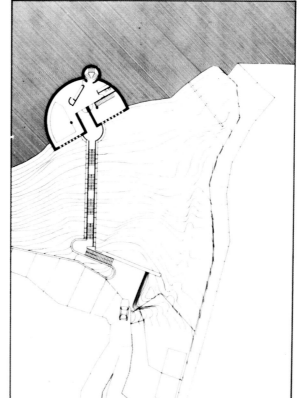

Ground floor

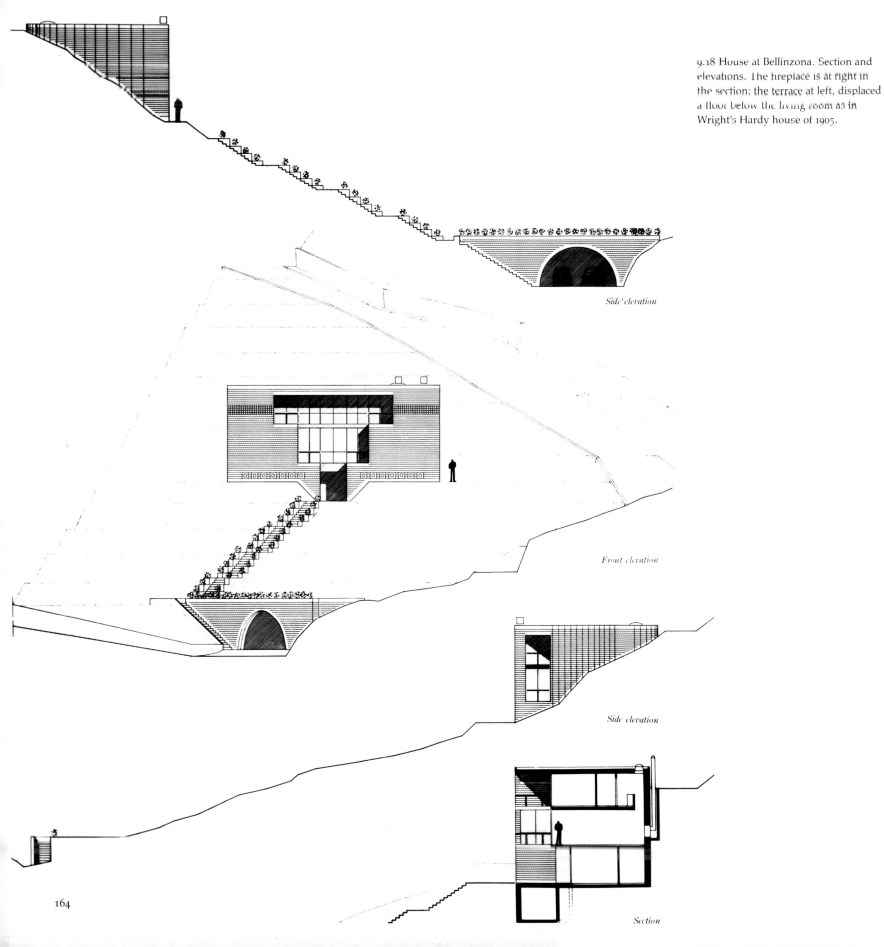

9.18 House at Bellinzona. Section and elevations. The fireplace is at right in the section; the terrace at left, displaced a floor below the living room as in Wright's Hardy house of 1905.

Side elevation

Front elevation

Side elevation

Section

The pattern, as exemplified in these and the many other houses by Wright that embody it, works its hypnotism by presenting conditions of habitation like those which, as a species, we have from our earliest beginnings found to be magnetically appealing. The exteriors of his houses convey rich symbols of both refuge and prospect, which irresistibly draw us to their interiors. They are reached by the narrow passageways through which, in our deepest ancestry, we withdrew from the world of the chase into the cave or grove, the protected and protecting sanctum. There, gathered around the fire hearth, seeing without being seen, we viewed and view the hunting ground beyond, and move from chamber to chamber within the filtered light of the narrow, overbowered forest path. Both the forms and the spaces are complex, far more so than in usual dwellings of similar size. But the relationships that reveal themselves around us, although atypical in terms of usual architectural experience, are intrinsically repetitive. The constant ceiling edges recall the external eaves under which we passed on entry—and so on, through the whole series of irresistible manipulations. Through half a century Wright continued to use, through endless permutations, these devices of prospect and refuge, complexity and order. They worked, and still work, with enormous effectiveness, because they stimulate those responses that are a part of why we are here.

The characteristics embodied in the pattern clearly varied in emphasis at different points in Wright's life. The work from 1902 to 1909 in the suburbs of Chicago represented a remarkable balance of both refuge from the community and contact with it. At Taliesin the role of refuge was paramount; Wright himself used the word in reference to its site. In the California houses of the 1920s this emphasis on refuge became still stronger. Yet in these same houses he began to create internal prospect conditions of unprecedented richness. Thus, at Fallingwater a balance was again struck in a rural, not urban, dwelling, but one blending conditions of refuge and prospect, complexity and order, with natural and manmade symbols of hazard, to create an unequalled drama of human appeal. At about this same time Wright, in old age, turned to the Arizona desert to build at Taliesin West the prospect-dominant creation one would have been tempted to associate with youth. At this time he also embarked on the Usonian houses, which embodied the familiar characteristics intensely, perhaps almost too intensely, in a series of quite small dwellings. And later still, at about the time of the Palmer house, he added to the Wisconsin Taliesin the cantilevered "bird walk" (fig. 9.19) which, like the balconies of Fallingwater, hovers over space in a bold juxtaposition of prospect and hazard. It has been easy enough to point out that these changing emphases often bore some correspondence to the changing conditions of Wright's own life.

Wright's pattern and the attributes that accrue to it explain why his popularity as an architect of houses persisted, and in a sense still persists, in spite of arrogance, outrageous budget excesses, leaking roofs, inadequate closets, late schedules, high maintenance, and all the rest of it. Wright's clients might claim that they put up with it all for the sake of beauty. But our current understanding of what that term means suggests that at least in domestic architecture, beauty in a fundamental sense is related to characteristics of prospect and refuge, complexity and order. Yet we have been able to make a distinction between these pairs of characteristics. Rich ladings of complexity and order, pervasive and inescapable, ally Wright's work with great art. Rich ladings of prospect and refuge, between which one can choose and adjust at will, make his houses continually magical spaces. And in the end it is this latter achievement, rather than the former, that gives Wright his place not only in history but in our continually astonished affection.

9.19 Taliesin. The "bird walk" from the hill to the north.

Notes

Introduction

1. Frank Lloyd Wright, *An Autobiography* (New York: Duell, Sloane, and Pearce, 1943), p. 253.

2. Robert Twombly, *Frank Lloyd Wright, His Life and His Architecture* (New York: Wiley, 1979), p. 260.

3. Kaufmann, *Fallingwater* (New York: Abbeville Press, 1986), p. 31. Wright, and others, have sometimes maintained that there has been considerable public antipathy to his work: see for example Wright, *Autobiography*, 1943, pp. 128, 132ff, 149–50, etc., or Donald Hoffman, *Frank Lloyd Wright's Robie House* (New York: Dover, 1984), p. 9, quoting Frederick Robie on this point. Such accounts need to be approached with caution, as in each case there is a self-serving motivation in emphasizing a *Sturm und Drang* view of Wright's career and in dramatizing the radical nature of his work. The Robie interview raises other questions as well; see Chap. 3, n. 32.

4. The Glasner house of 1905, an early example, has five openings into the living room, with traffic in all directions, and the fireplace adjacent to the kitchen door. The Roberts and Robie houses, La Miniatura, and many of the Usonians have similar problems, and all photos I have ever seen of these houses, under various owners, fail to show convincing conversational groupings, nor do such groupings seem easily obtained, at least to me. John Sergeant, *Frank Lloyd Wright's Usonian Houses* (New York: Watson-Guptill Publications, 1984), p. 30, discusses like problems with kitchen arrangements.

5. See H. Allen Brooks, *Writings on Wright* (Cambridge, Mass.: MIT Press, 1981), p. 66, in which Marjorie Leighey, at one time owner of a well-known Usonian, states, "The need for more storage space is felt almost to desperation." Nevertheless, Mrs. Leighey loved the house despite its problems. Twombly, *Life*, p. 243, argues that the Usonians had ample storage space, but a look at typical plans, for instance the first Jacobs house, more than confirms the observation quoted in Brooks. In 1934 Wright proposed a house (never built) for Stanley Marcus, with no closets at all. Marcus predictably enough objected, to which Wright replied: "Closets are rotten. They just accumulate junk" (Brendan Gill, *Many Masks* [New York: G. P. Putnam's Sons, 1987], p. 341). In fairness Wright seems to have practiced what he preached: the first Taliesin had just one bank of closets for the whole house. Where did he keep his capes, berets, ascots, scarves, white suits, and Cuban shoes?

6. Regarding leaking roofs, there is on record Wright's reply to Herbert Johnson to move his chair. A wittier comment was offered by Mrs. Richard Lloyd Jones, wife of one of Wright's distant cousins and owner of a Wright house in Tulsa, who explained a leak to a guest: "This is what happens when you leave a work of art out in the rain." Of examples of unserviceable detailing, the roof edge of Fallingwater is the most notable among many; as illustration see Edgar Kaufmann Jr., *Fallingwater* (New York: Abbeville Press, 1986), pp. 132–33 and 148–49. Regarding structural inadequacies see Chap. 6, n. 13.

7. Such examples as the Robie and first Jacobs house were close to budget, but these seem to have been as much the exception as the rule. The Hanna house was to have had a 1936 budget of $15,000; it cost $37,000. Fallingwater was to have been done for $25,000 and cost $150,000. Wright promised that the closetless house for Stanley Marcus (n. 5 above) would cost $10,000, though he later claimed he had said $25,000. No matter; bids came in at $150,000. Nor are such overages confined to domestic work; the Johnson's Wax building was originally estimated by Wright at $250,000; it cost $3,000,000, or twelve times the estimate. There are many other instances, and despite apologists, they are hardly trivial.

8. Lest this be thought to overstate the case, see e.g. Gill, *Masks*, pp. 148–63, 186–87, 248–50, 262–64, 274–84, 322–23; Herbert Jacobs with Katherine Jacobs, *Building with Frank Lloyd Wright* (San Francisco: Chronicle Books, 1978), pp. 90–97; Paul R. and Jean S. Hanna, *Frank Lloyd Wright's Hanna House* (Cambridge, Mass.: MIT Press, 1982), pp. 24–25, 47, 48; or Kaufmann, *Fallingwater*, pp. 46–47. Nevertheless these clients, too, forgave Wright in the end and came to love what he had built for them.

9. Jay Appleton, *The Experience of Landscape* (London: John Wiley & Sons, 1975). This edition is now out of print, but a paperback edition, a reprint of the original, is available from Hull University Press (1986).

Appleton is a graduate of Oxford and King's College, Newcastle, at which he took his degree in geography. He has spent his entire teaching career in that field at the University of Hull.

Typically he says of his intentions (p. ix): "I seek to prove nothing—merely to suggest." Nevertheless the suggestions put forward in *The Experience of Landscape* have been fruitful ones. Although less well known than it deserves to be, it has been able to claim both respect and durability. It has been the foundation of an important body of theory in landscape architecture; it has proven capable of suggesting related extensions of its fundamental ideas; and it has generated criticism and controversy. To respond constructively to this latter point Appleton wrote "Prospect and Refuge Revisited," (published in *Landscape Journal* 1984, pp. 91–103, and reprinted in Jack L. Nasar, ed., *Environmental Aesthetics: Theory, Research, and Applications* [Cambridge, England: Cambridge University Press, 1988], pp. 27–48). In that essay he addressed the various critiques generated by *The Experience of Landscape* during its first decade. One critique, however, that so far as I know did not emerge there, but has come out in seminars on the subject, has to do with the role of individual differences as they modify responses to genetically driven stimuli. Appleton, I believe, would not claim that such differences are less than vital. His autobiographical manuscript, "How I Made the World," is a major and extensive examination of the issue of varying individual predilections within a more universal preferential framework.

10. See for example Stephen Kaplan, "Aesthetics, Affect, and Cognition: Environmental Preference from an Evolutionary Perspective," *Environment and Behavior*, 19:1 (Jan. 1987), pp. 3–32; D. M. Woodcock, "A Functionalist Approach to Environmental Preference" (doctoral dissertation, University of Michigan, 1982), or J. Archea, "Visual Access and Exposure: An Architectural Basis for Interpersonal Behavior" (doctoral dissertation, Pennsylvania State University, 1984).

11. See for example Daniel E. Berlyne, *Aesthetics and Psychobiology* (New York: Appleton-Century-Crofts, 1971), pp. 143–57); John R. Platt, "Beauty: Pattern and Change," in D. W. Fishe and S. R. Madde, eds., *Functions of Varied Experience* (Homewood, Ill.: Dorsey, 1961); or Nicholas Humphrey, "Natural Aesthetics," and Peter F. Smith, "Urban Aesthetics," in Byron Mikellides, ed., *Architecture for People* (London: Studio Vista, 1980).

12. Kaplan, "Aesthetics," pp. 3–32.

13. An exact number is hard to determine; does one count remodelings, additions, gardeners' cottages? Does Taliesin count as one house, or three, or twenty? Are the cluster houses—Suntop, etc.—one unit or many? What of apartment buildings? The phrase "over 300 executed houses" arises from counting buildings cited as "residences" in William Allin Storrer, *The Architecture of Frank Lloyd Wright* (Cambridge, Mass.: MIT, 1978), and trying to apply common sense in answer to the above questions. Storrer is generally taken to be the most nearly complete available inventory of Wright's built work.

7 The Pattern

1. Classic sources for this period of Wright's career are Henry-Russell Hitchcock, *In The Nature of Materials* (New York: Da Capo Press, 1982, a reprinting of the 1942 edition) and Grant Manson, *Frank Lloyd Wright to 1910: The First Golden Age* (New York: Reinhold, 1958). More recently the pertinent volumes of the *Frank Lloyd Wright* monograph series by Yukio Futagawa, editor and photographer; text by Bruce Brooks Pfeiffer (Tokyo: ADA Edita, 1986–), offer an unprecedented wealth of drawings and photographs; hereafter this series is cited under Pfeiffer, *Frank Lloyd Wright*. . . .

2. Published in February of 1901.

3. Published in July of 1901.

4. Spellings vary; I follow that of William Allin Storrer, *The Architecture of Frank Lloyd Wright* (Cambridge, Mass.: MIT Press, 1978).

5. Subsequent examples of this approach include the Isabel Roberts house of 1908 in River Forest and its elegant close cousin, the Frank Baker house of 1909 in Wilmette.

6. The few exceptions in major houses from 1902 to 1906 are: the Dana house of 1903, the Gale house of 1904 (built 1909) and the Darwin Martin house of 1906; see Chap. 3. Thereafter the condition is virtually universal, the sole major exception, and that only a partial one, being Fallingwater; see Chap. 6. Furthermore, the condition is pervasive not only in Wright's houses; it is also a distinguishing characteristic of his non-domestic work. It occurs at Unity Temple, and at the later Madison First Unitarian Society and the Beth Sholem synagogue, although of course in religious buildings the condition is usual throughout history. But the condition also occurs at the Larkin Administration Building, the Imperial Hotel, the Johnson's Wax Corporate Headquarters, the Morris Gift Shop, the Arizona State Capitol project, the Guggenheim Museum, and the Marin County Civic Center, and these are building types in which it is not usual at all.

7. Wright's handling of the Heurtley house confers another important advantage as well, in providing a more dramatic viewing platform as a direct result of the elevated living floor. The advantage of height per se is better taken up in Chap. 3.

8. Vincent Scully, *Frank Lloyd Wright* (New York: George Braziller, 1960), p. 19, refers to the "taut, wood-stripped ceiling" as "a tent." This is a plausible interpretation, but is more appropriate to later versions of the device as it appears at Taliesin and Hollyhock House, where the wood trim is much more delicate. See Chaps. 4 and 5. As Chap. 4 notes, Wright himself referred to Taliesin's ceilings as "tent-like."

9. At some subsequent date the Heurtley terrace was enclosed by glazing and thus is no longer an outdoor space. In discussing the Heurtley house here and in Chap. 3, I deal with the characteristics presented by its original condition, and unless otherwise noted this will generally be the case with other examples as well.

10. The fundamental work on the Shingle Style is Vincent J. Scully, Jr., *The Shingle Style and the Stick Style* (New Haven and London: Yale University Press, 1976); see especially pp. 155–64. A detailed discussion of the sources for the inglenook in Wright's work is in Edgar Kaufmann Jr., "Precedent and Progress in the Work of Frank Lloyd Wright," *Journal of the Society of Architectural Historians* 39:2 (May 1980), pp. 145–49.

11. Including even the seemingly one-story Cheney house of 1904; see Chap. 3.

12. Meredith Clausen, "Frank Lloyd Wright, Vertical Space, and the Chicago School's Quest for Light," *Journal of the Society of Architectural Historians* 44:1 (Mar. 1985), argues that Wright's skylit spaces in public buildings, as for example the Larkin Building, Unity Temple, and the much later Johnson's Wax, were influenced by the skylit lobbies at the bases of light wells in Chicago's commercial buildings of Wright's early years. This is a valuable insight in terms of Wright's institutional and commercial buildings, but the houses seem to me to demand a different analysis. The Heurtley house was done in the same year as the Larkin Building, and Heurtley has a false skylight (not open to the sky) in the living room, but immediately thereafter even this feature is largely given up, as at the Cheney, Robie, and Roberts houses, Taliesin, the California series, Fallingwater, and others. There are skylights in the stairwells of Coonley and one above the fireplace at Hollyhock, and clearly Ocatillo and Taliesin West are brilliantly skylit—but generally, Wright's ceilings yield a sense of containment that is stronger than that of release, and with their opacity and their deep eaves, they create a notably dark space rather than a brightly lit one.

13. When Wright fled from Oak Park in 1909 he went to Fiesole in the hills above Florence, in the heart of the *piano nobile* tradition of the elevated living floor. But this was long after he had found his own format, whose primary importance is in getting the rooms under the roof for spatial drama, a characteristic the Italian *piano nobile* does not share.

14. The Glasner house of 1905 is a maverick on this point, if one accepts that its entry porch is a terrace of sorts—an interpretation I will offer in Chap. 3, but would not want to defend to the death. Before 1900 Wright used the conventional terrace/porch/piazza more commonly as entry, as for example in his own house of 1889 in Oak Park. Yet even by 1892, in the Allison W. Harlan house in Chicago, done while he was with Adler and Sullivan, Wright had set the terrace firmly apart from the entry sequence.

15. When this issue arises, there is often an inference that Wright's attraction to Japan was in some way unusual. It was not. Bruce Price, whose Shingle Style houses were a model for Wright's own house, was a Japanophile; so was Lyman Silsbee, Wright's first employer, through whom Wright probably was first introduced to Japanese tastes and artifacts. One could also cite Whistler, Wilde, and many others. It could be argued that Wright was rather late on the scene, for even by 1881 Japanophilia was sufficiently common that Gilbert and Sullivan could satirize it in *Patience*—"I do not long for all one sees that's Japanese"—and expect to be widely understood.

16. Manson, *Golden Age*, p. 31 (see n. 1).

17. Dimitri Tselos, "Exotic Influences in the Architecture of Frank Lloyd Wright," *Magazine of Art* 46 (Apr. 1953), pp. 160–84.

18. See for example Manson, *Golden Age*, pp. 34–40. The most recent discussion, however, and also the most perceptive, is that of David B. Stewart, *The Making of a Modern Japanese Architecture* (Tokyo and New York: Kodansha International, 1987), pp. 63–76. On Wright's involvement with the Japanese print see Julia Meech-Pekarik, "Frank Lloyd Wright's Other Passion" in Carol R. Bolon, Robert S. Nelson, and Linda Seidel, eds., *The Nature of Frank Lloyd Wright* (Chicago: University of Chicago Press, 1988), pp. 125–53.

19. See also Stewart, *The Making*, p. 10.

20. I will develop this point at greater length in Chap. 9.

21. Frank Lloyd Wright, *An Autobiography* (New York: Duell, Sloane, and Pearce, 1943), p. 141. This comment is repeated elsewhere in his writings.

22. Frank Lloyd Wright, *An Autobiography* (New York: Horizon, 1977), p. 166.

23. E.g., Wright, *Autobiography*, 1943, p. 142.

24. Frank Lloyd Wright, *The Natural House* (New York: Horizon Press, 1954), p. 15.

25. Christian Norberg-Schulz, *Genius Loci* (New York: Rizzoli, 1980), pp. 192–94.

26. Norberg-Schulz, *The Concept of Dwelling* (New York: Rizzoli, 1985), p. 99.

27. Ibid., pp. 128–29.

2. Complexity and Order, Prospect and Refuge

1. Nicholas Humphrey, "Natural Aesthetics," in Byron Mikellides, ed., *Architecture for People* (London, Studio Vista, 1980), p. 73.

2. Mario Gandelsonas, in the introduction to Peter Eisenman, *House X* (New York: Rizzoli International Publications, Inc., 1982), p. 7.

3. Discussion throughout this chapter and throughout this book presumes some primordial state of Homo sapiens. How deep in time was this state? Although "Lucy" appears to be dated to three million years ago, our current brain configuration and character appear to have much later origins. John R. Platt, "Beauty: Pattern and Change," in D. W. Fishe and S. R. Maddi, eds., *Functions of Varied Experience* (Homewood, Ill.: Dorsey, 1961), p. 411, cites views given at the 1959 Darwin Centennial Celebration at Chicago that the development of the brain "may have occurred in much less than 500,000 years." Other more recent work may reduce even that brief figure substantially; the current "Eve" theory holds that our particular genetic makeup had its origins about 200,000 years ago, and probably in the West African savannah. On an evolutionary calendar, and given the relatively long human generational interval, this is a very brief period indeed. That our instinctual reactions have remained virtually unchanged over that period is highly probable.

4. Roger S. Ulrich, "Aesthetic and Affective Response to Natural Environment," in I. Altman and J. F. Wohlwill, eds., *Behavior and the Natural Environment* (New York: Plenum, 1983), p. 87.

5. Peter F. Smith, "Urban Aesthetics," in Mikellides, *Architecture for People*, p. 74.

6. E. H. Gombrich, *The Sense of Order: A Study in the Psychology of Decorative Art* (Oxford: Phaidon Press, 1979), p. 1. Gombrich continues: "Thanks to the researches of ethologists during the last few decades more is known about inborn reactions for which animals are undoubtedly 'programmed' than even Darwin could have surmised. To speak schematically, an organism to survive must be equipped to solve two basic problems. It must be able to answer the questions 'what?' and 'where?' . . . . It goes without saying that in the lower stages of evolution these capacities cannot depend on that elusive entity we call consciousness. Even in man they are not so coupled." And on p. 6 he notes, "It is never without danger to draw analogies between nature and culture, but I believe that here, as elsewhere, such dangers must be faced if progress is to be made."

7. Humphrey, "Natural Aesthetics," p. 59.

8. John Dewey, *Art as Experience* (New York: Pentagon Books, 1934), pp. 4, 13.

9. Jay Appleton, "How I Made the World," unpublished MS, pp. 338–39, quoted by permission of the author.

10. But not becoming very well integrated with either criticism or practice in the environmental arts, with the exception, perhaps, of the field of landscape architecture.

11. Joachim Wohlwill, citing the position of Daniel Berlyne, in "Environmental Aesthetics," in *Human Behavior and Environment* (New York: Plenum Press, 1976), p. 41.

12. Appleton, "How I Made the World," draft p. 331.

13. Smith, "Urban Aesthetics," p. 84. See also Ulrich, "Aesthetic and Affective Response," pp. 95–97, and Daniel E. Berlyne, *Aesthetics and Psychobiology* (New York: Appleton-Century-Crofts, 1971), pp. 143–57.

14. Platt, "Beauty: Pattern and Change" (see n. 3).

15. Humphrey, "Natural Aesthetics," pp. 59–73.

16. Ibid., p. 63, referring to a phrase from the English poet Gerard Manley Hopkins.

17. Ibid., pp. 63–71. This may have something to do with the tendency for architectural historians to specialize. Far more importantly, it may be fundamental to the whole phenomenon of cultural preference and bias.

18. Appleton, "How I Made the World," draft p. 332.

19. Jay Appleton, *The Experience of Landscape* (London: John Wiley, 1975). Appleton presents his position in 262 pages of closely reasoned argument. What follows here can only be a brief synopsis, and one necessarily focusing on those aspects most clearly pertinent to architecture.

20. See especially D. M. Woodcock, "A Functionalist Approach to Environmental Preference" (doctoral dissertation, University of Michigan, 1982), especially Chap. 5, "Environmental Preference Theory: An Evolutionary Perspective." Woodcock breaks down Appleton's terms into primary and secondary prospect and refuge, in each case the primary being a condition actually occupied by the viewer, secondary being conditions apprehended at some distance. In architectural application, one is generally dealing with primary conditions; therefore, though Woodcock's terms are useful for landscape, I do not use them here. See also J. Archea, "Visual Access and Exposure: An Architectural Basis for Interpersonal Behavior" (doctoral dissertation, Pennsylvania State University, 1984). Archea approaches his study from a quite different direction and nowhere uses the terms *aesthetics* or *pleasure*; it is therefore all the more significant that his work leads to conclusions virtually identical to those of Appleton.

21. Mary Ann Kirkby, in an unpublished paper, "A Natural Place to Play: The Use of Refuge in a Pre-School Play Yard" (University of Washington Department of Landscape Architecture, 1984), in which she was investigating prospect and refuge behaviors in children's playground activities, cited an interview with a four-year-old boy who put the whole matter very tersely: "When asked why his hiding spot should have an opening, Ryan, age four, answered 'Because I would need to see if you were coming.' And on another occasion, when asked twice why he preferred one landscape over another, he answered, very matter of factly, 'Because I could see.' When asked why it was important to see he responded, without hesitating, 'Because there might be wolves out there.'"

22. Appleton, *Experience of Landscape*, p. 148.

23. Appleton, "How I Made the World," draft p. 356.

24. Charles Dickens, *Bleak House* (New York: W. W. Norton & Co., 1977), p. 228. But note that the currently handiest edition (New York: Bantam Classics, 1985), which unfortunately is the one on my own shelves, contains a bad typo in this passage, omitting two grammatically essential words (p. 236).

25. Appleton, *Experience of Landscape*, p. 69.

26. Ibid., p. 105.

27. Walter Creese, *The Crowning of the American Landscape* (Princeton: Princeton University Press, 1985), p. 241.

28. Thomas H. Beeby, "Wright and Landscape: A Mythical Interpretation," in Carol R. Bolon, Robert S. Nelson, and Linda Seidel, eds., *The Nature of Frank Lloyd Wright* (Chicago: University of Chicago Press, 1988), p. 144. An example of the sort of thing Beeby may be referring to can be found in Wright, "In the Cause of Architecture," *Architectural Record* 23:3 (March 1908), p. 155: "[Nature's] wealth of suggestion is inexhaustible; her riches are greater than any man's desire," but there are innumerable instances of the theme in his writings.

29. Other dates are commonly given, e.g., Grant Manson, *Frank Lloyd Wright to 1910: The First Golden Age* (New York: Reinhold, 1957), p. 93, gives 1895; Henry-Russell Hitchcock, *In the Nature of Materials* (New York: Da Capo Press, 1982), p. 29, gives 1896. Robert Twombly, *Frank Lloyd Wright, His Life and His Architecture* (New York: John Wiley & Sons, 1979), p. 57, has traced local primary sources which tie the date to September 1897.

30. Appleton, *Experience of Landscape*, pp. 125–27.

31. Wright, *An Autobiography* (New York: Duell, Sloan, and Pearce, 1943), p. 136.

32. An anonymous reader has kindly pointed out that this is true of "hundreds of 'eye-catchers' in 18th century gardens." But in those instances the notion of a climbable and habitable tower, or a symbol thereof, was the whole purpose. Wright's task, on the other hand, was to provide a working windmill for farm use. That he modified the program in this way suggests the importance to him of doing so. Another reader has suggested that the source of the windmill's name lies in analogies between the belvedere and Juliet's balcony, and that therefore the occupant of that balcony was intended to be seen, not hidden. But in Wright's lengthy discussion of the structure he nowhere uses the term "balcony," though he refers to "the little belvedere—named for Juliet" (Frank Lloyd Wright, *An Autobiography* [New York: Horizon, 1977], p. 160). But this seems not to have been the primary source, for he says at greater length (p. 159) "Romeo, as you will see, will do all the work and Juliet will cuddle alongside to support and exalt him. Romeo takes the side of the blast and Juliet will entertain the school children. Let's let it go at that. No symbol should ever be taken too far."

3. The Prairie Houses

1. See, e.g., Grant Manson, *Frank Lloyd Wright to 1910: The First Golden Age* (New York: Reinhold, 1958), pp. 103–108, in which he calls the *Ladies' Home Journal* houses "full-fledged Prairie Houses" and Bradley and Hickox "the first Prairie Houses to be erected." Henry-Russell Hitchcock, *In the Nature of Materials* (New York: Duell, Sloane, and Pearce, 1942, reprint, 1982), caption to fig. 73, and Vincent Scully, in Hitchcock et al., *The Rise of an American Architecture* (New York: Praeger, 1970), p. 188, give the Willits house the honor.

2. Vincent Scully, *Frank Lloyd Wright* (New York: George Braziller, Inc., 1960), p. 19.

3. Thomas H. Beeby, "Wright and Landscape: A Mythical Interpretation," in Carol R. Bolon, Robert S. Nelson, and Linda Seidel, eds., *The Nature of Frank Lloyd Wright* (Chicago: University of Chicago Press, 1988), p. 170.

4. Jay Appleton, *The Experience of Landscape* (London: John Wiley, 1975), p. 103.

5. Lisa Heschong, *Thermal Delight in Architecture* (Cambridge, Mass.: MIT Press, 1979), p. 34.

6. On this point see Philip Thiel, Ean Duane Harrison, and Richard S. Alden, "Perception of Spatial Enclosure as a Function of the Position of the Architectural Surfaces," *Environment and Behavior* 18:2 (March 1986), pp. 227–45, in which they make a convincing empirical demonstration of this point.

7. Jay Appleton, *Experience of Landscape*, pp. 118–19.

8. H. Allen Brooks, "Wright and the Destruction of the Box," *Journal of the Society of Architectural Historians* 38:2 (March 1979), pp. 7–14, notes also the importance of articulating elements between spaces. The article is an extremely important one for its vanguard discussion of Wright's spaces but is in some ways misleading. Brooks calls attention to rooms which join diagonally at the corners, implying that this was a condition of choice with Wright, and illustrating the Ross house of 1902 as an example. In fact in many of the great subsequent houses (Heurtley, Cheney, Coonley, Roberts, Robie, Taliesin I, Hollyhock, La Miniatura, and Fallingwater), the condition doesn't really occur in quite that way. It is a pervasive and effective feature of the Usonians, however; see Chap. 7. Brooks also emphasizes conditions where trim continues through a change of plane. He is entirely correct in noting that this is often done, but oddly enough it does not happen in what we have to assume were Wright's two early favorites, the Coonley house and Taliesin I. Finally, the first Taliesin and its contemporaries restate the box; see Chap. 4.

9. There is a practical reason for having the ground slope away from the house, as it minimizes the problem of foundation drainage, but this does not explain Wright's predilection. Many of his houses have floors at or below grade, e.g., the Cheney and Robie houses, but not the main living floors; and after 1902, in cases where such subordinate floors do not occur, the differential of elevation between Wright's main living floors and the overlooked terrain is usually far greater than is useful for drainage.

10. Manson, *Golden Age*, p. 127.

11. Appleton, *Experience of Landscape*, p. 95.

12. Frank Lloyd Wright, *The Natural House* (New York: Horizon Press, 1954), p. 15.

13. Other particularly clear instances: the Winslow, Williams, Thomas, and Dana houses.

14. Although from Edwin Cheney's point of view, a threat did find the way: the architect knew where the front door was.

15. This is less true of buildings in recent years because of increased interior light levels; as the amount of light on the interior approaches that of the exterior the glass becomes transparent from either side.

16. Appleton, *Experience of Landscape*, pp. 111–12.

17. Except the Glasner house, in which Wright took care to provide two equally removed surrogates in the veranda and the unbuilt tea house.

18. The working drawings for the Cheney house show that the dimension from grade to parapet was originally indicated as 10 feet.

19. Except by the houses across the street of course, but three conditions intervene: distance, foliage, and the upper zone of stained and leaded glass in the doors and windows, all of which mask such intrusions.

For his own work Wright was the measure of all things; see e.g., *An Autobiography* (New York: Duell, Sloane, and Pearce, 1943), p. 141. Accordingly, in this sectional diagram and that of the Robie house, I have drawn all human figures at 5 feet 8 inches. (Concerning Wright's own figure of 5 feet 8½ inches see Chap. 9, n. 4, though a half-inch at the scale of this drawing is meaningless.) For a more detailed discussion of Wright's sectional manipulation of sight lines, see Grant Hildebrand, "Privacy and Participation: Frank Lloyd Wright and the City Street," *The Frank Lloyd Wright Newsletter* 3:3 (third quarter 1980), pp. 4–9.

20. Appleton, *Experience of Landscape*, p. 175.

21. Colin St. John Wilson, "The Natural Imagination," *The Architectural Review* 185:1103 (Jan. 1989), p. 66.

22. Norris Kelly Smith, *Frank Lloyd Wright: A Study in Architectural Content* (Englewood Cliffs: Prentice-Hall, 1966), p. 77.

23. "Aesthetics, Affect, and Cognition: Environmental Preference from an Evolutionary Perspective," *Environment and Behavior* 19:1 (Jan. 1987), p. 3.

24. When the ceiling planes are designed to be the undersurface of a hipped or gabled roof, a structural issue arises. Since Wright was the first to design houses with this characteristic feature, he had to work out the structural issue for himself, and a brief discussion may help in understanding some of his problems and choices.

In the usual house with a gable or hip roof there is a flat ceiling suspended below horizontal cross-ties, occasionally, as in the case of the English cottage, the cross-tie structure may be left uncovered. Such cross-ties form chords that, in effect, make the gable or hip structure act as a truss that rests on the walls, exerting no lateral thrust. But when the ceiling ascends into the volume of the roof, as Wright had it do, the gable or hip is denied the horizontal cross-tie. The gable then acts approximately as an arch, and the hip as a dome—and as in an arch or a dome, a lateral thrust results, inducing a tendency to spread where the roof edge meets the wall. Wright had an uneven record in understanding this problem and devising measures to deal with it. In the Glasner house of 1905 and the Como Orchards cottages of 1909, he made no provision, and the consequent spreading has required expedient remedies: steel tie-rods at Glasner, 2×4s at Como Orchards. At the Heurtley and Cheney houses the problem does not arise because the chimney mass makes a formidable support at the apex of the roof. At the Coonley house the area of roof over the living room is large, while the chimney mass is far from the roof apex and therefore less efficient as support. Given the configuration of the scheme, and the obvious fact that the house has been stable and secure, it is reasonable to infer that each corner of the Coonley roof structure is very securely tied, and the horizontal "beams" at the open corners of the living room assist in maintaining a tension ring around the roof's perimeter. This tension ring, in combination with a degree of support from the fireplace mass and the intersecting corridor roofs to either side, would secure the diagonal ridge rafters against spreading, and they in turn would secure the remainder of the structure. Though all this would have had to be thought through pretty carefully, the whole thing would have been fairly simple to construct, and has obviously been durable. In this sense, and provided both the problem and the solution are properly understood, a hipped roof without cross-ties can be easier to manage than a gable, for which there are no equally tidy answers—with a gable, corner ties and tension rings are virtually useless. This in turn may help to explain, in part, Wright's loyalty to hipped roofs, and his avoidance of gables, once he had adopted the device of ceiling planes ascending deeply into the roof's volume. (If the roof is flat, of course, no such problem arises since no lateral thrust is generated.)

25. Walter Creese, *The Crowning of the American Landscape* (Princeton: Princeton University Press, 1985), p. 237.

26. Vincent Scully in Hitchcock et al., *The Rise*, p. 193 (see n. 1).

27. Appleton, *Experience of Landscape*, p. 196.

28. Beeby, "Landscape," p. 171 (see n. 3).

29. See for example Hitchcock, *Nature*, fig. 147 (see n. 1). This grid is of 4-foot-11-inch squares.

30. Bruce Brooks Pfeiffer, *Frank Lloyd Wright Monograph 1902–1906* (Tokyo: ADA Edita, 1986–) gives the date of the house as 1906, a date that appears occasionally elsewhere as well. One rendering of the house does boldly carry this date, but the drawing is from many years later and is known to have been dated by Wright at the time it was done. Robie bought the property in May of 1908, and the house could hardly have been done before; of all Wright's designs it is perhaps the most site-specific, coming right to the lot lines on two sides. Wright developed the design late in 1908, and working drawings were completed and signed in March 1909. The house was essentially completed late that year, although some minor work, especially furnishings, continued after Wright's departure for Europe in September (see Donald Hoffman, *Frank Lloyd Wright's Robie House* [New York: Dover, 1984], pp. 6, 19, 21, 25, 27). The date in this case has some importance in establishing the relationship to the Coonley house, and even more importantly to the Tomek house in Riverside, long agreed to date to 1907; see n. 32 below.

31. Vincent Scully's description of entry to the house is apt: "The Robie house rises, heavy as a mountain, buoyant as an airplane. Its interior spaces are caverns in the ground, platforms in the air. We find the entrance with some difficulty, enter into constriction and darkness, and are carried forward and upward to the light. . . ." (in Bolon et al., eds., *The Nature of Frank Lloyd Wright*, p. xiii, see n. 3).

32. As quoted in "Mr. Robie Knew What He Wanted," *Architectural Forum*, 109 (October 1958), p. 126. Hoffman, *Robie House*, pp. 8–9, excerpts the original tape of this interview, which in terms of the comment above gives a slightly different wording, although the meaning is unchanged. In either version this interview cannot be taken at face value. The meshing of the actual form of the house with Robie's supposed pre-design envisioning of it is so close that it leaves the impression that all Wright had to do was just draw the thing up. This must surely be Monday morning quarterbacking on Robie's part, especially since Wright had already (1907) done the similar Tomek house in Riverside. Hoffman (p. 9) makes the same point: "Robie so thoroughly absorbed Wright's views that when he looked back half a century later his mind wandered from memories of what he had asked for to memories of what Wright designed."

33. Other evidence also indicates that Wright considered such conditions in designing. A section through his project for Thaxter Shaw of 1906 reveals a line drawn to indicate and ensure just such a sight line from an upper bedroom across living room and terrace to a garden fountain. Serious attention to such sectional conditions was a constant with Wright; at a much later date, correspondence between Wright and Lloyd Lewis, quoted by Brendan Gill (*Many Masks* [New York: G. P. Putnams & Sons, 1987, p. 409), concerns sight lines established by balcony parapets. One phrase by Wright is especially germane: "I lifted the parapets to give you privacy from people entering from the road." With designs such as the Coonley house, however, where privacy was ensured by an extensive site, Wright did not hesitate to use open balcony rails.

34. Gaston Bachelard, *The Poetics of Space*, trans. Maria Jolas (Boston: Beacon Press, 1964), pp. 30–31.

35. William H. Jordy, *American Buildings and Their Architects*, vol. 4 (New York: Oxford University Press, 1972), p. 214.

36. Hoffman, *Robie House*, gives the fullest available portrayal of Robie as person and client. What emerges is not altogether appealing. Robie's own father apparently distrusted him, his wife divorced him less than three years after the house was finished because he was something of a libertine, and for the last fifty years of his life he avoided contact with his daughter, apparently deliberately (see Hoffman pp. 5, 89, and 12). But I do not think we have enough information to speculate whether Robie's character accounts for the contrast of mood between the Coonley and Robie houses, and furthermore I am inclined to agree with Norris Kelly Smith (*A Study*, p. 58) that Wright's houses really were created for himself.

37. Wright, *Autobiography*, 1943, p. 161. Wright continues "descriptions of ideals and the nature of my creative effort in house building already given apply particularly to this characteristic dwelling."

38. See, for example, Wright, *Autobiography*, 1943, pp. 141–48. The notion of the typical preoccupied Wright. He would later write of the Usonian as a type also, see ibid., pp. 489–96.

39. Smith, *A Study*, p. 58.

40. From "Modern Architecture" as quoted in Edgar Kaufmann and Ben Raeburn, *Frank Lloyd Wright: Buildings and Writings* (New York: World Publishing, 1960), p. 53.

41. Baker Brownell and Frank Lloyd Wright, *Architecture and Modern Life* (New York: Harper & Brothers, 1937), p. 23. For this point I am indebted to Neil Levine's essay "Frank Lloyd Wright's Own Houses . . ." in Bolon et al., eds., *The Nature of Frank Lloyd Wright*, p. 63 (see n. 3).

42. Some may infer that this position diminishes the significance of Wright's achievement. I think the opposite is true. A strong intention in architecture, whether conscious or not, is no guarantee of effective design, though generally, other things being equal, the ability consciously to articulate such an intention is often helpful to the designer. But the fundamental issue is that in either case one must have the talent to compose spaces and solids to achieve the intention. Wright was a spatial composer of enormous talent, and the probability that he used this talent to compose with astonishing effectiveness intentions only intuitively perceived is perhaps the greatest of all tributes.

4. Taliesin

1. The most readily available account of the Taliesin tale is in the Lady Charlotte Guest translation of *The Mabinogion*, available in facsimile edition by Academy Press, Chicago, 1978. The current Penguin edition does not include the Taliesin story. Taliesin as mythical hero also figures in Joseph Campbell's *The Hero of a Thousand Faces* (Princeton: Princeton University Press, 1949, 1968), much of which suggests Wright's own amazing life: "The hero, therefore, is the man or woman who has been able to battle past his personal and local historical limitations to the generally valid, normally human forms" (pp. 19–20).

2. The most completely researched account of these is in Robert Twombly, *Frank Lloyd Wright, His Life and His Architecture* (New York: John Wiley, 1979), pp. 119–43.

3. Norris Kelly Smith, *Frank Lloyd Wright: A Study in Architectural Content* (Englewood Cliffs: Prentice-Hall, 1966), pp. 104–106.

4. On this point see some of the most moving of Wright's prose, not his defense of his departure in *An Autobiography*, but pp. 392–93 of the 1977 edition (New York: Horizon). Under the headings "Memories" and "I Remember" occur, in reference to 1910–1913, such phrases as ". . . the familiar strains now gave me one of those moments of interior anguish when I would have given all I had lived to be able to begin reliving the old strains again . . . with such longing and sorrow as a man seldom knows, I hope. . . . whenever I would go to Chicago to keep track of my work I would take time somehow to go out to Oak Park: go there after dark, not wishing to be seen. Go to reassure myself that all was well there." But Wright's comments on this, as on other matters, must be approached with caution. If he retained a concern for the family, he failed to convince all of them that this was so. Brendan Gill (*Many Masks* [New York: G. P. Putnam's Sons, 1987], p. 499) quotes son David as saying to his father after the death of Catherine, David's mother and the woman to whom the above quotes refer: "You never gave a god-damn for her while she was alive." Wright's comments are to a degree self-serving, intending to show us a touching and endearing humility; but equally David's include an element of bitterness and were certainly spoken under stress.

5. Frank Lloyd Wright, *An Autobiography* (New York: Duell, Sloane, and Pearce, 1943), p. 162.

6. Ibid., pp. 167–68. The date is obviously in conflict with the 1910 date of the previous paragraph. Twombly, whose research is detailed, notes (*Life*, p. 122) that Wright sailed from Europe on Sept. 20, 1910, and arrived Oak Park Oct. 8. John Sergeant (*Frank Lloyd Wright's Usonian Houses* [New York: Watson-Guptill Publications, 1984] p. 175, n. 5) raises another question about this quote: "What evidence there is suggests that Mrs. Wright was at this time supported by her three children, Jane, Maginel, and Frank. It does not seem then that she was in a position to buy property." But she did, nevertheless: see Walter Creese, *The Crowning of the American Landscape* (Princeton: Princeton University Press, 1985), p. 250, n. 18, "[Anna Wright] bought the land . . . from Joseph Rieder on April 10, 1911, for $2,274.88 (Iowa County Registry of Deeds, Dodgeville, Wisconsin)." Wright's earliest extant drawing of Taliesin is of the same month and is titled "Cottage for Mrs. Anna Lloyd Wright."

7. Wright, *Autobiography*, 1943, p. 168. Italics are in the original.

8. One writer who has noticed is Reyner Banham, who discusses the hilltop site of the Ennis house in particular in "The Wilderness Years of Frank Lloyd Wright," *Royal Institute of British Architects Journal* 76:12 (Dec. 1969), p. 515. See also Gill, *Masks*, pp. 252, 279.

9. Wright, *Autobiography*, 1943, p. 137.

10. Wright, *Autobiography*, 1977, p. 254.

11. Nine photos of Taliesin, all exteriors, without text, were published in *Architectural Record* 33:1 (Jan. 1913), pp. 45–54. The other major source for exterior views is *The Work of Frank Lloyd Wright, the Wendingen Edition* (1925, reissued 1965 with text additions by Bramhall and Horizon, New York). This includes ten exteriors of the house before the fire of 1925, at which time the portions described here were little changed from the 1911 scheme. For interiors see Henry-Russell Hitchcock, *In the Nature of Materials* (New York: Da Capo Press, 1982), fig. 177, and Edgar Tafel, *Apprentice to Genius* (New York: McGraw-Hill, 1979), p. 111. Henry-Russell Hitchcock, *Frank Lloyd Wright* (Paris: Editions Cahiers d'Art, 1928), also includes four helpful exteriors. For plans and an unraveling of chronology, I am indebted to Sidney Robinson, *Life Imitates Architecture: Taliesin and Alden Dow's Studio* (Ann Arbor: Architectural Research Laboratory, University of Michigan, 1980).

12. Wright, *Autobiography*, 1943, p. 171.

13. Ibid., p. 171.

14. Ibid.

15. See H. Allen Brooks, *Writings on Wright* (Cambridge, Mass.: MIT Press, 1981), pp. 5–11.

16. Wright, *Autobiography*, 1943, pp. 170–71.

17. Thomas Beeby, "The Song of Taliesin," *Modulus, The University of Virginia School of Architecture Review* (1980–81), p. 7.

18. Wright, *Autobiography*, 1943, p. 173.

19. Among many instances, see *Autobiography*, 1943, p. 142.

20. Hitchcock, *Nature* (see n. 11), in the caption to fig. 179, says, "The late Prairie houses as a group are less interesting than those before 1910, nor are there many of them. The best, such as the Angster house, are more like Taliesin itself than like the earlier houses, with very open plans." The statement is ambiguous, but if Hitchcock means that Taliesin and the few other houses Wright did from 1911 to 1914 have "very open plans" this is simply not true, as a close look at the plans cited will reveal.

21. Wright, *Autobiography*, 1977, pp. 191, 194. Alexander Woollcott's comment on all this, following a visit to Taliesin in 1925, is a tribute of special pertinence here: "Of course that is the peculiar gift of Wright and his like in this world—to build freshly as though we had all just come out of Eden" (quoted in Brooks, *Writings*, p. 11).

22. Vincent Scully, *Frank Lloyd Wright* (New York: George Braziller, Inc., 1960), p. 22.

23. John Lloyd Wright, *My Father Who Is on Earth* (New York: G. P. Putnam's Sons, 1946, p. 86.

5. The California Houses

1. Wright first studied the idea of the concrete block house in 1906 in an unbuilt project for Harry E. Brown, to have been located in Genesco, Illinois. Among the California series the Storer, Freeman, and Ennis houses occasioned some shockingly acrimonious correspondence between Wright and his son Lloyd, who supervised them all during Wright's peregrinations. Lloyd deserves credit in architectural history for having played a vital, difficult, and thankless role in bringing to fruition these important houses.

2. See, e.g., Robert Twombly, *Frank Lloyd Wright, an Interpretive Biography* (New York: Harper & Row, 1973), p. 157: "[One] might easily imagine their interiors as silent mausoleums or eerie covens," and p. 159: "The concrete homes of the 1920s . . . were . . . meticulously executed essays in solitude and isolation."

3. See Brendan Gill, *Many Masks* (New York: G. P. Putnam's Sons, 1987), p. 268, referring to "the barbaric arrogance with which the Ennis house imposes itself between earth and sky . . . [threatening] to crush the hilltop on which it sprawls." Robert Twombly, *Frank Lloyd Wright, His Life and His Architecture* (New York: Wiley, 1979), p. 196, mentions its use as a setting for a 1958 horror movie. Henry-Russell Hitchcock, *In the Nature of Materials* (New York: Duell, Sloane, and Pearce, 1942, reprint 1982), writing with Wright at his side, is more restrained, but still calls it "rather undomestic" (caption to fig. 257).

4. Twombly, *Life*, p. 182.

5. Reyner Banham, "The Wilderness Years of Frank Lloyd Wright," *Royal Institute of British Architects Journal* 76:12 (Dec. 1969), p. 514.

6. In addition, in 1922, just as the Storer, Freeman, and Ennis houses were being started, Wright's extraordinarily doting mother entered a sanatorium, where in February of 1923 she died. Whether Wright was additionally distressed by this, or simply relieved, is hard to say; although he was in the United States at the time he seems not to have attended the funeral.

7. Frank Lloyd Wright, *An Autobiography* (New York: Horizon, 1977), p. 254.

8. Twombly (*Life*, p. 197) has said of the California houses that they "elevate detachment into seclusion and retreat into escape"; see also p. 192: "The few designs he did manage to execute from 1915 through the 1920s reflected the suspicion, frustration, and need for privacy in his personal life."

9. I am grateful to Kathryn Smith, "Frank Lloyd Wright, Hollyhock House, and Olive Hill, 1914–1924," *Journal of the Society of Architectural Historians* 38:1 (March 1979), p. 23, for describing this watercourse, and to Virginia Ernst Kazor, curator of the house, for pointing out that the water flows not as Ms. Smith describes it but as described here.

10. The best readily available reproduction of this drawing is in Bruce Brooks Pfeiffer, *Frank Lloyd Wright: Preliminary Studies 1917–1932* (Tokyo: ADA Edita, 1986), p. 1. The drawing is also reproduced in Arthur Drexler, *The Drawings of Frank Lloyd Wright* (New York: Horizon and Museum of Modern Art, 1962), fig. 63).

11. I am indebted to Norris Kelly Smith, *Frank Lloyd Wright: A Study in Architectural Content* (Englewood Cliffs: Prentice-Hall, 1966), p. 77, for the observation on Wright's rendering style quoted on p. 44.

12. A parallel instance occurred with the Paul Hanna house of 1936–37: perspectives showed plantings behind the house, open vista to the front: "Mr. Wright suggested that we establish a line of tall conifers along the rear of the property, but we rejected the idea." Paul R. and Jean S. Hanna, *Frank Lloyd Wright's Hanna House* (Cambridge, Mass.: MIT Press, 1982), p. 142.

13. Frank Lloyd Wright, *An Autobiography* (New York: Duell, Sloane, and Pearce, 1943), p. 231.

14. Ibid., p. 244.

15. John Sergeant, *Frank Lloyd Wright's Usonian Houses* (New York: Watson-Guptill Publications, 1984), p. 185, calls this a "diaphanous membrane"; in an otherwise perceptive discussion this phrase seems entirely wrong to me.

16. Hitchcock, *Nature*, p. 76.

17. Gill, *Masks*, p. 268.

18. Sergeant, *Usonian*, p. 185, notes the "glass-to-glass" corner of the Freeman house without noting this as its first usage, a point missed by others as well, but correctly noted by Gill, *Masks*, p. 282.

19. The Ennis house looks outward to two other architectural masterpieces, Hollyhock House to the south, and Richard Neutra's Lovell house to the north.

20. Gill, *Masks*, p. 199.

21. Rachel Levy, *The Gate of Horn* (London: Faber and Faber, 1948), p. 11.

22. The present ceilings throughout are flat with a dark exposed wood structure. Wright's original drawings show sloped ceilings not unlike those of Hollyhock House, which would have yielded a quite different mood. Virginia Ernst Kazor believes Mr. Ennis ordered the change against Wright's wishes. I am grateful to her for this and much other information on the California group.

23. Stephen Kaplan, "Aesthetics, Affect, and Cognition: Environmental Preference from an Evolutionary Perspective," *Environment and Behavior* 19:1 (Jan. 1987), pp. 3–32.

24. Twombly, *Life*, p. 192, says that between 1925 and 1932 Wright did only five executed buildings.

6. Fallingwater

1. See Jay Appleton, *The Experience of Landscape* (London: John Wiley & Sons, 1975), pp. 95 ff.

2. Ibid., pp. 98 and 118.

3. Ibid., p. 99.

4. Ibid., pp. 99–100.

5. Jay Appleton, "How I Made the World," unpublished MS, p. 352, quoted by permission of the author.

6. My edition is New York: Random House, 1930, in which this passage is on pp. 76–77.

7. Robert Twombly, *Frank Lloyd Wright, His Life and His Architecture* (New York: Wiley, 1979), p. 277.

8. According to Kaufmann, *Fallingwater* (New York: Abbeville Press, 1986), p. 51, "Wright himself after much deliberation believed [the parapets] helped carry the load, but not so effectively as he had hoped."

9. Fallingwater has occasionally been compared with Le Corbusier's Villa Savoye of 1929, the argument generally being that Wright did or did not derive something from it. Whatever his debt to Le Corbusier, on the question of refuge the two houses are worlds apart. Many differences contribute to this; the enclosed versus the free-standing fireplace, and the simple versus the complex outline of the architectural envelope are two that come easily to mind. Another is this eave condition. In each feature, the Villa Savoye emerges as the more dramatic prospect symbol and provision, but as far weaker in refuge than Fallingwater. The Villa Savoye conveys the magnificent excitement of an architecture open to light, the epitome of a dramatic seeing—but one is also seen. Given Wright's invariable provision of emphatic refuge conditions, and his well-known hostility to Le Corbusier's work, it is easy to speculate that he was actually offended by a habitation weak, and even deficient, in refuge symbols and provisions.

10. In very tall buildings subject to seismic and wind loads, for example, the structure is often made far stiffer than is necessary for prevention of absolute collapse in order that occupants are not made uncomfortable by lateral movement or whip. Thus structure in tall buildings is in part determined by prevention of psychological discomfort that might arise from excessive deflection.

11. Such a phrase, I realize, does not do justice to those from whose expertise Wright no doubt learned a great deal, especially, in early years, Paul Mueller at Adler and Sullivan and, of course, Dankmar Adler himself. Mueller was also with Wright during many of the Oak Park years and during design of the Imperial Hotel.

12. Frank Lloyd Wright, *An Autobiography* (New York: Horizon, 1977), p. 160.

13. Few of Wright's buildings have ever been at the threshold of actual collapse (although an exact number is impossible to determine because of revision during or after construction). An unusually large number, however, were genuinely and even necessarily innovative in structural concept (see, e.g., n. 24, Chap. 3) and the record is a strong testimony to his brilliance in understanding failure resistance. But many are badly flawed in deflection. A cursory sampling:

The roof projecting at third floor level west from the chimney of the Robie house droops many inches. When the Roberts house was rehabilitated in the mid-1950s, the eaves were sagging a foot and more. On deflection in the eaves of the Adams house of 1913 in Oak Park see Gill, *Many Masks* (New York: Putnam's Sons, 1987), p. 215; on p. 193 Gill also illustrates expedient props for the sagging eaves of the Gilmore house of 1908 in Madison. I have never seen the interior of the Glasner house, but an illustration in William J. R. Curtis, *Modern Architecture Since 1900* (Englewood Cliffs: Prentice-Hall, 1982), p. 83, shows steel tie-rods installed in the living room to prevent deflection of the roof due to an unresisted spreading force concentrated at the eaves. A similar problem demanded a similar expedient remedy—in this case rough 2×4s—at the one remaining cottage of the Como Orchards project of 1909; see Grant Hildebrand and Thomas Bosworth, "The Last Cottage of Wright's Como Orchards Complex," *Journal of the Society of Architectural Historians* 41:4 (Dec. 1982), pp. 326–27. Wright's predilection for omitting cross-ties in structures with a tendency to spread persisted throughout his life, and for good spatial reasons; sometimes he obtained secure structural provisions without tie members and sometimes not. Gill (*Masks*, 1987, p. 451) cites an instance in the construction of the house for Wright's son David near Phoenix in the 1950s: "While the wooden roof was in the course of being framed, Wright dropped in for a visit, glanced up at the short cross-pieces that conventionally stiffen rafters, and, pointing with his cane, said, 'Those braces must go.' David Wright looked at his father and said coolly, 'I don't think so.' And the braces remained." Apprentice Edgar Tafel (*Apprentice to Genius* [New York: McGraw-Hill, 1979], pp. 190–91) added steel to the roof structure of the Schwartz house out of obvious necessity. Wright was furious, but Tafel says that failure to do likewise for a house in "the South" (the Rosenbaum house?) actually did result in collapse. (John Sergeant, *Frank Lloyd Wright's Usonian Houses* [New York: Watson-Guptill Publications, 1984], p. 112, cites "an embarrassing sag" for that house but not collapse.) The carport of the Goetsch-Winkler house sags about three inches; this is clearly shown in Sergeant, *Usonian*, p. 54. On p. 118, he says of the Rosenbaum house: ". . . the long, 48-ft north wall could be made to bow by hand pressure." The Lewis house shows severe deflections in the roofs east and west of the living room; see Bruce Brooks Pfeiffer, *Frank Lloyd Wright Monograph 1937–1941* (Tokyo: ADA Edita, 1986), p. 172; p. 181 also shows obvious deflections in the Sondern house, another Usonian. In 1955 I visited the then eight-year-old Unitarian Church in Madison; repairs were underway to correct what, in distant memory, I recall as an appalling deflection of 18 inches or so in the balcony. Taliesin itself has innumerable disfiguring deflections; for an illustration of some of them, see Gill, *Masks*, p. 333. Bruce Brooks Pfeiffer, *Frank Lloyd Wright Monograph 1914–1923* (Tokyo: ADA Edita, 1986), p. 383, illustrates the retaining wall of the Ennis house which can be seen to be buckling severely. Apparently this condition is of long standing: in 1940 the then-owner of this house, John Nesbitt, corresponded with Wright about repairs to what was then a 100-foot-long bulge in the southern retaining wall (Gill, *Masks*, p. 279). There is considerable deflection in the trellis of Fallingwater, although this is not the crucial problem area. Many more examples in other of Wright's structures could be cited.

14. Kaufmann, *Fallingwater*, p. 49. Kaufmann points out that there were engineers in Wright's service. This is true, but there are two points of qualification: like all other staff at Taliesin they were dominated by Wright's will; and Wright's structures were genuinely innovative.

15. Donald Hoffman, *Frank Lloyd Wright's Fallingwater* (New York: Dover Publications, 1978), p. 34.

16. Hoffman, *Wright's Fallingwater*, pp. 13–14, 18. See also Kaufmann, *Fallingwater*, p. 31.

17. Wright claimed that his choice for the location of the fireplace (and therefore the house itself) was based on the fact that the boulder that is its hearth had been one of Kaufmann's favorite spots from which to enjoy the falls. That explanation can hardly be taken at face value. In building the house outward from that spot, Wright sacrificed the very view that Kaufmann valued. Furthermore, it can hardly be denied that had Wright wanted the house somewhere else, he could equally have used Kaufmann's predilection as support for an alternate location that would leave the chosen spot untouched. Therefore it seems reasonable to look on Wright's rationale as clever justification for a choice made for other reasons.

18. If one also assumes, as Wright clearly did, that doors and windows would often stand open, this argument becomes even stronger.

19. Wright, *Autobiography* (1977), p. 179.

20. John Dewey, *Art as Experience* (New York: Pentagon Books, 1934), p. 29.

7. Taliesin West

1. Other dates are given elsewhere, but Robert Twombly, *Frank Lloyd Wright, His Life and His Architecture* (New York: Wiley, 1979), has traced primary source accounts for the 1929 date; see p. 238, n. 15. See also Neil Levine, "Frank Lloyd Wright's Own Houses and His Changing Concept of Representation," in Carol R. Bolon, Robert S. Nelson, and Linda Seidel, eds., *The Nature of Frank Lloyd Wright* (Chicago: University of Chicago Press, 1988), p. 67, n. 44.

2. Edgar Tafel, *Apprentice to Genius* (New York: McGraw-Hill, 1979), p. 131. Henry-Russell Hitchcock, *In the Nature of Materials* (New York: Duell, Sloane, and Pearce, 1942, reprinted 1982), illustrates this as figs. 276–80, but refers to it as "Ocotillo." No one in fact seems agreed on the spelling: in Frank Lloyd Wright, *An Autobiography* (New York: Horizon, 1977), it occurs as both "Ocatillo" (p. 335) and "Ocatilla" (p. 479). I have simply used the first of Wright's spellings.

3. Frank Lloyd Wright, *An Autobiography* (New York: Duell, Sloane, and Pearce, 1943), p. 311.

4. Ibid.

5. Wright, *Autobiography*, 1977, p. 335.

6. Reyner Banham, "The Wilderness Years of Frank Lloyd Wright," *Royal Institute of British Architects Journal* 76:12 (Dec. 1969), p. 516.

7. Wright, *Autobiography*, 1977, pp. 334–37.

8. Ibid., p. 335, in which Wright says the structure was dismantled the following winter. Levine, in Bolon et al., *Nature of Frank Lloyd Wright*, p. 67, n. 44, indicates that the archaeologist Margerie Green, in discussion with a former apprentice, has discovered that the camp may have stood in place for many years. A probable scenario is not hard to imagine, the camp deteriorating and being slowly dismantled over the years, Wright returning in 1937 to find it almost all gone, and taking the most dramatic interpretation of its demise.

9. Bruce Brooks Pfeiffer, *Frank Lloyd Wright Monograph 1937–1941* (Tokyo: ADA Edita, 1986), quotes this comment by Wright on p. 45.

10. Tafel, *Apprentice*, pp. 199–200.

11. Cited by Jay Appleton, *The Experience of Landscape* (London: John Wiley & Sons, 1975), p. 1, from *Modern Painters*; see the edition of Cook and Wedderburn, 1903–12, v. 5, p. 234.

12. Among a wealth of such evidence, see the summarizing position of E. H. Zube, D. G. Pitt, and T. W. Anderson, *Landscape Assessment: Values, Perceptions and Resources* (Stroudsburg, Pa.: Dowden, Hutchinson and Ross, 1975), pp. 151–67.

13. The Coonley house has an extensive pool (see fig. 3.17); at Taliesin, Wright built a dam at considerable expense to widen the river in view to the east (figs. 4.6, 4.11); Hollyhock has both a subterranean cave pool around the fireplace (fig. 5.6) and the far larger exterior pools on axis in the garden and to the west (figs. 5.3, 5.7); La Miniatura has its pool in the ravine (fig. 5.10); the Storer house includes a pool as part of the entry terraces (see fig. 5.12); the second Jacobs house has a pool that is both interior and exterior (see fig. 8.34A); and of course there is the obvious example of Fallingwater.

14. Appleton, *Experience,* pp. 153–54.

15. Wright, *Autobiography,* 1977, p. 480.

16. In the late 1960s or early 1970s the superstructure was replaced by one of glass fiber panels and red-painted steel, apparently for maintenance reasons.

17. Wright, *Autobiography,* 1977, p. 166.

18. Ibid., p. 335.

19. Ibid., p. 480.

8. The Usonians

1. Wright claimed to have taken the name from the word "Usonia" in Samuel Butler's *Erewhon,* but no one has been able to find the word there.

2. The figure included the architect's fee of $450. The figure does not represent such a dramatic bargain when transferred to 1936 buying power; nevertheless for a custom house it was low at the time. Herbert Jacobs wrote a book about this and the second Jacobs house, the "solar hemicycle" of 1943–48; see Herbert Jacobs with Katherine Jacobs, *Building with Frank Lloyd Wright* (San Francisco: Chronicle Books, 1978).

3. This is one of the better-known features of the Usonians, but many, e.g., the Lewis, Pew, and Affleck houses, do not use it because of site conditions.

4. The house area is about 1,350 square feet, therefore the saving is on the order of 3 percent, a seemingly insignificant figure. But leveraging is at work here. The saving is mostly in the bedroom wing, which is about half the house, or ca. 700 square feet. Much of this area, however, is committed to fixed-size requirements: beds, bathtubs, toilets, and closets, which in turn take up, at a rough guess, half of that area. The corridor likewise has a fixed dimension. So the gain of 40 square feet is, in the end, apportioned to otherwise uncommitted room space, of which it represents upwards of 15 percent, a really sizable gain. Whether it offsets the cost of building the extra 40 square feet by conventional methods, however, is the crucial issue, to which there is no simple answer.

5. On this point see also the extended discussion by H. Allen Brooks, "Wright and the Destruction of the Box," *Journal of the Society of Architectural Historians* 38:1 (March 1979), pp. 7–14, reprinted in Brooks, *Writings on Wright* (Cambridge, Mass.: MIT Press, 1981). Brooks notes an early instance of this condition at the Charles S. Ross house, Delavan Lake, Wisconsin, of 1902. After a long hiatus the condition reappears as a very common feature of the Usonians.

6. Jay Appleton, *The Experience of Landscape* (London: John Wiley, 1975), p. 105.

7. The scheme for *Life* included a wood wall flanking the carport, prolonging the long axis of the house, and a swimming pool off the living room. Both were omitted from the Schwartz house, while the kitchen was enlarged, and the balcony, with its stepped edge, was introduced to overlook the living room. Otherwise the two schemes are virtually identical.

8. Loren Pope, quoted in Robert Twombly, *Frank Lloyd Wright: His Life and His Architecture* (New York: Wiley, 1979), p. 256.

9. Frank Lloyd Wright, *An Autobiography* (New York: Horizon, 1977), p. 522.

10. This is also a feature of the Rosenbaum and Schwartz houses and a number of others not discussed here, as, for example, the Loren Pope (Pope-Leighey) house of 1939 at Falls Church (now at Mt. Vernon), Virginia, or that for Melvyn Maxwell Smith of 1949, in Bloomfield Hills, Michigan.

11. His comments on the Coonley house have been noted in Chap. 3; in *Autobiography*, 1977, pp. 522–24, he devotes several pages to the Lewis house, pages which include a rare apology for shortcomings, especially with regard to the fireplace, which did not draw.

12. For correspondence on this point from both parties see Brendan Gill, *Many Masks* (New York: G. P. Putnam's Sons, 1987), pp. 408–409. Edgar Tafel, *Apprentice to Genius* (New York: McGraw-Hill, 1979), p. 190, says that Wright finally acquiesced to Lewis's wishes. But if so, that acquiescence somehow came to nothing. The parapets exist at the 3-foot height shown on working drawings (a more usual figure would be 2 feet 6 inches, roughly table-top height), and this cannot be a revision, as a higher location would have created an impossible juncture with the body of the house at either end. With Lloyd Lewis as with Edgar Kaufmann, Wright seems to have found his match for *bons mots*. The correspondence in each case is fascinating not only for its mutual feistiness but also for its mutually transparent affection, which says something about both clients, and something about Wright as well.

13. At 1,200 square feet. The smallest of them all, according to Sergeant's figures, is the atypical George Sturgis house of 1939 in Brentwood Heights near Los Angeles, at a mere 850 square feet. Sergeant suggests a parallel between Fallingwater and the Sturgis house but there are more analogies to the Pew house.

14. See chap. 6, n. 13, which lists such problems for the Schwartz, Rosenbaum, Goetsch-Winkler, Lewis, and Sondern houses; one could easily add to the list.

15. Other houses using Usonian features with a hexagonal plan grid include those for Leigh Stevens in Yamasee, South Carolina, and Sidney Bazett in Hillsborough, California, both of 1940, and the Carl Wall house of 1941 in Plymouth, Michigan. All are far smaller than the Hanna house. The Bazett house approaches, though it does not nearly equal, the spatial richness of the Hanna house. The Wall house, which Wright named "Snowflake," has an exquisite plan seen as pattern in two dimensions, and photographs beautifully from a distance, but the need for more spaciousness is felt in the interior.

16. Wright seems to have taken the Jacobses' pleas for economy seriously, but not those of the Hannas. Yet the Hannas were equally eloquent about their monetary constraints, as is painfully documented in Paul R. and Jean S. Hanna, *Frank Lloyd Wright's Hanna House* (Cambridge; MIT Press, 1982). The only conclusion I can draw is that with the Jacobs house Wright wanted to see what he could do with $5,500; with the Hanna house he wanted to see what he could do with a hexagonal module.

17. About 3,000 square feet originally in the house proper, as compared to 1,350 for Jacobs and Goetsch-Winkler and a mere 1,200 for the Pew house.

18. "Aesthetics, Affect, and Cognition: Environmental Preference from an Evolutionary Perspective," *Environment and Behavior* 19:1 (Jan. 1987), p. 8. See also Roger S. Ulrich, "Aesthetic and Affective Response to Natural Environment," in I. Altman and J. F. Wohlwill, *Behavior and the Natural Environment* (New York: Plenum, 1983), pp. 103–104, in which he maintains that the appeal of a deflected vista or "mystery condition" governs only when there is understood to be a high probability of delight rather than danger. The caveat is unimportant to the case of the Hanna house because there is obviously a very high probability that the space to which the vista leads is danger-free; but as a larger design consideration the point needs to be kept in mind.

19. John Sergeant, *Frank Lloyd Wright's Usonian Houses* (New York: Watson-Guptill Publications, 1984), pp. 86–87, includes the Palmer house among the Usonians but is not explicit about categorizing it as one.

9. Some Conclusions

1. The phrase is quoted in John Sergeant, *Frank Lloyd Wright's Usonian Houses* (New York: Watson-Guptill Publications, 1984), p. 86, from a client's comment in the *New York Times* of Feb. 6, 1972. Wright was by this time a walking illustration of Proust's observation: ". . . that is the age at which a great artist prefers to the company of original minds that of pupils who have nothing in common with him save the letter of his doctrine, who listen to him and offer incense"—but that had been the case for at least twenty years, and there is no indication that of itself it caused any waning of Wright's abilities.

2. Henry-Russell Hitchcock, Albert Fein, Winston Weisman, Vincent Scully, *The Rise of an American Architecture* (New York: Praeger, 1970), p. 193.

3. Philip Thiel, Ean Duane Harrison, and Richard S. Alden, "Perception of Spatial Enclosure . . .," *Environment and Behavior* 18:2 (Mar. 1986), pp. 227–45.

4. He claimed to be 5 feet 8½ inches; Gill (*Masks*, p. 47) thinks that like many of Wright's claims this was exaggerated, and that he was probably an inch or two shorter. The figure of 5 feet 8 inches seems to me to be as good as any other, although as the text indicates, a difference of even an inch would be of some importance in relation to a low ceiling dimension.

5. And blatantly said as much: see Frank Lloyd Wright, *An Autobiography* (New York: Horizon, 1977), p. 165.

6. It would be interesting to know the various heights of Wright's clients—difficult information to obtain—and which of them were happiest in the spaces for which he used his own dimension as the measure—impossible information to obtain. Still, there are a few things that can be said. Mamah Borthwick Cheney lived with Wright as his wife, and commonly in America the wife is no taller than the husband. If this were true in her case, then presumably the scale of ceiling dimension of her Oak Park house, and the early Taliesin as well, were pleasurable and effective for her. Early photographs of the Coonleys suggest Mrs. Coonley was of modest height. Both Aline Barnsdall of Hollyhock and Mrs. Millard of La Miniatura were petite, though the Barnsdall case tells us less than nothing since she was admittedly unhappy with the house. The Hannas, too, are small, and from all one can gather were enormously happy with the spaces they occupied, though in design stages they objected to many dimensions that seemed undersized to them. The Palmers also are of about Wright's stature, and are yet another instance of extraordinarily content owners.

7. The Lewis house is difficult to discuss in simple ratios because the floor plane changes as well as the ceiling. The same is true of the Ennis house which, in addition, presents a very wide range of ceiling heights from 6 feet 8 inches to 21 feet.

8. There is an interesting side issue here, however. Occasionally some rooms in Mackintosh's houses, e.g., the living room of Hill House, Helensburgh, have the upper wall and ceiling painted black, which at least to my eye creates an illusion of a more distant ceiling plane, and thus an effect similar to the elevated ceilings of Wright's houses.

9. Fundamental references for the work of the Prairie School are all by H. Allen Brooks. They are: *The Prairie School* (Toronto: University of Toronto Press, 1972); *Prairie School Architecture* (Toronto: University of Toronto Press, 1975); and *Frank Lloyd Wright and the Prairie School* (New York: Braziller, 1984). But see also Mark L. Peisch, *The Chicago School of Architecture* (London: Phaidon, 1964).

10. Willatsen (who also spelled his name Willatzen) left Oak Park to open a practice in Seattle with Byrne; the two worked together from 1908 to early 1914. During this period they did some work of high quality, the best known examples of which are the C. H. Clarke house of 1909 and the A. S. Kerry house of 1910–11, both in the Highlands, although the J. C. Black house in Seattle proper is perhaps finer than either. After Byrne's departure for independent practice in 1914, the quality of Willatsen's work slowly declined; by the mid-1930s he was producing work of absolutely no interest whatever, while Byrne went on to a career of considerable distinction. Therefore I am inclined to think that Byrne was the leader in the partnership.

11. Purcell had worked for a short time, Elmslie for a very long and poignantly loyal time, with Louis Sullivan.

12. The choice of Griffin is not entirely arbitrary. Of all employees at the Oak Park Studio, Griffin may well have carried the largest range of responsibility apart from Wright himself, and Griffin's subsequent career was one of considerable distinction. Peisch begins *Chicago School* by referring to "the pivotal character in our study . . . Walter Burley Griffin," and later (p. 62) says, "In developing a livable, economical, and aesthetically sound, small house, Griffin was more successful than most of his colleagues in the Chicago School, with, of course, the one great exception."

13. *The Prairie School*, p. 173.

14. Brooks, *The Prairie School*, p. 279, says that van Bergen "came close, perhaps closer than anyone, to actually imitating Wright's designs." A glance at van Bergen's work will confirm that this is true, but van Bergen also misses the point of Wright's pattern and therefore does not deploy its necessary features. In none of his homes, for example, are interior prospect conditions developed. Van Bergen, however, was one of the few Prairie School architects other than Wright to use porches and terraces consistently.

15. Neutra and his work are the subjects of many books including the recent and definitive work by Thomas S. Hines, *Richard Neutra and the Search for Modern Architecture* (New York/Oxford: Oxford University Press, 1982).

16. In somewhat later years, others who had trained under Wright would also find careers of note, though none achieved a place in the literature equal to that held by Schindler and Neutra. This group includes Bruce Goff and Alden Dow, among others. I am also unable to see within this group a consistent deployment of the pattern, but have not extended the text to a case-by-case examination, to avoid the tedium of what seems to me unnecessary repetition of argument.

One instance, however, strikes a personal note. The house Alden Dow did for A. W. Hodgkiss in 1939, in Petoskey, Michigan, was somewhat familiar to me as a child and adolescent, as the Hodgkisses were friends of my family. On reexamination, that house seems to me to more nearly replicate Wright's pattern than any other of Dow's work, and more nearly so than most work by others of Taliesin training. It was a house of some fame and distinction within that small and modest town, and I was thrilled by it on the few visits I paid there early in life. During the writing of this book I have wondered more than once whether my decades-long interest in Wright, and my current interest in an Appleton-based interpretation of Wright, are related to clear and vivid memories of that house as I encountered it at an impressionable age. This raises the larger point about the role of individual experience and memory in modifying our intuitive predilections, a point tackled straightforwardly by Appleton in "How I Made the World" (unpublished autobiography) and inferentially by Thomas H. Beeby in his essay "Wright and Landscape: A Mythical Interpretation" in Carol R. Bolon, Robert S. Nelson, and Linda Seidel, eds., *The Nature of Frank Lloyd Wright* (Chicago: University of Chicago Press, 1988).

17. Christian Norberg-Schulz, in the introduction of Mirko Zardini, *The Architecture of Mario Botta* (New York: Rizzoli, 1985), p. 12, cites the 1979 house in Pregassona as introducing Botta's "theme." It comes close, but it does not provide an elevated terrace off the major spaces. This, the last feature of Botta's pattern, appears at the Stabio house and is characteristic of his houses thereafter.

18. This in fact seems to me to be the spatial flaw in Botta's houses, for these large flat ceilings seem oppressive. But they are certainly forcefully countered by the high volumes which, typically skylit, contrast and release in the boldest way imaginable.

19. Stuart Wrede, *Mario Botta* (New York: Museum of Modern Art, 1986), p. 68.

20. Zardini, *Botta*, pp. 15–16.

21. The Taliesins offer some provision for small communities; still, their uses seem close enough to include them within the type.

It would also be worthwhile to weigh the question of whether the pattern and its attributes have anything to offer multiple-dwelling buildings, and especially high-rise buildings, an idea that I earlier tried to address. It proved unwieldy in this context, and I concluded that it needed a separate and more extensive treatment. But I might here at least mention Wright's own major work of that type, the H. C. Price Tower of 1953–55, in Bartlesville, Oklahoma.

The tower originally included eight dwelling units (now, I understand, remodeled to office space). Each of these units had a fireplace at the inner edge of the living room, under a low ceiling, with a built-in seating unit on the flank. Forward of the fire, the ceiling ascended to a double-story space like that of the Hardy house or La Miniatura. Opposite the fire was a vast expanse of glass. On the other hand, there were neither heavy overhanging eaves nor a conspicuous chimney—one could hardly expect them on such a building—but more was missing than that. The entry to each unit was straightforward. The ceiling did not return to the over-fireplace height at the windows. Nor was there a terrace from the major space. And the tightness of the plan denied it any real interior prospect, and certainly any component of mystery.

I do not think this means the pattern is incapable of multi-story application (in fact it occurs in almost its entirety in my own condominium in downtown Seattle, though not by conscious intention, and not in other units in the same building), but clearly the issue is a large one and deserves to be carried to a considerable level of detail in its own right.

22. There are, however, several others of almost this rank. Among these one might wish to include the Herbert Johnson house, "Wingspread," of 1937, and perhaps the Ralph Jester project of about the same year. Typically, within this second rank of Wright's work the pattern is also found, as it is in these two examples (although Wingspread has one atypical characteristic: the fireplaces—four of them grouped into one chimney mass at the center of the "great hall"—occur under a very high ceiling indeed).

Bibliography

This bibliography is intended to help, on the one hand, those who are familiar with Wright's career and would like to pursue further issues of psychobiology, and on the other, those familiar with literature in psychobiology who would like to know more of Wright's career, as well as those unfamiliar with either. The literature is formidable; this bibliography is by no means exhaustive. The annotations reflect my own opinions.

Sources on Aesthetics and Psychobiology

Those interested in this subject can probe an expanse of material ranging from the writings of Charles Darwin to those of Konrad Lorenz. The following is a concise selection of works whose direct architectural implications have been of particular importance to me.

Altman, I., and J. F. Wohlwill. *Behavior and the Natural Environment.* New York: Plenum, 1983.

One of a number of books by this publishing house on this general subject. Of particular interest is Roger S. Ulrich's essay "Aesthetic and Affective Response to Natural Environment."

Appleton, Jay. *The Experience of Landscape.* London: John Wiley & Sons, 1975.

This work is the product not only of Appleton's interest in geography but in a number of other fields; he states straightforwardly in the preface that he impinges on landscape architecture, landscape painting, landscape aesthetics, and landscape literature—to which I would add (although he does not), that his work also encompasses psychobiology and philosophy of aesthetics, at the least.

———. "How I Made the World." Unpublished manuscript.

A major address to the issue of varying individual predilections within a more universal preferential framework. Appleton examines the role of individual experience and memory in shaping the aesthetic responses of the person he knows best, himself.

Archea, J. "Visual Access and Exposure: An Architectural Basis for Interpersonal Behavior." Doctoral dissertation, Pennsylvania State University, 1984.

Archea uses the terms *visual access* (to see) and *visual exposure* (to be seen) rather than Appleton's refuge and prospect. He also omits aesthetics and pleasure from his terminology. Nevertheless his findings, tested empirically at the Philadelphia Geriatric Center, closely corroborate Appleton's position.

Bachelard, Gaston. *The Poetics of Space.* Trans. Maria Jolas. Boston: Beacon Press, 1964.

A penetrating and itself poetic analysis of the spatial images of dream, memory, association, and longing.

Berlyne, Daniel E. *Aesthetics and Psychobiology.* New York: Appleton-Century-Crofts, 1971.

A basic work that has served as a point of beginning for many subsequent studies.

Dewey, John. *Art as Experience.* New York: Pentagon Books, 1934.

A classic early approach to a modern philosophy of aesthetics, for which Dewey suggests the idea of a biological foundation.

Fishe, D. W., and S. R. Madde. *Functions of Varied Experience.* Homewood, Ill.: Dorsey, 1961.

See especially John R. Platt, "Beauty: Pattern and Change," a discussion of the relation between biology and aesthetics, with a wealth of detail impressive for this comparatively early date. Among other issues, Platt touches on the role of scanning eye movement in the perception of parallel lines, and our urge to complete in the mind geometrically incomplete shapes, this latter condition surely being one of the fascinations of ruins.

Gombrich, E. H. *The Sense of Order: A Study in the Psychology of Decorative Art.* Oxford: Phaidon Press, 1979; 2nd ed., 1984.

The introduction, "Order and Purpose in Nature," is of interest for its emphasis on the biological basis of ornament. The remainder of the work, however, returns to this theme infrequently, nor does the discussion include the concept of complexity.

Kaplan, Stephen. "Aesthetics, Affect, and Cognition: Environmental Preference from an Evolutionary Perspective." *Environment and Behavior* 19.1 (Jan. 1987) pp.3–32.

Empirical corroboration of much of Appleton's hypothesis, with some fine-tuning and modification; the characteristic of mystery is introduced and demonstrated.

Mikellides, Byron, ed. *Architecture for People.* London: Studio Vista, 1980.

A compilation of provocative recent work from a number of authors; of particular relevance are Nicholas Humphrey's essay, "Natural Aesthetics," in which he explores the biological rationale behind our enjoyment of complexity and order, and Peter F. Smith's essay, "Urban Aesthetics," which builds directly on that of Humphrey.

Norberg-Schulz, Christian. *The Concept of Dwelling*. New York: Rizzoli, 1985.

———. *Genius Loci*. New York: Rizzoli, 1980.

Norberg-Schulz's work aims for a philosophy of aesthetics, but at the same time is exclusively about architecture and urban form.

Thiel, Philip, Ean Duane Harrison, and Richard S. Alden. "Perception of Spatial Enclosure as a Function of the Position of the Architectural Surfaces." *Environment and Behavior* 18:2 (March 1986), pp. 227–45.

The investigators empirically examine the effect of change of position of the various architectural planes—walls, floor, ceiling—on the occupant's sense of enclosure, concluding that change of position of the ceiling plane is the most important variable, a conclusion valuable to an understanding of the effects of Wright's spaces. The authors' methodology could lead to further information about the effects of other architectural conditions.

Wilson, Colin St. John. "The Natural Imagination." *The Architectural Review* 185:1103, (Jan. 1989).

Wilson, building on the work of Adrian Stokes, discusses affective responses to architecture as a function of mutually complementary conditions that he terms *envelopment* and *exposure,* close cousins to Appleton's *refuge* and *prospect.* The article is of special interest for its direct discussion of these phenomena in a wide range of architectural examples including a number by Le Corbusier, although no buildings by Wright are cited.

Woodcock, D. M. "A Functionalist Approach to Environmental Preference." Doctoral dissertation, University of Michigan, 1982.

In part an empirical testing of Appleton's hypothesis, to which Woodstock adds the concepts of primary and secondary prospects and refuges.

Sources on Frank Lloyd Wright's Architecture and Life

Banham, Reyner. "The Wilderness Years of Frank Lloyd Wright." *Royal Institute of British Architects Journal* 76:12 (Dec. 1969).

A penetrating study of an often-neglected period of Wright's life, the 1920s and early 1930s. Includes discussion of the California houses and the Ocatillo camp.

Bolon, Carol R., Robert S. Nelson, and Linda Seidel, eds. *The Nature of Frank Lloyd Wright*. Chicago: University of Chicago Press, 1988.

Nine essays from a variety of viewpoints. Vincent Scully's introduction begins with an appreciation of the Robie house. Scully also provides a concise summary of the lacunae in Wrightian scholarship. Thomas Beeby's essay "Wright and Landscape: A Mythical Interpretation," is reprinted with minor changes from *Orion* 6:2 (Spring 1987; publication of the Myrin Institute). Beeby explores a relationship between Wright's houses and the landscape of his native central Wisconsin, invoking the role of personal memory in Wright's formal predilections. It is evocative and convincing, presented with an eloquence commensurate with the richness of Beeby's theme.

Brooks, H. Allen. *Writings on Wright*. Cambridge, Mass.: MIT Press, 1981.

Essays on Wright by (among others) Alexander Woollcott, Eric Mendelsohn, early Wright employee Charles Wright, Usonian owner Marjorie Leighey, and Brooks himself, who usefully reprints his "Wright and the Destruction of the Box." I feel that some aspects of Brooks's essay need qualification (see Chap. 3, n. 8), but it is an extraordinarily valuable vanguard analysis of Wright's management of space.

Clausen, Meredith. "Frank Lloyd Wright, Vertical Space, and the Chicago School's Quest for Light." *Journal of the Society of Architectural Historians* 44:1 (March 1985), pp. 66–67.

Clausen shows a convincing relationship between late nineteenth and early twentieth century skylit lobbies in Chicago's public buildings, and Wright's skylit spaces of the Larkin Building, Unity Temple, and the much later Johnson's Wax Corporate Headquarters, the link being of course Wright's remodeling of the Rookery lobby. The spatial management of the houses, however, which she does not address, seems to me to demand a different approach.

Creese, Walter. *The Crowning of the American Landscape*. Princeton: Princeton University Press, 1985.

An analysis of several interventions in the American landscape, among which are Wright's two Taliesins, and Olmsted's Riverside, the setting for the Coonley house, which is discussed at length.

Futagawa, Yukio, editor and photographer, text by Bruce Brooks Pfeiffer. *Frank Lloyd Wright*. 12 vols., Tokyo: ADA Edita, 1986–.

This monograph series constitutes the most complete documentation of Wright's buildings to date, an unequaled wealth of photographs and drawings done justice by the large format. Some plans, however, are unhelpful and information is sometimes inaccurate, as in the dating of the Robie house to 1906.

Gill, Brendan. *Many Masks*. New York: G. P. Putnam's Sons, 1987.

The most recent major biography of Wright. The focus is Wright's personal life, not his architecture, and is unmatched for its wealth of personal detail and correspondence. As an account that seeks to understand rather than to worship, it is now indispensable.

Hanna, Paul R. and Jean S. *Frank Lloyd Wright's Hanna House*. Cambridge, Mass.: MIT Press, 1982.

A client's detailed documentation of the conception, design development, cost inflation, and, at last, the construction, occupancy, and remodeling of one of Wright's most important houses.

Hines, Thomas S. "Frank Lloyd Wright: The Madison Years." *Journal of the Society of Architectural Historians* 26:4 (Dec. 1967).

A landmark article establishing Wright's true birthdate as 1867, and clarifying the facts of his parents' separation and his tenure at the University of Wisconsin.

Hitchcock, Henry-Russell. *In the Nature of Materials*. New York: Da Capo Press, 1982.

A facsimile of the same book published by Duell, Sloane, and Pearce in 1942, with a new foreword. Written with Wright very much by Hitchcock's side, it was done more or less as an accompanying volume to Wright's much-revised second edition of *An Autobiography* of 1943 by the same publisher in the same format. The text is occasionally outdated and is, infrequently, inaccurate. Treatment of the then-new Fallingwater and the early Usonians is frustratingly sketchy. Some plans, e.g., La Miniatura and especially the Storer house, are incorrect. But the book is nonetheless a classic and indispensable work.

Hitchcock, Henry-Russell, Albert Fein, Winston Weisman, and Vincent Scully. *The Rise of an American Architecture*. New York: Praeger and the Metropolitan Museum of Art, 1970.

In the present context this book is most useful for the portion by Vincent Scully, "American Houses: Thomas Jefferson to Frank Lloyd Wright," and especially pp. 188–206. Scully draws from his work on the Shingle Style (see below), but offers many fresh and perceptive observations.

Hoffman, Donald. *Frank Lloyd Wright's Robie House*. New York: Dover, 1984.

The most complete account of this building, with photographs, drawings, and correspondence which clearly dates the inception to 1908, completion to 1909. Many details of Robie's life are included, as is a verbatim version of the well-known 1958 interview undertaken by *Architectural Forum*.

Jacobs, Herbert, with Katherine Jacobs. *Building with Frank Lloyd Wright*. San Francisco: Chronicle Books, 1978.

The Jacobses secured three designs by Wright and built two of them, the first Usonian and the "solar hemicycle"; this is a detailed account of the whole series. Although several of Wright's clients built more than one house by his hand, this is the only book by such a client.

Kaufmann, Edgar, Jr. *Fallingwater*. New York: Abbeville Press, 1986.

An evocative text, and photographs of enviable magnificence. Written by the art historian who was briefly an apprentice at Taliesin, and who as a young man encouraged his father to have the house done by Wright. Introduction on the country house as a type by Mark Girouard.

———. "Precedent and Progress in the Work of Frank Lloyd Wright." *Journal of the Society of Architectural Historians* 39:2 (May 1980), pp. 145–49.

A tracing of precedent inglenook features as they may have influenced Wright's use of the device.

Manson, Grant. *Frank Lloyd Wright to 1910: The First Golden Age*. New York: Reinhold, 1958.

Written with Wright's cooperation. Intended as the first book of a never-completed trilogy dealing with Wright's whole career, it was in its time the most detailed treatment of the early period, and remains a valuable source.

Pfeiffer, Bruce Brooks. *See* Futagawa, Yukio.

Scully, Vincent. *Frank Lloyd Wright*. New York: George Braziller, 1960.

———. *The Shingle Style and the Stick Style*. New Haven and London: Yale University Press, 1976.

A reprint of the classic first serious modern work on its subject, published in 1955, it also treats Wright's debt to the Shingle Style in an analysis that has held up over time.

Sergeant, John. *Frank Lloyd Wright's Usonian Houses*. New York: Watson-Guptill Publications, 1984.

In the text generally, and even more in the notes, Sergeant ranges far beyond the Usonians per se.

Smith, Norris Kelly. *Frank Lloyd Wright: A Study in Architectural Content*. Englewood Cliffs: Prentice-Hall, 1966.

A biography of quality equal to Twombly's (see below). Smith argues convincingly that from one point of view Wright and his work can be seen not as radical but as conservative of traditional values.

Stewart, David. *The Making of a Modern Japanese Architecture*. Tokyo and New York: Kodansha International, 1987.

Primarily about Japanese architecture by Japanese architects, this book contains extraordinarily perceptive and soundly researched observations, the most helpful to date, about Wright's relationship to Japan.

Storrer, William Allin. *The Architecture of Frank Lloyd Wright.*
   Cambridge, Mass.: MIT Press, 1978.
   A listing as nearly complete as we have to date of
   Wright's built work. Includes disappointingly weak
   photographs and illustrations.
Tafel, Edgar. *Apprentice to Genius.* New York: McGraw-Hill,
   1979.
   Adulatory and anecdotal rather than analytical. The
   author was an apprentice at Taliesin during a Golden
   Age and was closely involved in the construction of
   Fallingwater.
Twombly, Robert. *Frank Lloyd Wright, An Interpretive
   Biography.* New York: Harper & Row, 1973.
   ————. *Frank Lloyd Wright, His Life and His Architecture.*
   New York: Wiley, 1979.
   A revision of the 1973 book. Twombly's careful re-
   search offers a wealth of material now indispensable to
   Wright scholarship, including the events surrounding
   his alliance with Mamah Borthwick Cheney, and an
   unsentimental view of life at Taliesin.
Wright, Frank Lloyd. *An Autobiography.* New York: Duell,
   Sloane, and Pearce, 1943.
   ————. *An Autobiography.* New York: Horizon, 1977.
   Wright originally wrote his autobiography in 1932. He
   made major and important changes for the 1943 edition,
   then continued to revise until his death in 1959. The
   work in its supposed 1959 state did not appear until 1977,
   and there is at least some question about the degree of
   revision that may have occurred between his death and
   the much-delayed publication. Therefore, where there
   are significant differences between the two editions,
   I have tried to use 1943; where differences are minor,
   I use 1977 because it is more easily available.
   In either edition the book is a primary source of enormous value, but it needs to be read with patience and
   critical judgment. As Gill, *Masks,* properly emphasizes,
   all editions suffer from casual editing. The writing style
   is markedly uneven, ranging from the lucidly eloquent
   descriptions of Taliesin's genesis to passages that seem
   confused and turgid beyond hope of comprehension. To
   make things more difficult still, what purports to be fact
   sometimes is not and cannot be. My own view is that the
   newcomer to Wright should precede the autobiography
   with either Twombly, *Life,* or Gill, *Masks,* or both.
   ————. *The Natural House.* New York: Horizon Press, 1954.
   An amalgamation of much of Wright's other writing,
   including a great deal from the autobiography.

Related Works

Brooks, H. Allen. *Frank Lloyd Wright and the Prairie School.*
   New York: Braziller, 1984.
   ————. *The Prairie School.* Toronto: University of Toronto
   Press, 1972.
   ————. *Prairie School Architecture.* Toronto: University
   of Toronto Press, 1975.
Curtis, William J. R. *Modern Architecture Since 1900.*
   Englewood Cliffs: Prentice-Hall, 1982.
   A first-rate work.
Hines, Thomas S. *Richard Neutra and the Search for Modern
   Architecture.* New York and Oxford: Oxford University
   Press, 1982.
   The definitive work on Neutra, with thoughtful
   observations on Wright as well.
Jordy, William H. *American Buildings and Their Architects.*
   Vol. 4, New York: Oxford University Press, 1972.
   The context of Wright's early work; it includes an
   entire chapter on the Robie house.
Peisch, Mark L. *The Chicago School of Architecture.* London:
   Phaidon, 1964.
   Done before the term *Chicago School* had been accepted
   as applying only to public architecture and the term
   Prairie School agreed on for residential work, this book
   deals with both fields; an early and fundamental work.
Wrede, Stuart. *Mario Botta.* New York: Museum of Modern
   Art, 1986.
Zardini, Mirko. *The Architecture of Mario Botta.* New York:
   Rizzoli, 1985.

Photo Credits

Figs. 1.6, 3.2, 3.23, 3.25, 3.27: University of Washington Photographic Services from *Ausgeführle Bauten und Entwürfe* (Berlin. Wasmuth, 1910)

Figs. 1.7, 1.8, 1.10: Special Collections Division, University of Washington Libraries

Figs. 1.11, 3.12, 3.13, 3.14, 3.17, 3.18, 3.21, 4.10, 4.11, 4.12, 5.32: National Center for the Study of Frank Lloyd Wright

Figs. 2.1, 5.3, 5.19: Norman J. Johnston

Fig. 2.2: University of Washington College of Architecture and Urban Planning

Figs. 3.5, 3.6, 9.8, 9.10, 9.11, 9.12: Christian Staub

Figs. 3.7, 3.8, 3.16, 8.21: John Savo

Fig. 3.15: Cal Kowal, courtesy Hermann Pundt

Fig. 3.20: University of Michigan College of Architecture and Urban Planning

Figs. 4.1, 4.2, 5.11, 7.1, 7.2, 7.3, 7.4: University of Washington Photographic Services from *Architectural Record*

Figs. 4.3, 4.4, 4.5, 4.6, 4.7, 5.8: University of Washington Photographic Services from Henricus T. Wijdeveld (ed.), *The Work of Frank Lloyd Wright* (Sandpoort, Holland: C. A. Mees, 1925)

Figs. 5.1, 5.5, 5.6, 5.7, 5.9, 5.13, 5.16, 5.17, 5.21, 5.22, 5.23, 5.26, 5.27, 5.28, 5.29, 5.31, 8.38: author/William Hook

Fig. 5.4: author/William Hook from Hollyhock House archives, courtesy Virginia Ernst Kazor

Figs. 5.14, 5.25, 5.30, 9.7: Julius Shulman

Figs. 5.33, 8.22, 8.23: State Historical Society of Wisconsin

Figs. 6.1, 6.3, 6.4, 6.5, 6.6, 6.7, 6.8, 6.9, 6.10, 6.12, 6.13: Scott Leff

Fig. 7.5: Ian Robertson

Figs. 7.7, 7.8, 7.9: Neil Levine

Figs. 7.10, 9.18: Gordon B. Varey

Figs. 7.11, 7.12, 7.13, 7.14, 8.2, 8.4, 8.5: Pedro Guerrero

Fig. 8.1: Steven Sartore, courtesy Hermann Pundt

Fig. 8.6: University of Washington Photographic Services from *Architectural Forum*

Figs. 8.31, 8.32, 8.33, 8.35, 8.36: Ezra Stoller/ESTO

Figs. 8.8, 8.9: Ellen Nibbelink

Figs. 8.11, 8.12, 8.25: Balthazar Korab

Figs. 8.14, 8.15, 8.16, 8.18, 8.19: Hedrich-Blessing

Figs. 8.26, 8.27, 8.28: Karl Greimel/Lawrence Technical University

Fig. 8.30: Peter Hildebrand

Figs. 8.37, 8.41, 8.42, 8.43, 8.44, 8.45: David Capps

Figs. 9.1, 9.2, 9.3, 9.4: Mary and Leigh Block Gallery, Northwestern University

Fig. 9.5: Library of Congress

Fig. 9.6: David Streatfield

Figs. 9.13, 9.14, 9.15, 9.16, 9.17: Mario Botta

Index